Markets in Chaos

Markets in Chaos

A History of Market Crises Around the World

Brendan Hughes

BEP

BUSINESS EXPERT PRESS

Leader in applied, concise business books

Markets in Chaos: A History of Market Crises Around the World

Copyright © Business Expert Press, LLC, 2024

Cover design by Charlene Kronstedt

Interior design by Exeter Premedia Services Private Ltd., Chennai, India

First published in 2023 by
Business Expert Press, LLC
222 East 46th Street, New York, NY 10017
www.businessexpertpress.com

ISBN-13: 978-1-63742-514-5 (paperback)
ISBN-13: 978-1-63742-515-2 (e-book)

Business Expert Press Economics and Public Policy Collection

First edition: 2023

10 9 8 7 6 5 4 3 2 1

Description

This book is useful for those seeking to learn about the history of market crises and individuals who want to learn about protection against downside risks for an investment portfolio.

The purpose of this book is not to convince the reader to attempt to anticipate the timing of the next market crash, but rather for the reader to be able to draw parallels (and some contrasts) between the different crises in history. The book reviews case studies related to specific macroeconomic event triggers ranging from COVID-19 to hyperinflation.

Readers will come away with extensive knowledge of different market crisis events spread across countries and timelines. The reader will be well versed on important macroeconomic topics such as the history of currencies. Perhaps most importantly, readers will feel better prepared to handle the next market catastrophe. Audiences such as business school students and those who are a part of organizations such as the Chartered Financial Analyst Institute will find this book of interest.

Keywords

financial crisis; government debt; fractional-reserve banking; gold standard; currency; money supply; inflation; economy; monetary policy; interest rates; crash

Contents

Testimonials

"Brendan Hughes follows the footsteps of legendary global investors like Jim Rogers and John Templeton in his writing about Market Crises around the world. Brendan goes many places most of us never will, and never would. He provides us a great set of examples of how markets (and the people participating in them) lose their way in regular and periodic ways.

Any serious investor/student would be well served by recreating some of Brendan's travels. Short of that, I recommend reading his book. It's way better to learn how to avoid making mistakes by reading about them than committing them and Brendan's book will help you to do so."—**Tom Gayner, Chief Executive Officer of Markel Group**

"'History doesn't repeat itself, but it often rhymes,' Mark Twain famously quipped. Those who have etched their names in the annals of successful investing, such as Sir John Templeton, are known to be avid students of history. Brendan Hughes's groundbreaking book, Markets in Chaos: A History of Market Crises Around the World, *is a must-read for any investor wishing to harness the potent lessons embedded in the annals of our financial past.*

From the far-reaching economic tremors of the Covid-19 pandemic to the historic collapse of the Mississippi Bubble, Hughes masterfully unravels the common threads that run through these global market crises. In doing so, he paints a compelling picture of the cyclicality of markets, shaped in no small part by the consistent irrationality of human behavior.

This book is not merely a chronicle of past financial shocks, but an illuminating guide to spotting and understanding patterns, valuable for predicting future market trends. Dive into Markets in Chaos *and discover how the echoes of history can provide keen insights for tomorrow's financial decisions."* —**Lauren Templeton, Founder and Principal of Templeton and Phillips Capital Management**

Acknowledgments

This book is the culmination of several years of research, writing, proofreading, and bringing the final product to market. I want to thank those that assisted me along the way.

I want to thank *Business Expert Press* for investing in this project and making it a reality. Thank you to my parents, Mark and Kelly Hughes, and wife, Paula Hughes, for assisting with some backend projects such as proofreading and source citations. I want to thank Drew Estes, Owner and Portfolio Manager of Banyan Capital Management, and Hui Sono, Professor of Finance and International Business at James Madison University, for providing professional reviews of the book. I want to thank Tom Gayner, Chief Executive Officer of Markel Group, and Lauren Templeton, Founder and Principal of Templeton and Phillips Capital Management, for providing review quotations.

Introduction

This book is a collection of 11 detailed case studies that document and discuss various market crises across countries in history. Spanning thousands of years dating back to the year 33 AD in Rome, this book covers classic financial crises directly tied to the banking systems in Iceland, Indonesia, Chile, the United States, and Rome, Italy. There are case studies that review asset bubbles in France and Japan. The book reviews case studies related to specific macroeconomic event triggers ranging from COVID-19 to hyperinflation with the United States (COVID-19 and the 1970s' energy crisis), Zimbabwe (hyperinflation), and Germany (hyperinflation). There are core underlying themes woven into the case studies such as flaws with the fractional-reserve banking business model, performance of fiat currencies versus currencies under the gold standard, and governments' response to crisis events.

The purpose of this book is not to convince the reader to attempt to anticipate the timing of the next market crash, but rather for the reader to be able to draw parallels (and some contrasts) between the different crises. It is likely that many would be surprised by the striking similarities between the events that are widely diversified in terms of geography and timeframe. In studying the historical context of what has gone awry in markets, one has a much better probability of protecting themselves for the moment that the next major crisis arrives. I am not of the view that it is a negative mindset to look back on what has gone wrong in history. With thousands of years of documented financial history, it would be irresponsible not to study what has happened. While financial history does not repeat in exact fashion, it is amazing how similar series of events have occurred throughout history. In studying these events, one can evaluate different risk factors that most never consider.

In addition to the 11 case studies, there is commentary on how this information can be used, along with a chapter on where we are now and what lies ahead. This book is differentiated from other historical accounts of market crisis events owing to my background as an investor. My view is that this piece weaves in analyses of topics such as flaws with the fractional-reserve banking business model in ways that economists have not done successfully in other works. Hopefully, it is clear that there is a more practical focus as to what one can do with this information compared to other historical accounts of market crises.

At a minimum, the reader should come away with extensive knowledge of different market crisis events spread across countries and timelines. The reader should become well versed on important macroeconomic topics such as the history of currencies. Perhaps most importantly, the reader should feel better prepared to handle the next market catastrophe.

CHAPTER 1

United States

COVID-19 (2020–2021)

Background and Market Impact

On January 4, 2020, the World Health Organization (WHO) issued its first public statement about what would later become known around the world as COVID-19, saying, "China has reported to WHO a cluster of pneumonia cases—with no deaths—in Wuhan, Hubei Province." Over the course of the next few months, information slowly started to trickle out about this illness. At first, the stock market shrugged off the news. On January 31, 2020, when we still knew very little about COVID-19, the United States suspended entry for most individuals who were present in mainland China in the previous 14 days. The S&P 500 continued to rise to a new all-time high on February 19, 2020. The stock market likely didn't have much of an initial reaction to the news about COVID-19 because most of the viral outbreaks in recent years did not end up having a significant impact on global business or the stock market. In fact, the S&P 500 showed the following six-month percentage increases: Middle East respiratory syndrome (MERS) in 2013, 10.74 percent; swine flu in 2009, 18.72 percent; and severe acute respiratory syndrome (SARS) in 2003, 14.59 percent.

The scope of the global damage that COVID-19 would inflict in terms of both health and economics would not become clear for a few months. At Fundsmith's annual meeting, which was held on February 25, 2020, Terry Smith, a world-renowned investor, stated, "If you think of our direct China exposure in the portfolio, it's like one-and-a-half of a holding. Imagine that we had one-and-a-half companies operating in China. Are you worried about that? I'm not worried about that."

Smith, like most others at the time, seemed to believe that the economic carnage would be mostly limited to China. He reminded the audience that the Spanish flu pandemic in 1918 infected 500 million people globally out of a population of 1.5 billion with 50 to 100 million deaths. Looking further back, the Black Death in the mid-1300s is estimated to have killed between 30 and 60 percent of all Europeans and between 75 million and 200 million people globally at a time when the prepandemic population was 475 million. Many in the news said that COVID-19 was unprecedented, but this was far from true. It wasn't until reports began to surface in Italy and other countries that investors started to feel on edge. On February 23, it was reported that COVID-19 had spread to more than 30 countries, and it was believed that Italy had the largest outbreak outside of China. This was the start of one of the most infamous stock market crashes in financial history. By the end of February, the S&P 500 was down nearly 13 percent from the all-time high reached on February 19.

I think that March 11, 2020, was the moment that all-out panic started to grip many Americans, U.S. media outlets, and the S&P 500. Moments before a National Basketball Association (NBA) game was set to begin, Rudy Gobert of the Utah Jazz was confirmed to have tested positive for COVID-19. The NBA immediately suspended the season. That same day, the United States banned most visitors traveling from Europe, and on March 13, President Trump declared a national emergency. On March 22, *The New York Times* declared that New York was now a global epicenter of COVID-19, and it was reported that New York City and its suburbs accounted for roughly 5 percent of the world's cases. It is important to note that statistics like this are highly debatable. I am not sure how you make a comparison of the United States to countries like Zimbabwe, where it is likely that little to no testing was being done, so we really don't know the extent of the virus spread in areas like this. On March 19, California issued the first statewide *stay at home* order, which would be followed by many other locations in the United States as well as around the world (lockdowns had already occurred in other countries such as Italy).

According to Bank of America Securities, it took a stunning 22 trading days for the S&P 500 to decline 30 percent from its record high set on

February 19. This was the quickest 30 percent decline in history, surpassing the market declines during the Great Depression. By March 23, the S&P 500 index had declined by 34 percent from the peak. Nobody knew it at the time, but this would mark the bottom of the violent market collapse. It is simply not the same to read about a market event such as this as to have lived through it as an investor. On March 9, which happened to be my birthday, the stock market circuit breakers went into effect for the first time since 1997. Stock trading was halted after the S&P plunged 7 percent in the first 15 minutes of trading. For those who aren't aware, circuit breakers halt trading activity when the overall market declines by 7, 13, and 20 percent to prevent uninterrupted falls in the stock market. With a 20 percent decline, trading stops for the day. In the span of two weeks in March, circuit breakers were triggered a stunning four times after not having done so in over 20 years. I will never forget what it felt like psychologically during this time. With the rise of computer trading and passive investments, stock market selloffs like this appear more vicious and nondiscriminatory than they were decades ago. In March of 2020, it was not unusual to look at your stock trading screen and see stocks of perfectly fine businesses down 30 percent in a single trading session. On March 18, in his now controversial interview, Bill Ackman went on CNBC in the middle of the trading day to say, "hell is coming," along with several other quotes that coincided with the stock market plunging further. This moment proved to be close to the turning point in the stock market decline. Perhaps even more stunning than the market decline in March 2020 was the rally that ensued afterward. The S&P 500 index closed out 2020 68 percent higher than the low point reached on March 23.

How Businesses Were Affected

The vast majority of businesses in the country and the world were negatively impacted by the effects of COVID-19, but industries that were particularly hit hard included airlines, cruise lines, restaurants, hotels, and live events. In the past, the government often allowed businesses such as airlines to go bankrupt during crises such as the global financial crisis in 2008 to 2009, but the United States government decided to use billions of taxpayer dollars to bailout airlines in the wake of the COVID-19 crisis. This does not make any sense to me because it is not as if you would wake up and see all the planes in the country grounded if the U.S. government opted not to bail out the airlines. Contrary to popular belief, if an airline goes bankrupt, they most often just recapitalize and continue with their business. I don't think these bailouts set a good precedent for the future because companies will have less incentive to behave responsibly if they know it is likely that they will just get a government bailout if their business falters in a material way. The situation with the airlines was particularly frustrating since most had spent years repurchasing vast quantities of stock prior to the government bailouts.

The COVID-19 crisis brought about a highly unusual business environment. Most executives, investors, and others did not take much time planning for a scenario where a particular business or industry literally had no revenues, or close to no revenues, for months on end. This put the spotlight on what I consider to be capital-intensive industries that require ongoing large cash outlays. I will again use the airlines as an example. In late March of 2020, Delta Air Lines was burning through $100 million of cash flow per day! This would equate to roughly $36.5 billion per year in lost cash.

What possibly stands out most about the COVID-19 economic impact is that the crisis disproportionally affected small businesses compared to large corporations. As an example, there are many families that had their entire net worth invested in a single restaurant or other service-oriented business. Many families did not have enough savings put aside to weather the storm of rolling lockdowns around the United States for a year where their businesses were either closed or not bringing in enough cash to pay the monthly bills. By contrast, a large and successful corporation, like Starbucks, can weather these conditions because they have no problem borrowing money in the short term. A company like Starbucks will likely become even stronger in the long term after this economic crisis because they will consolidate market share with small coffee shops going out of business. Additionally, large corporations like Starbucks had an enormous technological advantage over the smaller shops that showed through during the pandemic. Starbucks was able to near-seamlessly pivot their business model to mobile ordering, takeout, and drive-through. Most of the smaller coffee shops were not able to do this and suffered.

Prior to the COVID-19 pandemic, there was already a long-term shift underway from physical to digital. Business segments such as e-commerce had been growing rapidly for years at the expense of physical stores. The COVID-19 crisis significantly accelerated what I refer to as the digitization of everything. As an example, PayPal said on an earnings call that they believe a shift to e-commerce that would have taken three to five years happened in months. Many other companies had similar commentary. Businesses that previously had no online presence rushed to put their entire business online because they had no other option. Nike had been investing heavily in digitization for years prior to the COVID-19 crisis, but their CEO talked up the digital opportunity after COVID-19 in saying that, with digitization, business is open 24 hours a day, 365 days a year. Put more simply, I think that COVID-19 was really the moment that the physical and digital worlds became one from a business standpoint. Starbucks and Nike both said that they would meet the consumer wherever they are, whether in one of their stores or online. The digitization of everything was already one of the most powerful long-term trends in business, but the COVID-19 pandemic significantly accelerated this long-term shift.

COVID-19 made businesses fundamentally reimagine some aspects of their daily operations. For the first time ever for many companies, entire workforces were required to work from home for extended periods of time. Many companies found that remote work was effective, and a lot of employees enjoyed working from home. It isn't clear as of the time of this writing as to how much remote work will be done in a post-COVID-19 world, but it has been a growing trend, particularly in the technology industry, to allow employees to work remotely 100 percent of the time or at least part time. Some companies now see a future where offices are used for on-premises meetings but not as a location where employees hang out all day, five days per week. This fundamental change has led to issues related to commercial real estate demand. It is unclear at this time as to the magnitude of the commercial real estate losses banks will see on their loan portfolios, but I don't see how it won't be substantial. Effective remote work has been made possible owing to quality tools for virtual workplace collaboration such as Zoom and Microsoft Teams. In the future, with the rise of virtual and augmented reality technologies, it will likely be possible to feel as if you are physically present with other coworkers despite being on opposite sides of the world. Remote work should be an important long-term trend. Companies can save money by spending less on commercial real estate, employees can save time and reduce stress with more infrequent commutes in addition to money saved on transportation, and more remote work is better for the environment since less pollution is created.

In addition to the remote work aspect of business operations, many companies reconsidered business travel. With the rise of quality video chat solutions, many companies realized that a lot of the expensive and time-consuming business travel that they were paying for did not justify the cost. In a November 2020 interview, Bill Gates said, "My prediction would be that over 50 percent of business travel and over 30 percent of days in the office will go away." It is likely that critical high-dollar value deals and meetings of that nature will still be negotiated in person, but the bar for business travel will likely be a lot higher than it was in a pre-COVID-19 world.

At least in the short term, demand for household products soared as a result of COVID-19. People were spending more time at home and reallocating money that would normally be spent on discretionary areas such as travel and dining out to do home projects that had been put off for a while. Lowe's and Home Depot had record years in 2020 riding surging demand on nearly every household product. My prediction is that the demand for household products will remain elevated for years to come because of the rise in remote work. We saw a shift of people moving out of cities to more rural areas. During the pandemic, most individuals were working at home, and some thought that they might as well get out of high-rent cities if they weren't commuting to work or able to use the entertainment options in the city. It will be interesting to see how this develops in the long term. The extent to which companies continue to allow full-time remote work, or mostly remote work, will shape the long-term trend of moving from urban to rural areas. The same goes for high-tax states such as California and New York compared to Texas and Florida. During the COVID-19 crisis, people moved out of high-tax states such as California in favor of tax havens such as Texas. This could continue to happen if more remote work is allowed in the long term. From a financial perspective, it gets very difficult to justify living in a California city if you can work remotely for your job when the potential alternative is to live in a Texas suburb for a much lower cost.

The global financial crisis was shaped by the impact that it had on companies in the financial system. The collapse of Bear Stearns and Lehman Brothers, along with the possibility of others such as Goldman Sachs and Morgan Stanley, threatened the health of the entire financial system and business ecosystem more broadly. At least as of the time of this writing, this has not occurred as a result of the COVID-19 crisis. The lack of problems with the financial system is a result of the artificial backstop the Federal Reserve installed in terms of unprecedented easy monetary policy in response to the COVID-19 crisis, a topic that will be discussed further in the next section. It was widely believed heading into the current recession that banks were better capitalized as a result of lessons learned from the global financial crisis. Having said that, I have seen reports that a good portion of this capitalization has come from government relief. Additionally, the book, *The Lords of Easy Money: How the Federal Reserve Broke the American Economy*, lifted the veil on the bank capitalization myth in a discussion about Basel III, a bank capital adequacy framework passed in the wake of the global financial crisis. Basel III allows banks to use a risk-weighted formula to determine the value of balance sheet assets. Risk-weighted measures are complex and subjective and often lead to banks claiming to possess more capital than they have (especially under crisis scenarios) because banks are incentivized to report higher levels of capital. Having formerly worked as a consultant on banking loan portfolios, I know these games all too well. If there are laws that allow for large degrees of subjectivity, banks will push their asset value appraisals up to values they believe will seem at least within the realm of possibility to regulators. Basel III is used up until today and is likely making the banking system appear safer than reality. The government has continued to respond to the COVID-19 crisis by printing money and taking on more debt.

Macroeconomic Impact

As I write this chapter, the full scope of the long-term economic impact of COVID-19 on the United States economy is unclear. Some believe the total scope of the COVID-19 recession will make it the worst economic crisis since the Great Depression (this would prove untrue, but the lasting impact of the debt binge and subsequent inflation proved to be enormous). The U.S. economy officially entered a recession in 2020, which brought the longest economic expansion for the country on record to an end. Gross domestic product (GDP) in Quarter 2 of 2020 was estimated to have contracted by a breathtaking 32.9 percent on an annualized basis. The number of unemployed Americans soared by more than 14 million, rising from 6.2 million in February to 20.5 million just three months later. The unemployment rate rose from 3.8 percent in February to 13 percent in May, a stunning increase over such a short period of time. Some of these jobs would come back after lockdowns eased, but it was a significant blow, nonetheless. Inequality in the United States and globally increased as a result of the COVID-19 crisis not only because of large corporations benefitting at the expense of small businesses but also because wealthier families could much more seamlessly adapt to the COVID-19 world than families of lesser financial stature. When schools around the country went completely online, there were many families that didn't have access to reliable Internet, and their children lacked the ability to attend their online classes. This school example and the struggles of small businesses are just a couple instances of how inequality was accelerated by the COVID-19 pandemic.

To understand where we are today in terms of macroeconomic backdrop, we need to review what happened after the global financial crisis since the series of events that has developed over the last 15 years has set the table for where we stand today. From a high level, we have lived in an environment since the global financial crisis where for close to 15 years money has been free or close to free around the world. Low interest rates have boosted asset prices ranging from equities to houses because one of the main alternatives to these asset classes is to earn nothing in most bonds. There has been a self-reinforcing cycle of increased borrowing and risk-taking, all because money has been cheap for an unprecedented period in modern times.

Here are some implications of free money for a prolonged period:

- Very high levels of debt across governments, businesses (public and private), and consumers. We have gone into detail about the broad-based rise of government debts, but businesses and consumers have followed a similar trajectory. Consumer debt hit an inflation-adjusted record of $14 trillion in 2019. Corporate borrowing for U.S. nonfinancial companies increased from $6 trillion at the end of 2010 to $10 trillion by 2019.
- A focus on financial engineering as opposed to real productivity that helps explain the lack of wage growth up until recently. If a company pays a 2.5 percent dividend and is buying back shares, the company can borrow money for nothing and justify that this repurchase provides an immediate boost to shareholder value without the risk that something goes wrong with a capital investment. In some cases, this is perfectly rational behavior, given the monetary policy incentives.
- Rising income inequality because easy monetary policy stimulated asset values that mostly benefitted the wealthy (through rising values of stocks, houses, and so on) without the flow-through in terms of broad-based wage growth that is explained by the focus on financial engineering as opposed to real productivity. In the 1990s, before the era of free money and financial engineering, labor productivity in the United States averaged 2.3 percent. During the free money era, this figure declined to a 1.1 percent increase. This helps explain why, between 1989 and 2016, the wealth of the top 1 percent in the United States tripled, while the middle 20 percent saw an average rise in net worth of just 4 percent over the same period.
- Increased levels of risk-taking. Again, some of this has been rational behavior, given the incentives. The historical model for pension funds was that they would invest 60 percent in stocks and 40 percent in bonds. When many bonds are earning nothing, this is not going to be a feasible model for

many funds. Funds that were investing in bonds have been investing more in stocks, and funds that were investing more in stocks were suddenly investing in cryptocurrencies. You get the picture.

- Companies, particularly those backed by private equity money, have been piling on leverage often funded by loans where most of the money is due on the back end at variable interest rates. As an example, the U.S. market for collateralized loan obligations (CLOs) more than doubled between 2011 and 2018. Investors have been so desperate for yield that CLOs and other exotic debt instruments have been reducing or dropping covenants to protect investors, such as limitations that a borrower may have in raising more debt without permission. The increased levels of risk for investors owing to fewer covenants and protections have not impacted investor demand, given the dearth of other options for yield. Similar to the period prior to the global financial crisis, these leveraged loans have often been packaged together in a bundle and sold to third parties desperate for yield. The practice of rolling over large debts at variable rates worked great when money was free and was again at times rational behavior, given the incentives provided by the Federal Reserve.

I think that the global financial crisis marked a new era of easy monetary policy for the Federal Reserve. Investors and others hailed the philosophy that the Fed would do whatever it takes and provide a backstop for the economy. During the global financial crisis in 2008 and 2009, the Federal Reserve used aggressive interest rate cuts, quantitative easing (large-scale asset purchases), and provided targeted assistance to ailing financial institutions through the Troubled Asset Relief Program (TARP), along with other measures to support the economy. The combination of weak domestic economic growth and supportive monetary and fiscal policies caused the government debt levels to swell to 82 percent of GDP in 2009.

There were some fundamental differences in the macroeconomic backdrops leading up to the global financial crisis and the COVID-19 recession. One of the most significant differences was that, leading up to 2008 to 2009, the Federal Reserve had the ability to aggressively cut interest rates as the target federal funds rate was 5.25 percent in 2007. By comparison, the target federal funds rate in late 2019 leading up to the COVID-19 crisis was a range of 1.5 to 1.75 percent. In short, interest rates were already very low leading up to the COVID-19 crisis, where this was not the case leading up to 2008 to 2009. It is much more difficult for the Federal Reserve to use interest rate cuts to stimulate economic growth when rates are already at low levels.

While the steps taken by the Federal Reserve in 2008 and 2009 in response to the global financial crisis were considered aggressive, the policy responses in 2020 in reaction to the COVID-19 crisis were much more aggressive. As a comparison, starting in 2008, the Federal Reserve increased bond holdings by $3.7 trillion, which pushed the total balance sheet past $4.5 trillion in operations over six years. During the COVID-19 crisis, from mid-March to mid-June 2020, the Federal Reserve's holdings went from $4.2 to $7.1 trillion. It is estimated that, in a single week in March 2020, the Federal Reserve was purchasing $625 billion in Treasuries and mortgage-backed securities, which was more than the entire $600 billion second portion of the quantitative easing during the financial crisis, and this went on for eight months. As a more high-level long-term point of reference, between 1960 and 2007, the Federal Reserve increased the monetary base by a total of $788 billion. In short, the Federal Reserve's actions in response to the COVID-19 crisis in the span of a week was nearly as aggressive as close to 50 years of Fed operations leading up to the new era of easy monetary policy.

The Federal Reserve has gotten progressively more aggressive in the types of assets it purchases in bailout scenarios. For example, in response to the COVID-19 crisis, the Federal Reserve would for the first time purchase assets such as CLOs, corporate bonds, and junk debt. I believe the Federal Reserve has now effectively set the expectation that they will bail out almost any asset class during market crises. I do not believe this is a positive development. All the private equity companies that have for years piled on debt in an irresponsible manner to fund acquisitions and spinoffs should not receive a bailout. While not understood by most average citizens, a government bailout is effectively a tax via higher inflation.

These bailouts only further increase incentives to behave irresponsibly and at the same time increase inequality since bailing out these types of businesses disproportionally benefits the wealthy. In response to the COVID-19 crisis, the Federal Reserve even extended into the realm of providing direct credit to companies. The Federal Reserve has been putting itself even more at the center of the economy. The Federal Reserve is doing far more than it used to in what it believes are attempts to achieve the goals of, "maximum employment, stable prices, and moderate long-term interest rates."

I have seen some argue that banks held up well in response to the COVID-19 crisis because they were better capitalized than heading into the global financial crisis. This argument flies in the face of the facts about what happened in the dark days of March of 2020. There was a full-blown liquidity crisis covered up by the massive policy response of the Federal Reserve. For a few brief weeks in March of 2020, investors were selling anything they could as quickly as possible. There was a liquidity run on virtually every asset class, including Treasuries, often considered to be about the most safe and liquid asset on earth. Something highly unusual happened in March of 2020: Treasuries couldn't find a price. At one point, there were literally no buyers for a financial instrument that many investors consider to be the same as cash. Hedge funds, private equity companies, and others had to raise cash as quickly as possible to cover their leveraged bets that were going bad. Everyone needed cash at precisely the same moment. As referenced in the book, *Trillion Dollar Triage: How Jay Powell and the Fed Battled a President and a Pandemic—and Prevented Economic Disaster*, Warren Buffett stated, "We got to the point where the U.S. Treasury market, the deepest of all markets, got somewhat disorganized." Buffett later said that the financial system was, "very close to having a total freeze of credit to the largest companies in the world who were depending on it." In response to this liquidity crisis, the Federal Reserve executed $700 billion of quantitative easing in one weekend. There was an enormous cash injection that provided liquidity for a financial system that did not have any, even in historically highly liquid instruments such as Treasuries. The Federal Reserve's actions were likely the right moves given the options presented (if it is assumed that we will continue to use a fractional-reserve banking model without restrictions on the growth in the money supply), but these ongoing enormous bailouts since the global financial crisis have only been made possible because people have maintained confidence in the U.S. dollar and consumer price inflation has up until recently been mundane. We have recently seen high levels of consumer price inflation in light of the sustained massive money printing. It will be interesting to see how confidence in the U.S. dollar and other fiat currencies develops in the coming years, as the global financial system has been locked into a vicious cycle centered around enormous central bank bailouts to cover up problems that were never resolved from the global financial crisis.

What is the result of all this allegedly wonderful policy that the Federal Reserve has enacted? As of the time of this writing, the U.S. national debt is approximately $27 trillion, and for the first time since World War II, the national debt is larger than the economy. The skyrocketing national debt levels show no signs of slowing down, as President-Elect Biden just proposed another COVID-19 relief package that is close to $2 trillion. Economic policy has shifted to what is almost always done during times of severe economic distress: printing more money. Inevitably, this will cause fiat currency to be less valuable via monetary inflation (currency devaluation), even though we aren't seeing too much of an increase in inflation (consumer price inflation ultimately soared) as measured by the consumer price index (CPI). Few people realize that the CPI metric differs today from how it was measured in the 1970s, in that it does not include housing prices and substitutes a nonmarket rent for owners' housing costs. I would caution readers not to read too much into the CPI inflation figure, as it only captures price increases on consumer-related items and does not incorporate most asset price inflation. The former chair of the Federal Reserve, Alan Greenspan, effectively set the precedent for ignoring asset price inflation when the Fed thought about inflation measurements. Looking at the prices of asset classes such as stocks and real estate, I think it is safe to say that a decade of low interest rates and money printing has resulted in asset price inflation that is not being discussed. Money printing does not necessarily lead to higher inflation during periods of economic distress when the increase in money supply is not circulated within the economy. We have seen this happen during past crises such as the Great Depression where money velocity stalls and at least temporarily limits price growth even if there is a large increase in the money supply. As some believe was the case in the 1970s, the monetary policy in response to the COVID-19 crisis placed far more weight on maintaining full employment compared to maintaining price stability, and it is likely this policy was a direct result of how the Federal Reserve measures and views inflation. This turned out to be a costly error in the 1970s, and history looks set to repeat itself.

Some now believe that the central banks misdiagnosed the problem at the height of the COVID-19 pandemic in 2020. The central banks attempted to stimulate demand with their policy tools, and it looks like the real problem was the lack of supply in products such as semiconductor chips, fertilizer, and oil. The stimulus provided by the central banks did nothing to resolve the supply shocks, and when economies opened back up, there was too much capital chasing too few goods and services that ultimately sent consumer price inflation soaring around the world.

Some argue that the national debt will be reduced over time through stronger economic growth and other means such as increased taxation. As I will discuss later, the economic growth piece of the puzzle is not likely to replicate past periods of debt reduction. What I am particularly worried about is the health and stability of the U.S. dollar along with other fiat currencies. Without confidence in the finances of a national government, people will lose confidence in the currency being issued by that government. This leads to an unstable currency, and with an unstable currency, you have a lot of problems.

The biggest issue with an unstable currency is that people can lose faith in the currency altogether. We have seen this happen many times before such as the collapse of Zimbabwe's currency, which I discussed in my book, *The Wandering Investor*. Throughout history, every currency ultimately ceases to exist or becomes devalued over time. Thinking more broadly, how would you feel if time was measured in inflation-adjusted minutes, and the time of the day could swing by 10 percent depending on the level of inflation and other factors? It would lead to less overall confidence in the time system, and accomplishing tasks like meetings would become much more difficult because you would have people showing up at all different times. The same logic should be applied to currencies. As I also discussed in my book, *The Wandering Investor*, when I was attempting to acquire Indonesian rupiahs, the currency depreciated by about 12 percent over a six-day period against the U.S. dollar. There are much more extreme currency gyrations than this occurring around the world as we speak, but it is difficult for a consumer to place a value on products and services in local currency terms if there are constant wild fluctuations. The loss of confidence in a currency or hyperinflation eventually leads to countries abandoning their local currency altogether.

I am addressing the topic of unstable currencies in this chapter because I am concerned about the long-term health of the U.S. dollar along with just about every other fiat currency in the world. Ever since the global financial crisis, we have had over a decade of low interest rates, artificially inflated asset valuations, and soaring debt levels that were greatly accelerated after the COVID-19 pandemic, and now the United States, along with many other countries, has resorted to printing more money to address weak economic growth and high unemployment levels. I don't believe many people grasp the extent that monetary policy has changed since the global financial crisis. According to the book, *The Lords of Easy Money: How the Federal Reserve Broke the American Economy*, between 2007 and 2017, the Federal Reserve printed about five times as many dollars as had been printed in the previous 500 years. And this was before the incredible scale of money printing that happened after the outbreak of COVID-19. This grand monetary experiment will likely lead to problems with the global financial system. Contrary to what some believe, printing more money does not make people better off, as it inevitably makes the money less valuable via higher monetary inflation. This statement about printing more money resulting in higher inflation assumes that the money printed is circulated within the economy, which sometimes does not happen during periods of economic distress. It is highly unlikely that the United States will simply be able to grow its way out of the current deficit levels, even though this is what the government wants people to believe. One of the few remaining tools available will be higher taxes that could raise more federal income in the near term but would likely reduce long-term economic growth. Substantial sustained budget cuts are almost always politically unpopular, and politicians have no incentive to do this because most of the negative effects of running up deficits will happen long after they are gone. If the United States does not get its deficits under control, other countries will inevitably question the status of the U.S. dollar as the world's reserve currency. I think this is going to occur anyway, as countries are already trying to reduce reliance on the United States, which is at least partially attributable to the trade wars waged in recent years. Most people don't realize that country reserve currencies rise and fall as part of long-term cycles, and every reserve currency ultimately ceases to be a reserve currency.

In the long term, I think that the world is going to have to return to some form of gold standard. The gold standard era officially ended in 1971, when President Richard Nixon completely severed the link between the U.S. dollar and gold. Not often understood, 1971 was a moment when the United States ran out of money and effectively defaulted on its debts. The United States completely severed the link between the U.S. dollar and gold when it became obvious that the country couldn't keep its promises for the existing paper money. A country that is a fiat currency issuer will never default on its debts, but they can print money to the point that the local currency becomes worthless, as has happened often over the course of history. Historically, there has been a return to paper money linkages to hard assets such as gold when we have approached moments similar to where we are now in terms of there being a global monetary reset as a result of looming debt restructurings and defaults.

In addition to my advocacy for the return to a form of gold standard, I endorse Nobel laureate economist Milton Friedman's general view that central banks should target constant money supply growth where the ongoing growth rate of the money supply tracks GDP growth in an economy. Over the years, critics have noted that limits on money supply growth do not impact money velocity (an argument that stems from John Maynard Keynes' Keynesianism that believes demand for goods and services is the key to economic output), which is true, but as you will see from the case studies in this book, large increases in the money supply in excess of GDP growth ultimately destabilize the financial system. To quote Ray Dalio, "Where is the understanding of history and the common sense about the quantity of money and credit and the amount of inflation?" One of the critiques of Milton Friedman's school of thinking, called monetarism, is that there are many different definitions of the money supply. For example, M1 includes demand deposits at commercial banks, and M2 is the sum of M1 and other factors such as currency and coins held by the nonbank public, checkable deposits, and travelers' checks. It has become more difficult over the years to quantify the money supply with the rise of the shadow banking system and markets such as cryptocurrencies. Even with this limitation, it still makes sense to, as closely as possible, mirror money supply growth with economic growth. It has been alarming that Federal Reserve Chairman, Jerome Powell, has repeatedly publicly downplayed the correlation between money supply growth and inflation, likely aware that it was a major policy error to print so much money in 2020 long after conditions had stabilized. The Federal Reserve can publicly say as they please, but it is a fact that all else equal, when there is more money chasing an equal or lesser amount of goods and services, the result is that money becomes less valuable.

It is my view that a partial gold standard should be supplemented with a combination of limits on money supply growth tied to GDP growth and a full-reserve banking system. In response to the Great Depression, in 1933, a group of economists formed a proposal called the Chicago Plan that identified the culprit of the Great Depression as being the fractional-reserve banking system that is still employed today. Under a full-reserve banking system, there is a 1:1 ratio of loans to reserves, with every dollar in loans backed by a dollar in deposits. A full-reserve banking system coupled with rules related to money supply growth and a partial gold standard would dramatically limit the potential for extreme boom-and-bust cycles. I have not found any evidence that there is a benefit to printing massive piles of paper money in excess of GDP growth and having this activity incentivized at private banks with the allowance of fractional-reserve banking and government bailouts.

It will take years before we fully understand the effects COVID-19 had on the domestic and global economy. We have yet to see the long-term effects of the aggressive monetary and fiscal measures taken in response to the COVID-19 crisis, along with other developments such as broad-based bankruptcies of small businesses and potentially sustained high unemployment levels. It will almost certainly be much more difficult for the United States to bring down government debt levels than compared to the period after World War II. After World War II, debt to GDP fell by more than half to roughly 50 percent of GDP by 1959. The U.S. government was able to cut debt levels relatively quickly, thanks to rapid economic and population growth. U.S. GDP increased from $228 billion in 1945 to almost $1.7 trillion in 1975. Even those most optimistic about the U.S. economy going forward know that it is unrealistic to expect economic growth anywhere near these levels. Additionally, if the United States doesn't quickly reverse the protectionist immigration policies, population growth is going to be a major problem, given the low domestic birth rates. Even with the assumption of robust immigration, the United States would likely continue to model tepid population growth going forward. Making matters worse, mandatory spending (which includes items such as social security and Medicare) made up 61 percent of federal spending in 2019 compared to approximately 30 percent in 1970. It appears to me that the United States will either need to raise taxes (highly likely to happen) in the coming years to pay for the national debt and health care liabilities, restructure or default on the national debt, or continue to print large sums of money (almost certain to happen). Defaulting on the national debt isn't really an option for the United States since, as a currency issuer, the country could always just continue printing more money until it eventually becomes worthless. Given where the United States stands today, it is likely we will see higher taxes and more money printing that will devalue the U.S. dollar. Unlike during the post-World War II era, the United States has far less options going forward. The COVID-19 crisis has put already aggressive government spending into overdrive.

One of the largest long-term implications of the exploding global debt levels and potential decline of fiat currencies is the possibility that government debt instruments such as U.S. Treasuries will be devalued or completely wiped out. For most living today, such a concept would seem impossible. But, for some historical context, I will bring in Ray Dalio.

> While people tend to believe that a currency is pretty much a permanent thing and that *cash* is the safest asset to hold, that's not true. All currencies devalue or die, and when they do, cash and bonds (which are promises to receive currency) are devalued or

wiped out. That is because printing a lot of currency and devaluing debt is the most expedient way of reducing or wiping out debt burdens (Dalio 2022).

Most people living today in countries such as the United States have only ever known government debt to be stable, and as a result, they associate the low price volatility of government debt with a concept that the instruments are risk-free. This line of thinking is dangerous and ignores the history of government debt around the world. It is alarming to think about how many retirees have 80 percent of their total asset base parked in a single government's debt under the false belief that it could never be devalued or eliminated. Given the widespread assumption that government debt in countries such as the United States is risk-free, a scenario where government debt in developed countries was devalued would have a colossal impact that couldn't be overstated.

CHAPTER 2

Iceland

Global Financial Crisis (2008–2009)

Background and Market Impact

The reason I chose Iceland as a country case study for the global financial crisis is that I studied Iceland in my book, *The Wandering Investor*, and it was one of the hardest hit countries during this crisis. Leading up to the global financial crisis, Icelandic banks were offering international investors higher interest rates than could be received in their own domestic countries to achieve further growth. Iceland was offering interest rates as high as 18 percent, which encouraged carry trade, where investors borrow in a lower interest rate currency and use the proceeds to buy higher interest rate currencies. As would happen in the United States, a housing bubble was fueled by lenient lending, in some cases requiring no down payment for the purchase of a home. Homeowners assumed that their homes would continue to increase in value, which resulted in the overconsumption of other luxury items. Between 2003 and 2004, the Iceland stock market skyrocketed an astounding 900 percent. By 2006, the average Icelander was 300 percent wealthier than in 2003, at least on paper. Prior to the start of the global financial crisis, Iceland's three major privately held commercial banks were saddled with $85 billion in debt, and the total assets of the three banks were estimated to have been equal to over 10 times the national GDP. This was one of the largest banking sectors relative to GDP in the world. Making matters worse was the fact that the domestic banks made up most of the Icelandic stock exchange.

How quickly the financial crisis developed in Iceland in 2008 should alarm any investor or business owner. The entire banking system collapsed in a week. In a span of three days, the Icelandic government had essentially nationalized their three largest banks: Landsbanki, Glitnir, and Kaupthing. I have seen some textbooks say that the Icelandic government let the major banks fail, but this is a serious misunderstanding. The Icelandic government effectively bailed out the banking sector by nationalizing the banks.

What was the result? According to a report by *World Finance*:

> The stock market fell by around 95 percent, interest payments on loans soared to more than 300 percent, over 60 percent of bank assets were written off within a few months after the banks collapsed, and interest rates were hiked up to 18 percent in order to curb inflation rates.

The Icelandic króna collapsed by over 50 percent, and 25 percent of homeowners went into default. The Icelandic government attempted to stabilize the situation by initiating capital controls—limits on people taking money out of the financial system—on the króna reaching a debt agreement with the International Monetary Fund (IMF) and the other four Nordic countries (with $2.1 billion coming from the IMF and $2.5 billion from the other four Nordic countries) and guaranteeing all domestic deposits at Icelandic banks. It was not until 2017 that Iceland finally lifted the capital controls.

In the years following the global financial crisis, Iceland recovered much more quickly than other countries, such as Ireland, that were devastated by the crisis. I would caution against reading too much into this recovery. A large portion of the growth in Iceland in the years following the financial crisis was fueled by the tourism sector that exploded owing to a weakened currency and cheap international flights. This unsustainable model was exposed in the wake of the COVID-19 crisis when tourism came to a standstill.

How Businesses Were Affected

The business case study for Iceland during this period must focus on the banking sector. I don't think that what occurred in the Icelandic banking sector during the global financial crisis should be particularly surprising for anyone with an understanding of the fractional-reserve banking business model. I can think of few worse businesses on earth than a bank. The standard banking business model under fractional-reserve banking is to earn a 1 to 2 percent return on assets, and then leverage these returns 15 to one in order to earn what some consider to be an adequate return on equity (although I do not consider the returns to be adequate even with the heavy use of leverage). This business model arguably works fine when things are going well, but the extreme leverage required to operate the business is also the reason that banks go bust quickly when conditions deteriorate. Making matters worse, a run on a bank and the banking system occurs when credit dries up. With the rise of complex derivative products, it is near impossible to grasp what risks a bank of any size is exposed to. Having formerly worked as a consultant for larger banks, I can unfortunately say with certainty that the banks themselves don't have a better understanding of their risk exposures than an investor feebly trying to analyze the risk exposures of millions of complex derivative products. It is interesting that few people would consider it a prudent idea to lever up their retirement savings 15 to one, yet countless individuals don't flinch at the idea of allowing banks and investment banks to do this very practice in their respective operating businesses. Unlike a central bank that can devalue their claims if the claims are in the government issuing currency, private banks must resort to defaulting or getting a government bailout if they run into problems.

The fractional-reserve banking model, where banks lend money several multiples in excess of that in which they maintain in the form of cash deposits, is not much different from a legalized Ponzi scheme. Most rational individuals would assume that if they deposited their money into a bank, it would be guaranteed they could, at any time, retrieve this money. Under a fractional-reserve banking model that is still employed around the world today, this guarantee is not possible. If banks receive $100 in cash deposits, they will lend $1,500 by creating money out of thin air and lever the interest returns on the cash deposits to earn a return that some investors deem to be acceptable. The result of this terrifying series of events is that banks rely on the assumption that not too many people will retrieve their cash at the same time. When this assumption turns out to be false, as it has throughout history during periods of turmoil, the result is a bank run.

In the wake of thousands of bank failures during the Great Depression, the Federal Deposit Insurance Corporation (FDIC) was established in the United States under the Banking Act of 1933. The FDIC is an independent agency created by Congress but does not rely on funds from Congress, at least under what the agency declares is its standard operating model. The FDIC's income is generated from insurance premiums held on deposits at insured banks and from interest on premiums of government securities. As a backstop, the FDIC can borrow up to $100 billion from the U.S. Treasury. Today, the FDIC provides standard deposit insurance of up to $250,000 per insured bank for each account ownership category. What this basically means is that if an FDIC-insured bank in the United States fails, an individual has a guarantee from the FDIC they will be reimbursed up to $250,000 for their lost deposits. In Europe, there is currently a proposal for the EU to create a European Deposit Insurance Scheme (EDIS), a unified bank insurance scheme similar to the FDIC in the United States. Individual EU countries currently have their own bank insurance laws, but the EU has for years been working toward a more unified model for the bloc.

All these bank and savings institutions insurance schemes sound great on paper, but what has developed over the course of history has been more sinister. Banks, investment banks, and savings institutions inevitably get into financial trouble owing to their highly flawed business models. What then happens is governments look at these institutions and ask, "Is this company too big to fail?" If the answer is deemed to be no, these firms are often allowed to declare bankruptcy, and consumers are reimbursed up to a certain amount if this institution is insured by the FDIC or their local equivalent. If a given firm is deemed too big to fail, governments will often bail out these firms by borrowing massive amounts of newly created paper money and lend this money to the failing firm. While most consumers don't realize what has developed, they have just been taxed by their federal government in the form of higher inflation. What is most infuriating about this recurring cycle is that banks and lending institutions often get into these precarious positions with irresponsible lending and investment practices fueled by greed. The solution to this madness is to replace fractional-reserve banking with full-reserve banking and have limits on money supply growth that are tied to ongoing GDP growth. Under full-reserve bank-ing, banks do not lend from demand deposits and only lend from time deposits. There is a separation of the credit and monetary functions of the banking system. Iceland entertained the idea of ending fractional-reserve banking in the wake of the global financial crisis under a plan that would have removed the power to create new money from com-mercial banks, but this plan was never implemented. Supplementing a full-reserve banking system with a partial gold standard would provide a degree of decentralization of the monetary system, as the credibility of money would be less reliant on central banks.

In the wake of the Great Depression, famed economist Irving Fisher described the benefits of a full-reserve banking system that was supported by 235 economists from 157 universities and colleges, and later validated by a detailed working paper from the IMF in 2012:

- Not allowing for banks to create their own funds during a macroeconomic environment where there is a rise in credit, only to go on to get rid of these funds during a credit downturn. Fisher argued that this sequence of events is a primary source of business cycle fluctuations and putting such controls in place would allow for superior command of credit cycles.
- Full-reserve backing would eliminate bank runs.
- Allow the government to directly issue money at a cost of zero interest. This contrasts with the system where the government borrows money from banks and pays interest on the funds. Fisher argued that making this change would lead to a substantial reduction of government debt.
- The economy could see a pronounced curtailment of private debt levels, as the creation of money would no longer primarily be done at private banks.

Later in this book, I will elaborate more on the topics of full-reserve banking and limits on the money supply growth, but I wanted to include these details as a preface to the first detailed discussion on a banking system collapse.

Owing to the flawed incentives provided by a fractional-reserve banking system, the money supply in Iceland expanded by 10-fold in the 14-year period ending with the global financial crisis in 2008, with most of the money supply increase fueled by commercial banks. This dramatic increase in the money supply continued in the years leading up to the global financial crisis, even though Iceland was sharply increasing interest rates. Under a fractional-reserve banking model with insurance schemes and the implied assumption that the government will step in if there is a crisis, commercial banks compete primarily based on interest rates paid on deposits without much regard for the safety of investments and the overall financial institution. When customers lack the incentive to monitor the risks taken by commercial banks and the banks assume they will be bailed out by the government, banks will compete simply by offering the highest interest rates on deposits with little regard for risk. In order for the commercial banks to satisfy the higher rates paid, they take on more investment risk knowing that the government will likely step in for financial support if necessary, pummeling the average citizen with higher inflation in the process.

Adair Turner, the chairman of the UK's Financial Services Authority, provided his view of the cause of the global financial crisis: "The financial crisis of 2007/08 occurred because we failed to constrain the private financial system's creation of private credit and money." This unconstrained private credit creation happened in Iceland and around the world because, similar to the conditions that we have today, the rapid growth in the money supply was primarily funneling into the financial markets as opposed to the real economy. The government largely ignored the risks tied to the soaring money supply because consumer price inflation remained relatively mundane while asset price inflation skyrocketed. It has been a common error for central banks to underestimate the risks tied to asset price inflation. Between 1994 and 2008, the Icelandic banks expanded the money supply by a factor of 10, while nominal GDP tripled. When money supply growth dramatically outstrips GDP growth, the result is inflation (assuming the new money is spent), even if most of the inflation for some period of time only shows up in asset prices. It is stunning that to this day, central banks seem to not understand this concept.

It is critical to review why the Icelandic banks failed and what the triggers were. After all, the capital held at the banks was above international regulatory requirements. In a detailed 2017 study done by Brookings, they found that over 20 percent of the banks' combined loan portfolio at the time of failure was to six groups of related parties. This was a stunning revelation detailed after the fact when the Icelandic government went to great lengths to figure out the root causes of the issue by lifting bank secrecy laws and producing reports on their recount of what occurred. Leading up to the crisis, capital flows to Icelandic banks and the domestic economy more broadly exploded because of investors searching for yield with Iceland offering higher interest rates than other countries. This was occurring at a time when Iceland was undergoing a four-year hydroelectric dam and aluminum smelter project that equated to roughly 50 percent of Iceland's GDP, which likely gave the illusion of a booming and healthy economy. Much like was well documented in the U.S. market leading up to the global financial crisis, Icelandic banks were increasingly turning to exotic financing instruments such as collateralized debt obligations (CDOs) that resulted in shifting loan exposure off the bank balance sheet. The banks would essentially take various loans and package them together into one product without having much of an idea about the creditworthiness of the borrower and then seek to offload the packaged loans. This led to the overall weakening of credit standards much like what we saw in the United States leading up to the crisis. Another issue was the banks' increasing reliance on foreign deposits that were estimated to be 15 percent of the total balance sheets at the time of failure. Again, international investors were drawn to the generous yields being offered, and rating agencies had bought into this fictitious world where risks were minimal. The problem was that the banks had become reliant on this international funding source that was highly sensitive to interest rate changes. Bank deposit collections slowed in the latter half of 2007, so the banks borrowed from the European Central Bank and the Central Bank of Iceland. These authorities relied on rating agencies to determine the borrowing eligibility, and this was a problem, because rating agencies were treating rating products such as CDOs as being investment grade, even though the underlying loan portfolio could have contained toxic assets.

According to the book, *Iceland's Secret: The Untold Story of the World's Biggest Con*, for years leading up to the crash, the major Icelandic banks manipulated their share prices by purchasing large blocks of their own stock and dumping the shares into their own client's accounts and hiding them in offshore shell companies. For example, in August of 2008, it was estimated that Kaupthing purchased a staggering 67 percent of its own trading volume while not disclosing that the bank was effectively making the market in their own shares. Several Icelandic banking executives ultimately went to prison, but the sentences were more for public display, with the sentences being short and, in many cases, nonexistent.

One of the triggers for the ultimate demise of the Icelandic banking system was when international banks and investment companies started to request margin calls to businesses in Iceland when global liquidity was drying up. Naturally, these Icelandic businesses then went to the domestic banks to refinance their loans. The Icelandic banks ultimately decided to pile on yet more leverage to satisfy these claims, but this was just staving off the banking system collapse a bit longer as opposed to providing any solution for the underlying problems that had been bubbling for years. As Terry Smith said in his 2020 Fundsmith annual letter to shareholders in reference to a famous quote by Warren Buffett, this was, "yet another illustration of the rule that it is only when the tide goes out that you find out who has been swimming naked." This is another example of why banks are such horrible businesses. A liquidity crisis can emanate somewhere else around the world and be the trigger for a bank or banking system collapse in a completely separate country. The Icelandic banks obviously were a large part of the problem with lending to a concentrated group of parties, piling on insane debt levels, increasingly turning to more exotic debt instruments and lowering overall credit standards, and becoming overly reliant on international funding, but the reality is that the ultimate trigger for the collapse was a liquidity issue that didn't even start in the country. This should be terrifying but certainly not surprising for anyone who has taken a few moments to study the history of financial crises.

Iceland is the smallest economy in the world to have its own floating currency, and the króna has a history of instability. In addition to other problems a volatile currency can have on an economy, this piece of information was also relevant in the demise of the Icelandic banking system. As previously stated, leading up to the crisis, the Icelandic banking system had become reliant on international funding. International funding is done in currencies that are not the domestic currency. You would think that a small country with a history of currency instability would have strict regulations for foreign currency reserves, but this was not the case leading up to the global financial crisis. In the study done by Brookings, it is estimated that the foreign deposits at the time were as much as eight times the currency reserves set aside by the Central Bank of Iceland. In short, the banks did not have enough international currency to return to international individuals and businesses that were now making margin calls, and the Central Bank of Iceland barely had any international currency in reserve, either. Once the banks failed, this led to a devaluation of the Icelandic króna. The currency devaluation produced a rise in monetary inflation that forced an increase in interest rates and in turn triggered mass mortgage defaults. The capital controls put in place to stem the run on the króna were removed only in 2017. As an international investor, if you have seen that a country is willing to lock your money up for close to a decade, I am not sure how you ever achieve any level of confidence that you will be able to retrieve your money. In that sense, the weak domestic currency should become somewhat of a self-fulfilling prophecy, even though the capital controls were put in place to stabilize the currency.

In summary, as it relates to banks under fractional-reserve banking, these are just a few of the things that can go wrong with the business. An individual bank itself can be doing everything right, which was not the case in Iceland leading up to the financial crisis but can be brought down by a liquidity crisis brewing across the world, an issue with the domestic currency, and many other developments, of which we probably still understand only a fraction today. Anyone who can say with certainty as to what the ultimate impacts will be of the money printing, piling on of debt at the government and corporate levels, paired with global economic weakness in response to the COVID-19 crisis, is lying to him/herself.

Macroeconomic Impact

We studied several macroeconomic effects of the banking system in the previous section, but I wanted to talk about the alleged miraculous recovery that Iceland experienced in the years following the global financial crisis. Iceland returned to growth within just two years and was one of the biggest success stories in terms of European economic growth in the years following the financial crisis. In addition to the previously discussed government actions and policies, taxes were increased, spending was reduced in areas such as education and health, public sector payments were reduced, and debt relief and austerity measures were applied to both the public and private sectors. It may be true that these government policies contributed to some degree to the economic recovery of Iceland in the years following the crisis, but I would attribute the overwhelming amount of the recovery to a single factor: the tourism boom. Tourism alone was estimated to have accounted for 40 to 50 percent of the economic recovery of Iceland from 2010 to 2016. In 2019, prior to the COVID-19 crisis, it was reported that tourism accounted for 42 percent of Iceland's economy, which was an increase from 27 percent in 2013. As of 2018, Iceland was receiving over 2.3 million visitors per year compared to approximately 350,000 people living in Iceland. To put this into perspective, Iceland received about 490,000 visitors in 2010 when tourism growth really started to take off. This torrid growth in the tourism sector equated to a near five-fold increase in international visitors over just an eight-year period. This overnight explosion in international tourism can be attributed to the weak currency, low oil prices, and cheap international flights. Put simply, it was cheap to travel to Iceland. When I purchased my airfare ticket to Iceland in 2015, the cost was $500. I, too, had been attracted to the competitive rates being offered by domestic discount airlines such as WOW Air (which later went bankrupt in 2019).

As I had warned in *The Wandering Investor*, the Iceland economic model that fueled growth for years following the financial crisis was not sustainable, which became apparent in the wake of the COVID-19 crisis. The economy has been far too reliant on one sector, and this sector happens to be one that is not a utility, either. What I mean by this is that people do not have to travel like they need to eat, drink, or use the Internet. During times of economic distress, consumers will cut back on discretionary travel spend. It is far more favorable for a domestic economy to be built upon an industry that has relatively stable and growing demand across the business cycle. Additionally, it has been reported that high levels of tourism in recent years have impacted the environment to some extent, and this could affect future travel demand, because Iceland's tourism demand is primarily due to the natural beauty offered by the country. In future years, Iceland will have to delicately balance tourism growth with preserving the environment while diversifying the overall economy.

I remain convinced that Iceland having a floating currency does not make any sense. A country with a little over 360,000 people with a total GDP of nearly $25 billion (as of 2019) that relies on tourism, fishing, and aluminum smelting should not have a floating currency. The reality is that the currency crash that occurred during the global financial crisis would have been much worse if it weren't for the capital controls put in place that remained for nearly a decade. There will always be potential for extreme currency volatility and financial devastation with a country profile such as what we have with Iceland. In 2017, the Icelandic finance minister said that the country was considering pegging the domestic currency to another currency such as the euro. This never happened, and I suppose they are waiting for a worse financial crisis to occur to make the move.

I don't believe that Iceland learned much from their devastating experience during the global financial crisis. I have had this view for years, and it has been controversial, with editorials being published, such as the 2015 article in *The Washington Post* titled, "The Miraculous Story of Iceland," that ran counter to my personal diagnosis. Iceland has maintained a floating currency and has failed to diversify the economy in any material way. I think a good comparison for Iceland following the financial crisis would be an economy such as Brazil that rode the oil boom from 2000 to 2012, when it was one of the fastest growing major economies in the world. Brazil's economy has never recovered since oil prices declined. The underlying economic issues in Brazil were covered up for a period of time owing to high oil prices. The same can be said for Iceland as it relates to tourism. The Icelandic banks are reportedly much better prepared for a crisis scenario than they were leading up to the global financial crisis, but Iceland is likely to have additional problems associated with the slowdown in the tourism sector. Aside from dramatically curtailing overall GDP growth and rising unemployment, the cooling tourism sector is making it increasingly likely that there could have been dramatic overbuilding in the tourism infrastructure market that has the potential for a significant rise in bad loans and issues for the overall Icelandic housing market. A 2020 report by Fitch estimated that the hotel capacity in the capital was estimated to increase by 25 percent over a three-year period when it was unclear as to how demand would rebound from the COVID-19 crisis.

Fortunately for Iceland, despite the lack of ability to diversify the overall economy, they have maintained a strong environment for business. There has historically been a high correlation between the long-term success of a given economy and how friendly the country is in terms of business protections. Iceland ranked 13th globally in the 2022 Index of Economic Freedom. Despite the positive marks, as it relates to upholding the rule of law and providing for efficient regulations, I believe Iceland will eternally be at risk of another major crisis with a small and undiversified economy that has a floating currency. Unlike during the last crisis, Iceland likely won't have one exploding industry to bail them out.

CHAPTER 3

Indonesia

Asian Financial Crisis (1997–1998)

Background and Market Impact

Our journey back through history and around the world brings us to Southeast Asia in the 1990s. During the period of the late 1980s and early 1990s, several Southeast Asian economies such as Indonesia, Thailand, Singapore, Malaysia, and South Korea were on fire and racking up annual GDP gains in the range of 8 to 12 percent. Despite the strong growth, there were issues brewing underneath the surface. Much like what we saw with China in the 2000s, these hot Southeast Asian economies were primarily being supported by export growth and areas such as foreign investment (although some studies argue that other factors such as improved school systems contributed to the outsized growth rates). These economies had exchange rates tied to the U.S. dollar (with the exchange rate pegs, trading bands, and managed float systems varying in degrees of commitment) and were using high interest rates that brought a flood of investments into the countries. As is almost always the case leading up to financial crises, there was a credit boom that was attributable to the influx of foreign investment. The flood of money led to rising valuations in real estate and equities. These countries were financing a portion of their operations with short-term debt that was issued in international currencies. Financing operations with short-term loans issued in foreign currencies is fine if you assume a stable currency and have proper foreign currency reserves, but it can lead to disaster if these are false assumptions.

In the mid-1990s, the United States began to raise interest rates to combat inflation. This had a dual impact for the Southeast Asian economies of making their exports less attractive and causing less foreign investment, as money was drawn to the U.S. market. This ultimately led to a sharp depreciation in the currencies of Southeast Asian economies such as Indonesia, Thailand, Singapore, Malaysia, and South Korea.

As a quick summary, according to *Federal Reserve History:*

> On July 2, 1997, Thailand devalued its currency relative to the U.S. dollar. This development, which followed months of speculative pressures that had substantially depleted Thailand's official foreign exchange reserves, marked the beginning of a deep financial crisis across much of East Asia. In subsequent months, Thailand's currency, equity, and property markets weakened further as its difficulties evolved into a twin balance-of-payments and banking crisis. Malaysia, the Philippines, and Indonesia also allowed their currencies to weaken substantially in the face of market pressures, with Indonesia gradually falling into a multifaceted financial and political crisis.

Capital that had been pouring into the Southeast Asian economies quickly fled, and this led to sharp currency devaluations and issues in the banking sector. The Thailand stock market declined by 80 percent, with Indonesia's equities plunging by 60 percent. Given the lack of foreign exchange reserves, Indonesia abandoned their managed float system (where central banks attempt to influence their countries' exchange rates by buying and selling currencies to maintain a certain range) and allowed the rupiah to float freely. The rupiah declined by 75 percent, real per capita GDP dropped by 13 percent, and prices for basic food staples skyrocketed by as much as 80 percent, along with the unleashed inflation.

How Businesses Were Affected

We will once again start by looking at the financial sector, because this is where we can usually learn the most from crises. In the years leading up to the Asian financial crisis, Indonesia had reduced regulations in the financial sector. The Indonesian banking sector had traditionally been dominated by state-run banks, but policy changes in the 1980s paved the way for the rise of private commercial banks. Between 1983 and 1984,

Indonesia introduced its first financial deregulation policies. This initial financial deregulation allowed for commercial banks to set their own interest rates along with the removal of restrictions on commercial bank loans. The result was a rise in interest rates and a large increase in commercial bank loans and deposits. The second round of financial deregulation in Indonesia occurred in 1988. These policies encouraged new banks to start by providing for a reduction in commercial bank minimum paid capital and legalizing foreign joint ventures with local banks. The financial deregulation in Indonesia was happening at a time when the local and regional economies were booming, as is usually the case.

A 1999 study conducted by the University of Pennsylvania concluded that, leading up to the Asian financial crisis, the Indonesian banking sector had rapid credit growth, a large amount of poorly capitalized private banks, intense competition for customers, high exposure to related and affiliate parties, and an overall lack of oversight and guardrails. There were clues leading up to the crisis that the banks needed more oversight and higher capital requirements. As an example, Bank Summa, which was a top-10 bank in Indonesia, collapsed in 1992, and upon liquidation, it was revealed that a staggering 70 percent of the total loan portfolio was nonperforming loans, and that many of the bad loans had been made to affiliate companies, similar to what we saw happen in Iceland. This was just one of the more high-profile examples of issues in the Indonesian financial sector leading up to the Asian financial crisis. The reality was that the banks were undercapitalized, and the balance sheets had large exposures to loans of poor quality. These issues were covered up when the economy was flourishing, but the Indonesian financial system was not prepared to weather a financial shock.

Thinking high level about comparisons between Iceland during the global financial crisis and Indonesia during the Asian financial crisis, we can arrive at these conclusions: both were characterized by a banking system with high debt levels with poor regulation and loose oversight, both had high loan exposure to affiliate parties, both had rapid credit growth leading up to the crises, both had a currency-mismatch problem where they were borrowing in international currency and lending in domestic currency without proper reserving, and both had hot economies leading up to the financial crises that masked the underlying issues and led to rising values in the equity and real estate markets. The rapid credit growth and rising equity and real estate valuations are near-universal characteristics of all markets leading up to financial crises. One of the major differences between Iceland and Indonesia was that Iceland had a floating currency, and Indonesia had a managed float system with a trading band that was U.S. dollar-denominated (although the Indonesia currency system was opaque and didn't clearly spell out the exchange rate band links to foreign currencies). Both ended up resulting in currency crashes.

I would argue that the issue with the Asian currencies during the Asian financial crisis had to do with the lack of foreign currency reserving as opposed to the overall strategy of managing their currencies relative to foreign currencies. The Asian countries did not have proper reserves on hand to defend the currency linkages, which resulted in the currency crashes. The most sensible strategy a country can employ to defend their currency peg, band, or managed float system is for the central bank to purchase more of the domestic currency during a time where there is potential for a crisis. The ability of a central bank to buy their own domestic currency depends on the size of liquid foreign currency reserves along with the size of the current and capital account surplus or deficit. In order for a central bank to purchase their own domestic currency, they must have foreign currency to sell in order to fund these purchases. If Indonesia had proper foreign currency reserves on hand leading up to the crisis, it could have mitigated the effects by quickly moving to stabilize the rupiah by selling foreign currency and buying the Indonesian rupiah on a large scale to provide for temporary stabilization. I personally don't agree with those who argue against currency bands, pegs, and managed float systems for emerging countries with volatile economies. As support for this line of thinking, examine what Iceland had to do during the global financial crisis to support the króna. Capital controls were implemented for nearly a decade to provide support for the currency. Having seen that, no sensible international investor would ever place a dollar of investment in the country again, knowing that they may not ever be able to take the money out. To be clear, capital controls are also an option for countries such as Indonesia that have used currency pegs, bands, and managed float systems, but I believe it is easier to maintain domestic currency stability if a country with a volatile economy maintains a peg or band to a relatively stable basket of currencies and keeps proper foreign currency reserves. What if COVID-19 had only existed in Iceland and tourism, which the economy heavily relies on, was banned for years? Assuming that only Iceland was impacted and larger and more stable economies such as the United States were doing just fine, the Icelandic currency would have an epic crash, rivaling the worst we have seen in history. This extreme situation could be mitigated with an effective currency peg or band assuming sensible policies on foreign exchange reserves and quick reaction by the central bank to sell international currencies in favor of the domestic currency on a massive scale.

One of the reasons the Indonesian banking sector was hit so hard during the Asian financial crisis, aside from the reasons already stated, was that an estimated 25 percent of the bank loans in 1997 were going to the real estate sector. Like many other periods in history, the combination of too much money chasing too few quality opportunities, high real estate prices bringing additional real estate investment, and weak financial regulation ultimately led to the demise of the domestic banking sector. What was happening in the Indonesian real estate sector leading up to the crisis could have even been worse than what we experienced in markets like the United States leading up to the global financial crisis. Some estimates say that 95 percent of Indonesian real estate development during the run-up to the Asian financial crisis was being financed by loans from the banking sector. It doesn't take an economic expert to see how this ended badly. When real estate prices declined, and the domestic currency and interest rates increased, there were mass loan defaults in the property sector that caused severe stress in the Indonesian banking system. Making this financial implosion worse was the fact that domestic banks had financed long-term loans to property developers with short-term international financing denominated in foreign currency. These loans had both the currency and timing mismatch issues that were previously touched upon. Many of these international loans were unhedged in nature, so when the Indonesian rupiah collapsed, the amount to be repaid became much more expensive for the domestic Indonesian banks, and many international funding sources stopped making new loans to the now distressed Indonesian banking sector. Similar to what we studied in the case of

Iceland, foreign exchange reserves were not adequate to weather this crisis scenario. In June of 1997, it was estimated that Indonesia's short-term debt relative to foreign exchange reserves stood at 180 percent, which was only behind Korea in terms of exposure. Just as international funding for the Indonesian banking sector was drying up, there was limited liquidity domestically. The plunging rupiah and significant increase in interest rates led to a surge in loan defaults in many other areas of the economy. Terrified Indonesians created a run on the banks by withdrawing money from the local banks, with some individuals reallocating funds to international banks and others to perceived safer state-controlled domestic banks. By late 1997, a large portion of the Indonesian banking sector was considered insolvent.

Outside of the banking sector, one of the most impacted industries was construction. Almost overnight, this went from a burgeoning industry with rapid job gains to one with massive layoffs. Manufacturing was another hard-hit industry. Given the steep decline in the Indonesian rupiah, exports were now more expensive and not as competitive. Demand for manufacturing exports disappeared, resulting in huge layoffs and a large decline in production activity. One of the other business impacts that occurred as a result of this crisis was the amendment to the Bankruptcy Act in 1998 to a law that was created in 1905 and had remained largely unchanged for nearly a century. Prior to amendments to the bankruptcy legislation, there were virtually zero domestic bankruptcy court cases likely owing to a lack of confidence that the court system would successfully resolve the issue. The bankruptcy law amendments sought to speed up bankruptcy court proceedings along with providing for remedies such as the creation of a commercial court to improve the credibility of potential bankruptcy court proceedings.

Macroeconomic Impact

Let us look at the role of the IMF in the wake of the Asian financial crisis in Indonesia. In November of 1997, Indonesia entered into a three-year agreement with the IMF for $10 billion. The IMF deal would ultimately swell to over $40 billion. The IMF rescue packages had attached contingencies such as the bankruptcy law amendments discussed earlier. Additionally, the Indonesian government agreed to close insolvent banks,

15 major government-subsidized projects were halted, and reforms were put in place to eliminate monopolies, among other measures.

When thinking about IMF support during times of severe crises, I always wonder who is going to bail out the IMF. In the wake of the global COVID-19 crisis, the IMF reported that half of the world's countries had requested a bailout. To provide a quick review, the IMF acquires its budget from member states that pay subscriptions with the amounts paid in accordance with the size of the economy. The amount a country pays to the IMF determines the voting rights it has along with the eligible financing it can receive from the IMF. The IMF can borrow money under separate agreements with the participating countries. As discussed in the chapter on the United States related to COVID-19, I think that, after COVID-19, even countries such as the United States are now caught in an unsustainable debt spiral without strong economic and population growth to provide for a bailout scenario like in the past. With the world facing significant financial challenges, it is right to question how international organizations such as the IMF will be financed in the future. It is not a long-term solution to simply print more money to finance these organizations, because printing more money will ultimately lead to the underlying fiat currencies becoming worthless if done with enough length and severity.

To recover from the Asian financial crisis, Indonesia implemented reforms in the banking sector that included, along with amendments to the bankruptcy law previously discussed, other measures: expanded oversight and bank restructuring efforts, which increased capitalization requirements. The food crisis that was exacerbated by soaring inflation was assuaged with emergency imports and temporary subsidies. Interest rates were increased, which dampened inflation and facilitated recovery in foreign reserves.

When I visited Indonesia in late 2019, it was readily apparent that the country had a long way to go in terms of Copyright laws. As stated in my book, *The Wandering Investor*:

If you spend time in Indonesia, you likely will notice brands and stores that are infringing on the patents of global brands. For example, I saw a "Popeye" fast food chain that was clearly ripping off the Popeyes name and brand. We were told of stories about various trademark pirates that have been responsible for stealing the Polo Ralph Lauren intellectual property and brand in Indonesia (this was confirmed by my independent research). Driving around the country and conducting even the most basic Internet searches, you will find that Indonesia has had long-running problems in regard to the regulation and enforcement of Copyright laws.

This discussion is relevant here because it tells you that, even though regulatory reforms put in place in the aftermath of the Asian financial crisis were improvements, Indonesia still has a long way to go in terms of catching up to the Western world. It would be difficult for me to trust many of these alleged business environment improvements if, 20 years after the Asian financial crisis, the government is completely unwilling to uphold basic business protections such as Copyright laws.

In 2018, the Indonesian rupiah fell to its lowest levels since the Asian financial crisis, and the currency has remained volatile over the years. Unlike leading up to the crisis, the rupiah is not managed in a band against other currencies but floated against a basket of currencies of Indonesia's major trading partners. A 2018 report on Indonesia's currency stated, "The high foreign ownership on bonds coupled with Indonesian corporates' increased USD debt are also rendering (the Indonesian rupiah) prone to more weakness." At that time, in 2018, it was estimated that 41 percent of the debt was denominated in foreign currencies. The high foreign ownership of domestic debt is a problem, because if the domestic currency depreciates, it makes it more expensive to pay off the debts denominated in foreign currency, which has been a large figure for Indonesia. Additionally, if all the foreign-denominated currency funding were to leave, it would substantially hit Indonesia's foreign exchange reserves. In recent years, the Indonesian government has tried to diversify the economy away from areas such as oil and gas toward sectors such as manufacturing and tourism. To the extent that the Indonesian economy continues to be more diversified and stable across the business cycle, the domestic currency will naturally become less volatile. I believe that pegging the rupiah or responsibly managing the currency relative to a basket of currencies while maintaining conservative levels of foreign exchange reserves and reducing the reliance on foreign money for the debt markets would go a long way toward reducing the ongoing currency volatility. A problem that emerging currencies have is that they just aren't very liquid. As an example, I investigated acquiring Colombian pesos and found out that the cost of acquisition was an 8 percent spread on each end of the trade. This is incredibly expensive and standard across emerging currencies. I think that many emerging currencies have been artificially deflated owing to a massive disadvantage in the form of illiquidity. To the extent that services such as WhatsApp follow through on their goals of reducing cross-border currency transactions to zero over time, this should provide for more stability for emerging currencies.

Despite some negative commentary, Indonesia has come a long way since the Asian financial crisis. According to 2020 data produced by the World Bank, the country has reduced the poverty rate by more than half since 1999. The GDP per capita has risen dramatically, soaring from $459 in 1998 to $4,151 in 2019. Even though Indonesia significantly lags in terms of business normalization conditions in comparison to much of the Western world, the country has been trending in the right direction in recent years in rankings such as the Index of Economic Freedom. Indonesia has a similar story to India but is earlier on in terms of the growth trajectory: the country has a large and growing youthful population that is very early on in terms of rising consumption. As I wrote in *The Wandering Investor*:

> The lingering question will be if Indonesia can overcome corruption, insufficient infrastructure, poor education and health care systems, and a less favorable regulatory environment compared to more developed countries to fully take advantage of enormous consumer growth opportunities? Time will tell.

Indonesia needs to do a lot more to shore up their ongoing issues related to currency volatility. Indonesia must also reduce its reliance on foreign debt, as this becomes a significantly higher risk when factoring in the volatile domestic currency. The country must continue to push to diversify the economy, as the historically undiversified nature of the local economy has exacerbated the ongoing currency issues and made crisis scenarios more likely. Indonesia's historical reliance on selling products and services abroad has been a major contributor to the issues they have constantly faced in terms of a reliance on international funding and currency gyrations. To reduce risk, Indonesia must further turn its attention inward and focus on cultivating the country's biggest asset that is its large and youthful population. As I have written about at length before, this all starts with education, and Indonesia needs to improve its education system and provide better opportunities and incentives to start and maintain higher value chain businesses that would encourage additional domestic consumption.

CHAPTER 4

Zimbabwe

Hyperinflation (2007–2009)

Background and Market Impact

I wanted to cover the hyperinflation crisis in Zimbabwe not only because it is a good case study for any business class, but also because it is fundamentally different than many other crises that began with a banking crisis. While still a contributing factor, the hyperinflation situation in Zimbabwe did not begin with a banking crisis. This bout of hyperinflation is ranked as the second most severe period of hyperinflation in modern history behind Hungary in the 1940s.

I need to begin this discussion with defining hyperinflation: a period of rapidly rising prices for goods and services when price increases usually measure over 50 percent per month. To quote the book *When Money Destroys Nations: How Hyperinflation Ruined Zimbabwe, How Ordinary People Survived, and Warnings for Nations that Print Money* in reference to hyperinflation, "it is the dramatic process of an established currency losing its usefulness as money." Hyperinflation usually occurs as a result of some combination of war, economic turmoil, high national debt levels, excessive money printing, political instability, and a loss of confidence in the monetary system. While relatively rare in history, these extreme cases of hyperinflation have often resulted in efforts such as the abandonment of a currency altogether or adjustments such as new currency pegs being enacted. Some of the most famous hyperinflation cases in history include Hungary in the 1940s, Yugoslavia in the 1990s, Germany in the 1920s, and Greece in the 1940s.

I have torn into the Zimbabwean government in the past because this crisis was mostly self-inflicted and induced by disastrous government policy. As I write this chapter in 2021, Zimbabwe has never really recovered from the hyperinflation crisis in the 2000s. It is hard to believe now, but Zimbabwe was once known by locals as the *breadbasket* of Africa because it provided food for the continent. Some argue that depicting Zimbabwe as the breadbasket of the continent is an overstatement, but at the least, Zimbabwe used to be self-sufficient when it came to food. Those arguing against the breadbasket claims will point to data such as the fact that Zimbabwe never surpassed a 10 percent market share in Africa in terms of maize and wheat production between 1961 and 2013. Zimbabwe may never have been the true breadbasket as has often been depicted, but the country was still a net exporter of maize and food self-sufficient prior to the infamous land reforms. In the early 2000s, Robert Mugabe (who was president of Zimbabwe at the time) launched land reforms that ultimately resulted in seizing White-owned farms and transferring this property to local Black individuals. One of the main issues with this policy was that many of the Black individuals that inherited the property did not have any experience with farming. Most of the country's over 4,000 White farmers were forced from their land and fled to surrounding countries. To be clear, not all of Zimbabwe's agricultural decline was policy-related. The country suffered from two severe droughts in 1992 and 1995 that impacted domestic production and the local economy overall. Having said that, these droughts in the 1990s do not explain the plunging domestic agricultural production in the 2000s. Between 2000 and 2007, domestic commercial farming production plummeted 50 percent. Only in 2020 did Zimbabwe try and offer to return land and compensate individuals who were impacted by these disastrous policies. The economic carnage has long persisted as a result. Not only has the local agricultural sector never recovered, but other segments such as real estate and foreign investment overall have suffered lasting impacts. Would a sensible investor buy a piece of property in Zimbabwe knowing that in the past, the government has confiscated property on a large scale without providing compensation? I would think not. As I have written in *The Wandering Investor:*

> Estimates have the country pegged at $600 to $700 a year per capita GDP. To get a sense of how poor this is, England would have been in a better economic state at the start of the Industrial Revolution in the late 1700s.

What developed in Zimbabwe as a result of these land reforms had a similar economic impact as the Natives Land Act of 1913 in South Africa. With the Natives Land Act, 7 percent of arable land was allocated to Africans, and the remainder was allocated to the White population. Over 80 percent of the land went to the White population who made up less than 20 percent of the total population. Similar to what happened later on in Zimbabwe, this forced land distribution removed economic incentives and had disastrous long-term consequences for the economy and standard of living.

Thinking high level, the seeds of Zimbabwe's hyperinflation were planted when the government confiscated the farmland, which set off a chain of negative events. Foreign investment dried up, lending to farmers plunged owing to the lack of enforcement of land ownership (along with the fact that most of the farmers who received the confiscated land did not have much agricultural experience), which resulted in a long-term decline in domestic agricultural production, and real estate values were negatively impacted by the land reforms. In short, the land reforms had the dual impact of reducing country wealth due to declining value in agriculture and real estate, which had a dramatic effect on the overall GDP and average household wealth. When thinking about the recipes for hyperinflation, the land reforms set in motion ingredients like economic turmoil and political instability. The land reforms also raised prices for food, as agricultural production declined. We will now discuss some of the other lethal ingredients of this deadly cocktail.

As is almost always the case with periods of elevated inflation, the Zimbabwean government was increasing the national debt. They financed these debt issuances with money printing, which caused the domestic currency to become less valuable. In 1997, the Zimbabwean government financed direct payments and pension payments to war veterans who equated to approximately 3 percent of the total GDP. The budget deficit in 1997 soared 55 percent from 1996, and the World Bank withdrew an outstanding credit line to Zimbabwe. At least part of these payments to war veterans were supposed to be covered by tax increases in 1998, but mass protests caused the government to renege on this plan.

In 1998, the Zimbabwean government sent troops into the Democratic Republic of Congo to prop up their leader who was under assault from rebels backed by Rwanda and Uganda. The official figures are believed to have greatly understated the total cost of this effort, but the monthly war costs in 1998 were reported to have equated to 0.4 percent of the total GDP, and this was before additional troops were deployed in 1999. This costly act of war was not done just out of the goodness of Zimbabwe's heart but was rather meant to enrich Zimbabwe's politicians with a deal for mineral concessions in exchange for the military support. This is just one example in a very long list of government corruption occurrences in Zimbabwe's history. To give you an idea as to how corrupt the Zimbabwean government has been, in January of 2000, there was a lottery put on by a partially owned state bank. President Robert Mugabe was the winner of the top cash prize, $100,000 in local currency (documented in the book *Why Nations Fail: The Origins of Power, Prosperity, and Poverty*). The fact that he was even eligible to win this prize tells you everything about the government's moral compass and priorities.

While still a decade prior to the hyperinflation, most consider *Black Friday* to be the moment when Zimbabwe's economy collapsed. On November 14, 1997, the Zimbabwean dollar lost nearly 72 percent of its value against the U.S. dollar. The domestic stock market plunged 46 percent in sympathy with the stunning collapse of the local currency. The series of events detailed above are believed to have contributed to the currency collapse. Additionally, there were rumors at the time that Zimbabwe did not have enough foreign exchange holdings to cover a few months of imports. As deficits rose, agricultural production declined, money printing increased, the currency collapsed, and inflation increased. The rise in inflation further hurt agricultural production and domestic consumption because it made importing farming equipment more expensive and encouraged more exporting of agricultural products because of currency devaluation, causing further food shortages.

At the time of the collapse of the Zimbabwean dollar in 1997, the domestic currency was operating under a managed float system comparable to what we studied in the chapter on Indonesia. The Zimbabwean government went on to peg the local currency to the U.S. dollar in 1999, and the currency ended up disintegrating despite the peg. The combination of a currency peg or managed float system, prudent fiscal management, confidence in the local government, and adequate foreign exchange reserves, along with the ability and willingness to shore up the local currency in the event of a major destabilizing event and increasing economic diversification, will dramatically mitigate the chance of an unstable domestic currency. The best way for a country to have a high probability of maintaining a sound currency is to have the fiscal and economic qualities listed previously while supplementing this with a currency peg or managed float system and conservative foreign exchange reserves. I believe it is best if a country like Zimbabwe manages its currency to a diversified basket of assets such as the U.S. dollar, the euro, the Japanese yen, the Chinese renminbi, the British pound, the Australian dollar, and gold. Owing to the soaring debt levels and ongoing weak economic growth, I have become increasingly worried about the health even of currencies such as the U.S. dollar that have long been considered safe havens. I would attribute the destabilization of the Zimbabwean dollar as being just as much responsible for the economic catastrophe in Zimbabwe as other causes such as the land reforms and the war in the Democratic Republic of Congo.

In the 2000s, as Zimbabwe's economy slumped, basic consumer staples were in short supply, inflation increased, confidence in the local government eroded, and people started leaving Zimbabwe in large numbers. In 2005, approximately 6 percent of the population is estimated to have left the country. The emigration further exacerbated the food and consumer staple supply issue and led to higher inflation. The disaster flywheel was in full swing, as the emigration out of Zimbabwe reduced the country's taxable base, and this resulted in the printing of more money and further devaluation of the domestic currency. The Zimbabwean government again made the situation worse when they decided to implement price controls on goods sold with the goal of taming the soaring inflation. Anyone who has spent time studying economics will know how this turned out. Production of consumer staples was further reduced given the decline in incentive to produce the goods. Inflation soared to new highs as a result.

In 2008, inflation in Zimbabwe was estimated to have been 79.6 billion percent month-over-month! This is a daily inflation rate of around 98 percent. In other words, prices would roughly double every day. Imagine going to the supermarket and buying a bag of tomatoes for $3 at the beginning of the week and then returning a week later to find that the price has increased to $192. In 2009, Zimbabwe stopped printing its own currency and other currencies were used. In 2015, the Zimbabwean central bank announced that Zimbabwean dollars would be exchanged for U.S. dollars. The dollarization process that was started in 2009 was taken further with the local currency being scrapped altogether in 2015.

When hyperinflation roars to the degree that it did in Zimbabwe during this period, it is extremely confusing to figure out how much products cost in terms of real purchasing power. Most calculators don't even possess the ability to include enough zeros to figure out the cost of consumer staples. When hyperinflation gets this out of control, governments typically respond by removing zeros from the currency, which only further compounds the confusion about the real cost of consumer staples. As we have recently seen in Turkey, related to their high rates of inflation, the Zimbabwean government underreported inflation in an attempt to make people believe that inflation is lower than it really is, with the goal of lowering future inflation expectations. This is all part of the classic hyperinflation response playbook. Unfortunately, for Zimbabwe and its citizens, most of the government efforts proved futile, and the country has never really recovered from this period of hyperinflation.

How Businesses Were Affected

As is the case with pretty much every financial crisis situation in modern history, the banking sector played a role in the demise of Zimbabwe. The reason that banks almost always play a large role in these stories is that businesses rely on lending to produce goods and services. In modern history, banks have mainly served the role as being the primary lender to businesses, and more recently, we have seen micro-lenders and financial technology companies rising in importance. Later in this book, we are going to look at another case study in ancient history to see what happened when banks were more primitive.

As we have learned in this chapter, the seeds for the hyperinflation in Zimbabwe in the 2000s were planted by a series of events that began in the 1990s. In the 1990s, Zimbabwe initiated financial liberalization reforms, and banks such as United Merchant Bank of Zimbabwe Ltd.

were granted operating licenses. This bank was declared insolvent after it was revealed that it sold promissory notes to other banks and deposited the proceeds in an offshore bank account that happened to be owned by the head of the bank. United Merchant Bank of Zimbabwe Ltd. was intertwined with the entire Zimbabwean banking system, so the government had to step in to bail out other banks to prevent a total system collapse. This was all happening in the late 1990s when inflation was ramping up and the central bank was raising interest rates in an attempt to rein in inflation.

There was a second wave of banking failures in the 2000s that followed the chaos described above in the late 1990s. In the 2003 to 2004 period, it is estimated that at least 12 domestic banking institutions were either placed under curatorship or liquidated. These failures were in addition to asset management businesses that failed. I think that most would consider this to essentially be a total financial system collapse.

One of the main causes of the widespread banking failures in Zimbabwe was the rampant corruption. Another example of corruption in the Zimbabwean banking sector happening during that time was at Royal Bank. Executives at Royal Bank were said to have defrauded the bank of billions of Zimbabwean dollars. They allegedly awarded contracts for goods and services in which they had an interest. This type of corruption was going on throughout the financial sector and government.

By 2004, annual inflation had soared to 600 percent. The Reserve Bank of Zimbabwe (the central bank) responded by aggressively raising interest rates to combat the runaway inflation. One of the major problems with hyperinflation scenarios is that people often respond by hoarding durable goods. For example, in a country like Zimbabwe seeing hyperinflation, you would see locals hoarding farming equipment. People stop depositing money into banks and financial institutions because the currency has become worth substantially less or is worthless altogether. Banks dramatically curtail lending or stop lending money because they can't be sure that the interest incurred will compensate for the rise in inflation. At this point, a barter or black-market economy emerges. This is exactly what we saw happen in Zimbabwe between 2007 and 2009, as Zimbabwe went back to an economy where bartering and foreign currencies were used. Citizens spend the paper money where it is accepted as quickly as possible, with the expectation that the money is going to be worth less in the future than today. Later, I will review the history of banking and currencies along with why they are critical to the success of a given economy.

In the 2007 to 2009 period, hyperinflation took off, money velocity stalled, banks failed, the domestic currency became worthless, and food shortages were rampant. When you have a scenario like this, every business and individual is negatively impacted. According to the book *When Money Destroys Nations: How Hyperinflation Ruined Zimbabwe, How Ordinary People Survived, and Warnings for Nations that Print Money*, after the domestic currency became worthless and Zimbabwe attempted dollarization, some economists estimate that between 75 and 90 percent of the local population was unemployed. Zimbabwe had to import 60,000 tons of wheat in an attempt to ease the bread shortage but still fell short of their annual requirements.

Another industry that was particularly impacted during the Zimbabwe hyperinflation saga between 2007 and 2009 was the mining sector. Just as economic chaos was raining down everywhere, former President Robert Mugabe thought it was a good idea to institute a new law stating that foreign-owned local mines must present an offer for the companies to be 51 percent Zimbabwean Black-owned. Even though there was already little chance that any rational foreign investor would place a dollar of investment in a Zimbabwean mine at this point, this 2008 declaration sent those chances to essentially zero. By 2021, the Zimbabwean government had allegedly removed the mining restrictions, and foreign investors could fully own Zimbabwean mines. Even if that were the case, I am not sure how a foreign company could ever have confidence that the Zimbabwean government won't wake up one day in the future and decide to steal all their assets. This is unfortunate because Zimbabwe has a vast and diverse mineral base with close to 40 different minerals. Even with the ongoing industry headwinds that are mostly self-inflicted, the mining industry accounted for 12 percent of the GDP in 2022.

Government-related industries were perhaps even more affected than businesses in the private world. As happens during periods of hyperinflation, the government's tax revenue was effectively wiped out. The tax revenue due at year end has depreciated to such a degree that it is essentially worthless. To compensate for the lost tax revenue, the government resorts to printing more money, which further stimulates inflation. Many municipal businesses went bankrupt owing to the bureaucracy related to municipal wages and trade unions. As a result, there are stories of shortages of daily necessities that we take for granted, such as water and electricity.

Macroeconomic Impact

To this day, Zimbabwe has never really recovered from its tumultuous period that began in the 1990s. At the core of the problems has been political instability. In 2017, a coup forced out longtime President Robert Mugabe, and Emmerson Mnangagwa took over. Optimists had hoped that Mnangagwa would usher in a new era of prosperity for Zimbabwe, but it has been much of the same. The 2018 election was reportedly ravaged by vote rigging and intimidation. The 2018 inflation rate hit its highest since 2008, which prompted another new currency called the Real-Time Gross Settlement (RTGS) dollar to be declared as the sole legal currency. Ever since the inflation saga that began in the 1990s, Zimbabwe has tinkered with its currency. Just like every other effort in the past few decades, it does not look like the RTGS dollar era is going well. Reports in 2021 state that there is a continued existence of illegal foreign currency market, with 60 to 90 percent premiums being paid on the black market at the end of 2021 compared to the official market for the currency. In other words, people do not have confidence in the value of the currency.

Proponents of the so-called modern monetary theory (MMT) argue that governments that issue their own currencies are essentially monopolists who don't have to worry about rising national deficit levels because taxes and transactions are done with the government-issued currency. The line of thinking is essentially that a government that issues their own currency can never default on the national debt because the government can always just choose to print more of the domestic currency. While this is true, what has happened at various points in history such as what we saw with Zimbabwe is that people ultimately end up losing confidence in the domestic government-issued currency altogether if it becomes the consensus view that the debts won't be repaid, or excessive inflation essentially renders the currency worthless. An alternate scenario, which we will study later, is what has happened in Japan where the government has had high deficit levels and money printing coupled with deflation due to individuals and businesses hoarding cash. Both scenarios are problematic and refute the core arguments of MMT. Instead of rallying around this disproven theory, I would recommend MMT enthusiasts spend some time examining past case studies.

Unfortunately for Zimbabwe, I do not see much changing until the government instills confidence in the system. The government needs to prove that they are willing to uphold basic forms of the rule of law such as property rights. Emmerson Mnangagwa has taken some steps to reverse the disastrous land reforms enacted under Mugabe, but it will take years, if not decades, of improvement before foreign investment returns in a meaningful way. It was good to see the Zimbabwean government finally agree to compensate the evicted White farmers two decades later (I am looking at this purely through a financial and investment lens), but it takes a long time to root out such deep-seated corruption and decay.

I want to address Zimbabwe's pervasive debt problem. Zimbabwe officially gained independence as a country in 1980. Upon being granted independence, Zimbabwe inherited sizeable debts from Rhodesia (the former unrecognized state in Southern Africa). Government debts expanded throughout the 1980s owing to loans for development, military, and a drought. By the end of the 1980s, Zimbabwe was spending 25 percent of the government revenue on debt repayments. Zimbabwe received bailout loans from the IMF and the World Bank in the early 1990s. As we previously studied, Zimbabwe's debts rose throughout the 1990s because of wars, droughts, and other factors. In 2000, Zimbabwe defaulted on debt repayments, and the World Bank announced that it would no longer be extending loans to Zimbabwe. As of 2020, the World Bank's lending program to Zimbabwe is still listed as being suspended due to arrears. Unfortunately, Zimbabwe has never recovered from its debt problems that started in the 1990s. A 2020 *Business Times* article stated, "Zimbabwe is now sitting on a sovereign debt time bomb that could trigger at any time due to the ballooning external and domestic debts." The key factors cited for this government debt distress were depreciation of the local currency, penalties on overdue external debt, and overall budget deficits. This sounds exactly like the Zimbabwe that saw its currency collapse in the late 1990s when it was recovering from two severe droughts and waging a costly war in the Democratic Republic of Congo. If you are an international lender and see that a country has faced decades of debt problems that have only been compounded by economic turbulence and deep-rooted political corruption, why would you ever lend money to that country? Unfortunately, this is the reason that it is only more likely that Zimbabwe will keep printing money and devaluing the domestic currency. After struggling mightily for decades, Zimbabwe is still stuck in this vicious cycle of hell.

CHAPTER 5

United States

Energy Crisis (1973–1980)

Background and Market Impact

I chose to write another chapter on the United States because the country was a major player during the 1970s energy crisis, but also so that I could make references to learnings from the chapter on COVID-19 and discuss how the energy crisis of the 1970s shaped the world we live in today. One of the more important developments in the history of the oil market was the creation of Organization of the Petroleum Exporting Nations (OPEC) in 1960. Representatives from Saudi Arabia, Venezuela, Kuwait, Iraq, and Iran decided to form this coalition with the goal of supporting oil prices. At the time, these countries represented 80 percent of the world's oil exports, and their economies were heavily dependent on oil revenues. For the first several years, OPEC did not carry much influence, but that began to change in 1971 when the consortium decided to restructure how foreign oil companies could negotiate with OPEC. Negotiations between OPEC and foreign oil companies were now split into separate regional areas, and this resulted in higher oil prices.

We have already discussed price controls earlier in this book, but this subject again arose during the 1970s. In an effort to tame inflation, President Nixon imposed wage and price controls in 1971, with oil and gas being among the commodities impacted. Reported inflation was slightly above 4 percent when the price controls were initiated, and 1,000 days later, when the price controls were scrapped, the reported inflation was in double-digit territory. When you enact price controls, this reduces the incentive to create a product or service. You then have a reduction in supply of a particular product or service because there are fewer individuals and businesses willing to produce that product or service. In this particular instance of disastrous price control policy, the United States only became more reliant on foreign oil and energy because American businesses did not have much incentive to produce these commodities with the price controls in place. It is amazing to me that similar stories have repeated themselves throughout history, with the result being more or less the same each time. Let the free markets run their course. U.S. domestic oil production peaked in 1970 until a technological revolution took hold around 2010.

The insane price control policies enacted on oil and gas only compounded issues that were related to a policy created in 1959. The Mandatory Oil Import Quota program (MOIP) restricted the amount of imported crude oil and refined products allowed into the United States. With the combination of the oil price controls and oil import quota program, you had a reduced incentive for domestic businesses to produce oil and restrictions on the amount of foreign oil that could be imported. President Nixon announced the end of the MOIP in 1973, but these measures were taken too late to stave off the energy crisis.

In 1973, Syria and Egypt attacked Israel in what would become known as the Yom Kippur War. Oil supplies were reduced in the wake of the war when Arab states suspended oil shipments to countries that were supporting Israel. The result was a 14 percent reduction in internationally traded oil. Between 1973 and 1974, the price of oil per barrel skyrocketed from $2.50 to $11.50. There were widespread gasoline shortages across the United States during this time, and it could take hours to get gasoline.

It was also in 1973 that President Nixon announced *Project Independence*, which was supposed to be a plan for the United States to achieve energy independence with the timeline goal of 1980. Nixon was just a few years off in his timeline, as America didn't materially alter the oil landscape until the shale oil revolution took place nearly 40 years later.

Over the ensuing years, various energy conservation policies were put in place to try and conserve oil and other energy supplies. Unfortunately, United States oil demand continued to rise, and between 1974 and 1978, U.S. consumption of oil imports almost doubled. At this point, the United States was at the mercy of foreign oil. This was long before the days where an electric vehicle was close to being economically viable.

The Iranian Revolution between 1978 and 1979 only compounded all the previously discussed issues. President Jimmy Carter responded to the storming of the U.S. embassy in Iran by placing an embargo on Iranian oil imports. This was at a time that Iranian oil production was in turmoil because of protests and unrest. The result was a doubling of oil prices between 1979 and 1980.

The energy turmoil of the 1970s set the stage for a U.S. emphasis on offshore oil drilling in the 1980s. President Reagan finally fully deregulated oil prices in 1981, and this led to lower prices as non-OPEC production ramped up in response to a renewed incentive to produce oil. President Reagan waged a war on labor unions in an attempt to reduce inflation. Many attribute the early 1980s as the start of the long decline of labor unions, which has only recently been reversed.

The United States oil market today looks substantially different than the landscape in the 1970s when foreign oil wreaked havoc on the American economy. U.S. oil output peaked in 1970 until the global oil market was reshaped with the U.S. shale revolution around the turn of the decade in 2010. The U.S. Energy Information Administration (EIA) released a report in 2019 showing that U.S. crude oil imports from OPEC had hit a 30-year low. Once unthinkable, the United States was estimated to have become the world's largest crude oil producer in 2018, thanks to the rise of shale production. Shale oil is found in shale rock formations and is produced through a combination of hydraulic fracturing and horizontal drilling. It was long believed that it was not possible to extract oil from shale rocks because of the tightly packed nature of the minerals. Those in the oil industry believed that oil could not flow through shale rocks because the hydrocarbon size of oil was too big. Later research studies revealed that this conventional wisdom was untrue, and that oil could in fact flow through the small openings in shale rocks. Once this groundbreaking research had been proven, hydraulic fracturing and horizontal drilling that had been previously applied to gas extraction were applied to oil, and the U.S. shale oil industry was born.

It will be interesting to see what happens long term with the shale market. One of the main problems with shale oil production is the cost relative to more conventional oil extraction. A 2020 report estimated that only 16 U.S. shale oil companies operated in fields where the average new well costs were below $35 per barrel. In comparison, ExxonMobil was estimated to have been profitable on its New Mexico oil wells at a price of $26.90 per barrel. Aside from cost, shale production also faces environmental headwinds. I will leave the climate debate for someone else to cover and focus on the impact being seen in the form of regulations. At the time of this writing, it is unclear as to how the regulatory landscape will develop, but it is believed that President Biden will enact legislation such as limiting the reserves that *frackers* can use and raising the cost of overall oil production to lessen the incentive to extract oil. With the economics of shale already challenged at best, regulations such as these could kill the shale oil industry.

The 1970s period is often defined as being one of *stagflation* (I will elaborate more in the section on macroeconomic impacts). Stagflation is an environment where there is a combination of weak business activity and high inflation. It took nearly 10 years for the Dow Jones Industrial Average to reach its peak in the first few years of the 1970s after inflation took off, and there was a prolonged period of economic malaise. Between 1973 and 1982, there were three technical recessions.

How Businesses Were Affected

This discussion should begin with the U.S. oil companies. These companies were obviously negatively impacted by the price controls imposed during this era. Under free market economics, the domestic oil companies would have responded to large price increases in oil by producing more oil to capture excess profits until enough oil was produced to create a more balanced demand and supply scenario. In the world of price controls, these oil companies never receive this incentive to produce more oil because there is a cap on how much they can make for each barrel of oil. The long lines at gas stations around the United States during this time provide support to the claim that price controls do not work. Making matters worse for the domestic oil companies was the fact that the 1970s era was an inflationary environment. This means that their input costs were increasing at a time when there was a maximum price that could be paid for their finished product. It is no mystery as to why the domestic oil businesses were challenged, and there was an oil shortage.

In addition to Nixon's perilous price control policies, he introduced wage controls. In his warped world of economics (some reports show that Nixon understood the economic downsides of price controls, but initiated them to secure reelection in 1972), price and wage controls would tame inflation. History shows that these policies always do the opposite. The wage controls led to less incentive for people to work and caused a labor shortage. In turn, there was a shortage of consumer goods available and a rise in bankruptcies and unemployment. The vast majority of operating businesses were impacted by these policies during this time.

One of the U.S. industries most impacted by the economic tumult of the 1970s was the automobile industry. With soaring oil prices, U.S. consumers almost overnight went from buying gas guzzling American automobiles to demanding more fuel-efficient vehicles. Unfortunately for U.S. manufacturers, such as General Motors and Ford, they had not anticipated the shift to more fuel-efficient vehicles. Japanese car manufacturers had anticipated this shift and had been focusing on more fuel-efficient vehicles and gained at the expense of the U.S. companies. The U.S. automobile manufacturer's challenges were exacerbated by new federal mandates such as new regulations requiring specific fuel economy standards in response to soaring oil prices. U.S. automobile manufacturers quickly went from big annual profits to posting losses and laying off workers.

Macroeconomic Impact

When most economists think about the economy in the 1970s, the first word that comes to mind is stagflation. This isn't a term that many today were familiar with until recently when inflation fears arose for the first time in many years. Up until the 1970s, most economists believed that there was a constant inverse relationship between inflation and unemployment levels. The supporting rationale for this line of thinking was that inflation was the result of strong economic activity that drove up prices and would be accompanied by low unemployment levels. This is true in what we now refer to as *demand-pull* inflation. The inflation that plagued the 1970s was deemed to be driven by *cost-push* inflation, which was not previously considered by most economists. Instead of inflation being driven by strong economic activity, it was largely being driven by soaring oil prices that would spill over into everyday consumer goods after the wage controls put in place limited the incentive to work and produce goods. The reason that wage controls were particularly impactful during this period of rising inflation was that most rational individuals were demanding higher wages to compensate for the loss of money purchasing power. The cost-push inflation became somewhat of a self-fulfilling prophecy with currency devaluation, import quotas, and embargos. The cost of overall business remained high, workers didn't have as much incentive to work and unemployment levels remained elevated, companies went out of business, and the price of everyday consumer staples was high. You can see how this was not an ideal situation.

Another important development that contributed to the inflationary period of the 1970s was the severed link between the value of the currency and gold in 1971. The gold standard is a monetary system where a country's currency is linked to the value of gold. England became the first known country in modern times to adopt the gold standard in 1821. The United States adopted the gold standard in 1879, and there was a fixed price of currency to gold of $20.67 per ounce until 1933 (the fixed price of gold was set in 1834, and some argue that was when the United States shifted to a gold standard). The period between 1880 and 1914 is known as the classical gold standard. In 1933, FDR at least partially took the United States off the gold standard in wake of the Great Depression. FDR called for all gold coins and certificates in excess of $100 to be exchanged for other forms of money. Gold was redeemed for a set price of $20.67 per ounce. A year later, the government set the price of gold at $35 per ounce. The increase in the set price of gold allowed the federal government to increase the money supply, thus helping the United States cover costs associated with getting the economy back on track. The fixed gold price of $35 per ounce would remain until President Nixon completely severed the price link to gold in 1971.

Nixon's policy decision in 1971 related to gold convertibility led to the beginning of the demise of the Bretton Woods system that was created in 1944. The Bretton Woods system was established to create an international monetary framework with an adjustable peg system based on the U.S. dollar convertible into gold at $35 per ounce along with capital controls. What pushed the ultimate decision for the United States to sever the link between the U.S. dollar and gold in 1971 was the combination of inflation and the fact that it was believed the British and French governments were going to exchange their U.S. dollars for gold. Extreme and sudden selling of the U.S. dollar in favor of gold in large quantities could quickly devalue the U.S. currency and deplete U.S. gold reserves at the same time. I think Nixon was referring to this potential international threat to the U.S. dollar when he said, "We must protect the dollar from the attacks of international money speculators."

Why is the history lesson on the gold standard relevant to the 1970s inflation era along with the prolonged era of easy monetary and fiscal policy that we have today? Without the requirement that governments hold gold reserves to support their currencies or limits on money supply growth tied to GDP growth, governments have printed a lot more money. It is ironic that one of Nixon's perceived goals in severing the link between the U.S. dollar and gold was to keep inflation in check. I don't think it should be in any way surprising that this policy decision ended up having the opposite effect. When governments print more of their own currency, this makes the currency less valuable (again assuming the additional currency is put into the economy). This is basic economics, and it is strange to see some people failing to grasp this concept today when we are seeing waves of direct payments to individuals as part of COVID-19 relief. Even more stunning, in mid-2022, U.S. states such as California are preparing to send stimulus checks to families for *inflation relief*. The money created out of thin air to finance these direct payments will ultimately lead to higher prices due to currency devaluation and does not leave people better off than they were before. In order to create more wealth, a society must be more productive.

As I write this chapter, America's national debt is in excess of $27 trillion. Money printing on an enormous scale has been possible because the U.S. dollar is not linked to gold or any other hard asset. As we have seen throughout history, the problem with this level of money printing is that faith can be lost in a country's currency altogether. As we studied with Zimbabwe, this is just one example of many. One of my primary concerns with the world in the future is that people will ultimately lose confidence in the U.S. dollar. We are heading down that path with the level of money printing and the lack of productivity and population growth to compensate for the soaring debt levels like we had after World War II. The global implications of a scenario where confidence is lost in the U.S. dollar would be enormous. Think of all the countries, some of which we have studied in this book, that have their currencies pegged or managed in relation to the U.S. dollar and use fiat currency as the primary method of exchange. I think what is ultimately going to happen is that we are going to have to return to a partial gold standard, which I will discuss later. Gold has proven to be a reserve currency for thousands of years, and I believe it will be needed to restore confidence in currencies that could come under pressure on a massive scale because of insane global monetary policy decisions enabled by a lack of accountability.

To supplement the proposed partial gold standard, there needs to be limits on the money supply growth tied to ongoing GDP growth. For example, if an economy grows at an inflation-adjusted 2 percent compound annual growth rate over a 10-year period, the money supply should not grow much more than 2 percent per year over that period. If money supply growth limits were enacted, governments would need to show restraint during the good times and save the money supply growth for an event such as a war that has traditionally been a major disruptor of monetary policy. To the extent that the money supply growth in an economy is supported by GDP growth, there is a dramatic reduction in the possibility of boom–bust cycles and financial crises. I endorse a full-reserve banking system where there are 100 percent reserves backed by deposits and the monetary and credit functions of the financial system are separated. Countless financial crises have been the result of irresponsible commercial bank money creation that has been incentivized with government bailouts and insurance schemes. Using a partial gold standard would only further shore up confidence in the domestic currency by supporting the paper money with a universally accepted store of value that has been coveted for thousands of years. A partial gold standard would provide an element of decentralization to the monetary system where full-reserve banking is employed, as confidence in the domestic currency would be less reliant on the central banks.

CHAPTER 6

Chile

Latin American Debt Crisis
(1982–1989)

Background and Market Impact

Up to this point, we have covered various crisis scenarios in history spread across four different continents, with two case studies on the United States that were separated by 50 years. This chapter is the first case study on the Latin American region, and many refer to this period for Latin America as the *lost decade*. You will later see the term lost decade was also used to reference Japan in the 1990s.

The crisis in the 1970s covered in the previous chapter is a perfect transition to the Latin American debt crisis of the 1980s. The oil price shocks in the 1970s planted the seeds for this crisis. The soaring oil prices led to current account deficits for countries in the Latin American region that were net oil importers. The result was skyrocketing debt levels across Latin America in the 1980s. At the end of 1970, the estimated total Latin American borrowing from U.S. commercial banks was $29 billion, and this figure exploded to $327 billion by 1982. The trigger for the start of the Latin American debt crisis was in 1982, when Mexico declared that the country was unable to service its debt. This development sent shockwaves across the region, with 16 countries in Latin America ultimately rescheduling their debts.

Specific to Chile, the country had a buildup in private debt between 1975 and 1982, with private foreign debt increasing from 10.5 percent of GDP to 41.8 percent over this period. In the section on how the crises impacted specific businesses, we will further discuss the banking system collapse that resulted from issues related to private debt, exacerbated by the currency mismatch problems that were brought to the forefront when the domestic currency was devalued. Unlike some of the other cases that we have previously examined, the rise in private debts was not accompanied by an increase in federal deficits.

After a military coup overthrew the Chilean government in 1973, the new government embarked on an agenda that was focused on deregulation, which is interesting because usually when there is a military coup, the new government seeks to consolidate state power. Sticking with a common theme similar to what we saw with Iceland and Indonesia, the government was focused on financial liberalization but did not put enough oversight measures in place to prevent a financial crisis. Banks and other firms that had been nationalized under the prior regime were sold to the private sector. The number of publicly held firms declined from 620 in 1973 to 66 in 1981. In general, privatization and allowing businesses to operate in free private markets is a positive development. Having said that, additional care needs to be taken when privatizing and providing financial liberalization reforms in the banking and financial sectors because of the inherent flaws in the business models and how a collapse in the banking sector can take down the entire economy of a country.

The Chilean crisis that began in 1982 was the result of loose financial oversight and an extended period of booming credit creation. For years, Chileans had been buying cheap imported goods on credit because the artificially high exchange rate had made imported goods cheap to purchase. Then came the recession in 1982 that devalued the Chilean peso and sent the country into a tailspin. The result of the severe recession and exchange rate devaluation was that banks could not repay their foreign loans. Chile's reliance on copper for export earnings and for the overall economy caused problems when there was a decline in copper prices. What essentially happened was that Chile had been able to borrow international funds freely from 1977 to 1981, and this easy international credit dried up overnight. Chile had not prepared for a rainy day when international credit was harder to come by and copper demand was not as high. They should have been shoring up their foreign exchange reserves at least in part by diversifying their export earnings streams, but this did not happen.

The 1970s era had been marred by the energy crisis (which we previously covered) that stimulated inflation in many international markets. This inflation had boosted commodity prices, and in turn, Chile's international business for exports such as copper. A combination of a global recession in the early 1980s coupled with deflationary supply-side commodity trends hurt countries that were reliant on commodity exports, such as Chile. Once Chile had to devalue its artificially high exchange rate, it caused problems, because the high exchange rate had encouraged the buying of cheap imported goods on credit that were not being supported by Chile's export business.

Chile suffered a recession during the 1982 to 1983 period. Economic output fell by over 20 percent between 1981 and 1983. By late 1983, unemployment soared to over 30 percent of the total workforce with the number of people living in poverty greatly increasing during the recession. Domestic measured inflation—as measured by CPI, which I believe is a flawed metric, as it doesn't incorporate most asset price inflation or other measures—more than doubled.

How Businesses Were Affected

As we know by now, it is usually important to study what happened to the banking sector when we are thinking about a shock to the financial system. The financial case study of Chile is fundamentally different from our studies of Iceland and Indonesia. Unlike Indonesia and Iceland, Chile did not have a buildup of debt in the public sector leading up to the financial crisis in 1982. In fact, Chile ran a budget surplus in 1980. The debt problems experienced in Chile were tied to the private sector. Like we saw in Iceland and Indonesia, the period leading up to the financial crisis was characterized by a banking system with high debt levels paired with poor regulation and loose oversight, rapid credit growth, a currency mismatch problem (borrowing in international currency and lending in domestic currency without proper reserving), undiversified economies that became a problem when there was a shock, and hot economies that masked underlying problems.

A fixed currency exchange rate was introduced in Chile in 1979 when the Chilean peso was pegged to the U.S. dollar at a fixed rate of 39 pesos per dollar. By 1979, Chile was still seeing high inflation rates of around 39 percent. The government wanted to lower inflation, so they instituted a fixed currency peg exchange rate to try and bring down inflation. The fixed exchange rate policy initially worked well while the U.S. dollar remained weak, as investors bought Chilean pesos to take advantage of the higher relative interest rates. Things changed quickly when President Reagan took office in the United States in 1981. U.S. monetary policy shifted toward tightening to combat the domestic U.S. inflation problem, and this caused a strengthening of the U.S. dollar. Once the U.S. dollar appreciated, the money that had rushed into Chile to take advantage of the higher relative interest rates fled. Iceland and Indonesia should have studied what happened in Chile, because similar developments occurred in their respective countries at a later date. In simple terms, a lot of the money that was flowing into Chile leading up to the crisis was speculative capital taking advantage of the relative strength in the local currency. This type of capital is fundamentally different than long-term investment capital because it will most likely leave the country quickly if conditions change. Countries that see this happening must be prepared and have sufficient foreign exchange reserves on hand to weather a sudden large outflow of international capital. It is estimated that Chile had to increase the money supply by approximately 70 billion pesos to purchase international currency and compensate for the outflow of foreign money. This ultimately caused problems for the financial system, such as increased inflation. If Chile had been more conservative with their foreign reserving prior to the outflow of foreign capital, I may not be writing this chapter today. One of the primary downsides of fixed currency exchange rates is that it can lead to increased speculation as we saw happen here. If a country is going to employ a fixed exchange rate, they must be prepared with sufficient foreign exchange reserves or be prepared for disaster.

The fixed exchange rate era collapsed in June of 1982. At this point, Chile was in the midst of a major economic crisis, and the implosion of the fixed currency exchange rate led to a sharp devaluation of the Chilean peso. Basically, what happened here in terms of the currency mismatch problem taking down the banking system was very similar to what later happened in Indonesia. When there was a sharp devaluation of the domestic currency, the amount to be repaid became much more expensive for the domestic Chilean banks. When international lenders see this happening, they stop making new loans to the banks facing the currency mismatch problem, and it leads to a sudden violent collapse of the financial system. It is amazing how near-identical scenarios have occurred throughout history, and yet people today will again seem to be surprised when an undiversified economy reliant on international funding has issues with their currency, which results in the collapse of the banking system.

The start of the fall of the Chilean banking system occurred in May of 1981 when Compañía de Refinería de Azúcar de Viña del Mar (CRAV), one of the largest private companies in Chile, declared bankruptcy. Later in 1981, it was revealed that Chile's domestic financial businesses had debt that was more than double the amount of capital on hand. This compounded the problems related to the currency and evaporating credit. Between 1982 and 1985, the central bank initiated various debt restructuring programs designed to ease the strain on the financial system. The economic cost of the debt restructuring programs was huge, with an estimate for 1985 coming in at close to 8 percent of the total GDP. Similar to what later happened in Iceland, Chile ultimately decided to nationalize the banks to save the financial system. By 1985, it is estimated that 14 of the 26 domestic banks were under state control.

Aside from the issues related to the financial sector, businesses that had benefitted for years from high foreign inflation suffered when international inflation started to decline in the early 1980s. There was a farming crisis during the early 1980s in the United States that affected Chile. It was described as the worst farming crisis since the Great Depression. For years, farmers had been able to acquire easy debt to purchase land, equipment, and supplies. When commodity prices declined in the early 1980s, the farming industry in Chile and other countries was adversely affected.

The majority of industrial businesses were negatively impacted by the declining inflation, with businesses such as copper producers being particularly impacted and having a dramatic effect on the overall Chilean economy.

Macroeconomic Impact

The policy decisions made in response to the banking crises in Iceland and Chile were similar, and both countries had successful recoveries in comparison to many others during these times of financial distress. Both Iceland and Chile decided to nationalize the banks and inject massive liquidity into the financial system. The debt restructuring programs employed by Chile were absorbed by the treasury and central bank. To avoid further problems with the financial system, Chile responded with a lot of model policy decisions. Chile employed conservative fiscal policies and mostly generated fiscal surpluses between 1987 and 2017. The excellent fiscal discipline allowed for Chile to keep domestic inflation in check in the years following the crisis. In addition to the admirable fiscal restraint, Chile learned from its prior mistakes and improved its international reserves. By 1992, it was estimated that Chile had enough international reserves on hand to fund a year of imports, and the foreign reserves were equal to roughly half of Chile's foreign debt balance. Part of Chile's successful recovery is attributable to the endorsement of free market economics in response to the crisis. Chilean exports became more competitive once the artificially high fixed exchange rate was scrapped, and the Chilean peso was able to depreciate to reflect economic reality. This made Chile's exports less expensive to other countries. Chile reduced tariffs on imports, which made the country more attractive to do business with. In short, Chile responded to the crisis by employing policies that reflected free market economics paired with fiscal restraint. It should not in any way be surprising that Chile had one of the more successful economic recoveries in history in the wake of a major crisis, and the country has largely been an economic success story ever since.

As previously noted, debts at the government level were not responsible for the Chilean banking collapse in the 1980s, but rather the private sector debts were the root cause. So, while the exemplary fiscal restraint employed by Chile in the years following the crisis helped the country keep inflation manageable and reduce the chances of another financial crisis, we can't point to this factor as being responsible for Chile getting through the global financial crisis relatively unscathed. The changes made to foreign reserving, the currency exchange rate, and the free market economic policies employed were all important factors. Chile's lack of reliance on external funding to support the domestic banking system was another important factor. The IMF estimated that, during the time of the global financial crisis, Chile's banking system was only relying on external funding for 5 percent of its total assets. This greatly reduced the risk factor that played a critical role in taking down the banking systems in Iceland and Indonesia.

Aside from the recent economic troubles Chile has faced related to COVID-19 and the protests concerning inequality, Chile has largely been an economic success story in recent decades. Despite the ongoing issues related to inequality, Chile has been the best performing and most stable economy in South America for a long time now. How has Chile achieved relative economic stability in a notoriously volatile region? Chile has been fiscally conservative, a champion of free trade, a supporter of policies that enforce local laws and regulations, has employed more conservative financing in the banking and overall financial sector, and has had a lack of significant issues tied to their currency since the crisis in the 1980s.

An ongoing problem that Chile will face is tied to their ongoing reliance on copper. Chile is the world's largest copper producer and remains reliant on mining for exports. As of 2021, mining still accounted for approximately 62 percent of the total country exports and close to 15 percent of Chile's GDP. While Chile has benefitted from their role in being a champion of free trade in recent decades, their major challenge going forward will be further developing domestic industries to reduce reliance on international businesses and financing. Like we studied before, Iceland and Indonesia remain heavily reliant on international business that makes it more likely that a crisis scenario will occur in the future. According to the 2018 Global Entrepreneurship Index, Chile clocked in at 19, which was well ahead of more established countries such as China. Chile should double down on entrepreneurial businesses by offering business and educational incentives to provide products and services that stimulate domestic demand. Chile has done a lot of the right things in recent decades at least as it relates to economic policy. However, reducing risks related to reliance on foreign business (which is also highly volatile, given the nature of copper demand) and financing would take Chile to the next level of economic health.

CHAPTER 7

Japan

Lost Decade (1991–2001)

Background and Market Impact

I thought it was appropriate to include Japan in this book so that we could explore some topics not previously covered such as deflation and declining population growth. Young people today may not believe it, but back in the 1980s, Japan was the modern-day China-equivalent, and many were projecting that Japan could ultimately overtake the United States in terms of economic strength. I use China as a parallel because both countries rode export-led growth to years of economic success. The obvious economic difference between Japan in the 1980s and modern-day China relates to demographic trends, which we will discuss later in this chapter. As we have previously discussed in this book, the economic model dependent on export growth is fragile and comes with risks related to demand, currency, and the financial system.

As we know by now, most crisis situations are preceded by periods of strong economic growth that masks underlying issues. This was the case for Japan in the 1970s and 1980s. Over this period, the Japanese economy grew at an average rate of 4 percent. Like many market bubbles, contributing factors to the ultimate Japanese collapse in the late 1980s were financial deregulation paired with aggressive lending and poor risk management by companies in the financial sector, an extended period of low interest rates and rapid credit growth, and an artificially low domestic currency. While history doesn't repeat itself, it often rhymes. I hope it has become clear by now that most financial crises have had similar characteristics in the period leading up to the crisis and were ultimately triggered by monetary tightening or a change in the direction of the currency.

One of the important events to note was the Plaza Accord, an agreement signed in 1985. The agreement between Japan, the United Kingdom, France, West Germany, and the United States was supposed to help adjust for trade imbalances between the nations. Because of the weak Japanese yen, demand for Japanese exports had surged in the years leading up to the Plaza Accord. This agreement was significant because it was at least partially responsible for the sharp rise in the Japanese yen that, in turn, caused lower demand for Japanese exports. Given its reliance on exports for overall GDP, Japan slid into recession in 1986. By the end of 1986, the Japanese yen had appreciated by 46 percent relative to the U.S. dollar in the months following the signing of the Plaza Accord. The weak economic activity led the central bank to support easy monetary conditions that were responsible for the broad domestic asset bubble, which peaked in 1989.

Terry Smith at Fundsmith reflected on the Japanese market bubble in 1989 when he said that the Japanese stock market peaked with a price-to-earnings (P/E) ratio of over 60. At the time, it was argued that Japanese accounting was more conservative than other countries, but, as it turned out, the stock market was just vastly overvalued. As is the case with most market crashes, the Japanese crash was triggered in 1989 when a new central bank head started to sharply raise interest rates out of fear that inflation was set to accelerate. The higher interest rates reversed years of easy credit and led to a now-infamous crash in real estate and stock market valuations. The inflated valuations across asset classes in Japan in the 1980s were the result of an extended period of low interest rates and rapid credit growth. This is a phenomenon that we have seen repeat itself throughout history.

Japan's stock exchange, the Nikkei 225, soared more than 900 percent in the 15 years preceding the ultimate collapse. As I previously noted, the Japanese stock market peaked with a P/E ratio of over 60. This is a stratospheric valuation multiple, as an average figure in the mid-20s would be considered high as judged by U.S. history. While the bubble in the Japanese stock market was unreasonable, the real estate market was far more irrational. Japan's total land area is around 4 percent of the size of the United States, yet the value of the Japanese real estate market at the peak of the bubble was four times that of the United States! Tokyo real estate per square foot was more than 350 times as valuable as Manhattan real estate. To get a sense of how insane the bubble in Japan was at the time, the Imperial Palace (the residence of the emperor of Japan) was reported to have been worth more than the state of California. At the end of 1992, the Nikkei 225 index was still down by nearly 60 percent from the end of 1989. After the bubble started to deflate upon peaking in 1989, equity prices declined, and real estate prices plunged and remained 70 percent lower in 2001 relative to the peak of the bubble. As of early 2023, the Nikkei 225 index has yet to reach the levels touched during the asset bubble in 1989. Having such a protracted period of dismal equity price performance in a period of low interest rates is extremely painful for retirees as it relates to retirement savings (we will discuss this further in the section on macroeconomics). Some consider the Japanese market bubble to be the greatest in history in terms of total market capitalization impact and recovery time.

How Businesses Were Affected

I want to again summarize what has happened throughout history as it relates to the banking sector contributing to the collapse of financial systems. The process usually begins with deregulation of the financial industry paired with poor oversight and lenient laws related to lending. Financial deregulation is almost always done during times of economic success as we have seen with Japan, Iceland, Indonesia, and Chile. Somewhere along the line, there is usually a weakening of credit standards. Borrowers with little to no assets can acquire loans from banks and financial institutions that are competing to make a return. This situation becomes particularly problematic when lenders are relying more heavily on collateral, which is tied to inflated asset prices such as real estate. This is what happened in Japan in the early 1990s and in the United States leading up to the global financial crisis. In the case of Japan, Iceland, Indonesia, and Chile, the currency played a major role in the collapse of the financial systems. As the currency relates to Japan, the weak Japanese yen had stimulated export growth that had an outsized impact on the overall economy, given the reliance on foreign demand. After the signing of the Plaza Accord, the yen appreciated significantly, and this sent the economy into recession and led to the easy monetary policy that inflated asset valuations, ultimately causing the demise of the financial system once there was monetary tightening.

One of the largest problems for the Japanese financial system in the 1990s was the fact that loan portfolios were concentrated in property-related businesses that had wildly inflated valuations. Many of these loans were collateralized by property valuations, and the loans became nonperforming loans when the bubble burst, and real estate values were torpedoed. As we saw with the United States during the global financial crisis, it is a serious problem for bank lending to be overly reliant on real estate, especially when property valuations are out of touch with economic value. Another problem was that the rising equity valuations had made bank balance sheets appear healthier than they were. Equities were being counted as part of a bank's capital base, and once the valuations declined, banks were in weak financial condition and had problems servicing existing loans. The decline in the banking sector's capital base also limited the sector's ability to extend new loans, which hampered overall economic activity. It is dangerous that the banking sector was overly reliant on stock price valuations for their capital reserves. In the wake of the global financial crisis, regulations such as the Dodd–Frank Act were passed in the United States that put additional capital requirements on the financial sector. In the case of Japan, banks should have had more readily liquid capital on hand, as in cash or short-term bonds. This series of events was similar to that in the United States during the global financial crisis, and I believe that, as I write this chapter, countries such as Australia are at risk of the domestic banking sector being overly reliant on loans to the real estate sector collateralized by inflated valuations.

What makes the situation with the banking system different in the case of Japan as compared to our previous examples is the amount of time it took the collapse to develop. While the Japanese asset bubble burst in 1989, it really wasn't until 1997 that the domestic banking crisis came to fruition. This was the year when financial crises were sweeping Asia triggered by currency devaluations tied to monetary tightening in the United States (refer to the chapter on Indonesia). The broad-based Asian financial crises combined with domestic monetary tightening and other factors previously discussed were the nail in the coffin for the Japanese financial system.

Similar to policy responses that happened in countries such as Iceland and Chile (and the United States in response to the global financial crisis), Japan used government funds to inject massive liquidity into the financial system. It is estimated that Japan injected an equivalent of more than 12 percent of the 1998 domestic GDP into the financial system to provide a backstop for banks. Public proceeds were given to 21 domestic banks in 1998 to help ensure that capital requirements were met. Similar to the policy responses we studied in Iceland and Chile, Japan temporarily nationalized two banks in 1998. Iceland and Chile went much further in terms of taking banks under state control in the wake of their financial crises, but the policy responses were similar, nonetheless. Additional public proceeds were injected into 15 banks in 1999 to provide further stability for the financial system. While costly, the swift policy responses by the Japanese government prevented a worst-case scenario akin to something we saw in Zimbabwe.

Outside of banking and other financial businesses that were heavily impacted by this crisis, one of the other obvious industries affected was real estate. As we have seen throughout history and in our examples related to countries such as Indonesia and Iceland, during the boom times when credit is flowing, and real estate prices are rising rapidly, too much real estate is developed to meet the demand.

What follows is a period of excess real estate supply combined with an environment where loans are more difficult to obtain. There is also the psychological effect that impacts the overall real estate market. If you are a property owner or prospective property owner and see an overall market decline by two-thirds in value over a relatively short period of time, it may give you second thoughts about the safety of such an investment. The result is a period of weak real estate performance.

When you have a series of events that impact the financial system such as what we saw in Japan, this impacts every business and citizen, but the impact on small businesses is disproportionate. Larger companies can more readily access capital through avenues such as public markets and in aggregate are more self-sufficient when it comes to having business models that don't rely as much on external financing. It was estimated that 75 percent of the loans being made during the bubble period were to small businesses that were often backed by real estate. When access to capital dries up, you have a scenario where there are widespread bankruptcies and job losses tied to small businesses.

Macroeconomic Impact

I wanted to cover a topic that we have yet to address in this book: deflation. The opposite of inflation, deflation is the general decrease in the level of the price of goods and services. Throughout most of history, we have more often worried about inflation getting out of hand and ultimately having people lose confidence in a given currency as a result. So, how can a deflationary macroeconomic environment be harmful? Japan has largely been in a deflationary macroeconomic environment since the mid-1990s, and we can examine the causes and effects and compare those to other cases in history.

One of the main problems with an environment of persistent deflation is that households and investors can hoard cash, because an expectation is created that cash will be worth more tomorrow than it is today. This leads to high overall savings rates and a lack of money flowing through the economy. A recurring cycle is then created where businesses hire fewer people and invest less money, which has a further negative impact on the overall economy. Deflation can also be a problem for banks because falling asset prices can have a negative impact on collateralized loans and lead to losses for the financial sector. As a result, you can have a situation where the financial sector is less willing to lend money. One of the other effects of a deflationary environment is on monetary policy and domestic savings. At this point, Japan has effectively had a zero or near-zero interest rate policy for over 20 years in an effort to stimulate demand and inflation. The persistently low interest rate environment has been a massive problem for Japanese retirees because they haven't been able to get adequate returns from neither stocks nor bonds for decades. As previously noted, deflation can create a recurring cycle of underinvestment and lead to long periods of weak economic growth, which is what we have seen happen in Japan for decades. A deflationary environment leads to a greater real value of debt that is a significant burden for borrowers and leads to less demand for borrowing, which is another major reason for a recurring cycle of underinvestment when there is a protracted period of deflation.

A critical macroeconomic factor that must be discussed as it relates to Japan is the aging population. While there has been some degree of immigration policy liberalization in the past few years, Japan has long been one of the world's least hospitable countries to immigrants. With low domestic birthrates and few immigrants entering the country, Japan has battled with a declining overall population and an aging population. I have seen current estimates show that Japan is expected to have 30 percent fewer people in 2065 than it did in 2015. This estimate would have to assume that Japan does not push a lot further in terms of allowing more immigrants into the country. The other demographic component is Japan's aging population. Roughly 28 percent of Japan's population is currently over 65, and this figure is expected to surge to 40 percent by 2060, unless Japan either starts allowing far more immigrants to enter the country or produces a lot more babies. There are several problems related to an aging population that other developed countries such as the United States will grapple with in the coming years. Some of the more important challenges related to an aging population include rising federal health care costs (which is especially worrisome for countries that already have high deficit levels and low GDP growth) and pension costs, lower productivity because a lower percentage of people will be working and at least some portion of the older population that is working won't be as productive as younger workers, and lower consumer demand since many older families aren't buying as many things as younger consumers.

I have seen some arguments against Japan's aging population and population decline being tied to deflation, but I am going to argue that these theories are off target. In most cases, when a government prints a lot of money and enacts easy monetary policies, this results in inflation. As I have previously mentioned, it is a common misconception that the act of printing money causes consumer price inflation. It is only when the government prints more money, and this additional currency gets put into circulation within the economy, that there is consumer price inflation. After all, consumer price inflation is the result of the amount of spending exceeding the quantity of things such as goods and services, and the

quantity of money can be inflated with money printing that will stimulate consumer price inflation if this additional money is used to purchase
goods and services. So, how is this relevant to the topic of Japan's aging
population and population decline? Japan's psychology toward money has
resulted in what I would call a deflationary trap for decades. Basically,
what has happened is that a lot of money has been printed, but businesses
and individuals have not been convinced to invest this money because
they have come to believe that cash will be worth more tomorrow than it
is today owing to deflationary pressures. The reason that the aging population factor has compounded these problems is that Japan's retirees have
seen what it is like to have a situation where domestic stocks and bonds
essentially yielded nothing in aggregate for over 20 years. If you are a
75-year-old Japanese retiree and have seen this happen, you are probably
going to be more likely to keep a higher percentage of money in cash and
to invest more money internationally. As we have seen with Japan, once
you get into this vicious deflationary cycle, it is very difficult to break out
of it.

How does Japan's deflation compare to other instances of deflation in
history? While we have not experienced deflation in the United States in
the 2010s and 2020s, it has been argued that technological advances and
modern monopolies have kept inflation low. While I think there is some
degree of truth to this theory, the Federal Reserve has long been measur-
ing inflation incorrectly. In recent years, the low interest rate environment
has caused inflation in the prices of basically every asset class ranging from
stocks to cryptocurrencies. The Federal Reserve has not incorporated this
development into their inflation calculation, but this asset price inflation
is very real. What has happened in most cases throughout history following eras of easy monetary policy is that the central banks ultimately raise
interest rates to stave off inflationary pressures, which lowers the prices of
inflated assets. The key difference in what has happened in Japan has been
that businesses and individuals have been hoarding cash and not investing, which has kept the country in a deflationary environment.

I think an interesting case of deflation in U.S. history is the period
of the 1870s and 1880s when the economy was growing yet prices were
declining. Between 1873 and 1879, prices declined by nearly 3 percent
each year, yet overall growth was nearly 7 percent over this period.

Despite displaying overall GDP growth, this period of time has been called the *Long Depression* because of the deflationary pressures. This is a very different scenario from other deflationary environments such as the Great Depression that were similar in nature to Japan where people and businesses stopped investing in the economy. So, what was the cause of deflation in the United States in the 1870s and 1880s? The IMF argues that the price declines were tied to relatively favorable supply shocks. The late 1800s in the United States was an economic environment that is not too dissimilar from the U.S. in the 2010s. There was widespread use of new technologies such as railroads that were lowering costs. The late 1800s was a period dominated by monopolies in oil, steel, and railroads run by John Rockefeller, Andrew Carnegie, and Jay Gould. What all these business luminaries and industries had in common was that they kept prices low. Some may be perplexed by the idea that the 1800s monopolies translated to lower consumer prices, but this was because these companies opted to take additional market share instead of raising prices, which is a similar dynamic to the U.S. technology stalwarts of today. Rockefeller's strategy of essentially buying out all the competition can be compared to technology companies in the United States in the 2010s, so when studies are done on Standard Oil and others during the late 1800s, it becomes obvious why these references are made. Today, you have companies such as Meta Platforms and Alphabet offer their services for *free* (the cost of course is in the data these companies collect in exchange for their services offered at no monetary cost), and they have consolidated their market position over the years by purchasing various competitors similar to Rockefeller in the 1800s. I would consider the deflationary environment of the United States in the 1870s and 1880s to be supply-side deflation and the low inflation of the United States in the 2010s (at least when looking at CPI) to be driven by the supply side of the equation. In short, new technology and productivity gains made goods and services less expensive. This is very different from demand-side deflation such as Japan for the last few decades and the United States during the Great Depression. Demand-driven deflation is far more dangerous, and as we have seen with Japan, it can last for protracted periods. Unlike some economists, I do not view the consumer receiving low prices due to technological advances as being a negative development. I have yet to complain about placing an Amazon order with free shipping and often receiving my package within a day. On the other hand, a scenario such as in Japan where people and businesses lose confidence can cripple an economy for a long time, and there isn't always a clear solution. The jury is still out on what Japan will do to break this deflationary trap (as I am editing this chapter in 2022, consumer price inflation in Japan hit a 33-year high and could be one of the few countries where inflation is at a desirable level).

A thought-provoking question relates to Japan's deficit levels. Japan has been the most indebted major economy in the world, and their public debt was more than 250 percent of the GDP in 2021. Japan has remained highly indebted since their problems faced with the *Lost Decade* required massive government spending to shore up the financial system along with attempts to stimulate growth. Many would ask why Japan has yet to default on their debt, as they have consistently carried enormous deficit levels in recent years. As we have previously studied, a country that acts as a currency issuer will never default on their debt. Having said that, what has usually been the risk throughout history is that governments such as Zimbabwe have resorted to money printing on a massive scale, resulting in high inflation and ultimately a loss of confidence in the domestic currency. Japan has not experienced these high levels of consumer price inflation because individuals and businesses have opted not to invest the money that has been printed. So, while Japan has not experienced the inflation problem, they have been stuck with a low growth economy for decades. In fact, as of the end of 2020, Japan recorded less than 1 percent average annual growth over the past three decades. This is the choice that most countries face when they run huge public deficit levels: print a lot of money to stimulate the economy, which can result in high consumer price inflation, or have a scenario where a lot of money is printed but nobody invests the money and growth remains low. Neither of these scenarios is desirable, and these case studies provide further evidence as to why proponents of the modern monetary theory are misguided.

Going forward, the easiest solution for Japan would be to allow more young immigrants into the country. Japan has continued to have more elderly citizens soaking up government resources by taking advantage of social net resources while not contributing much in the way of productivity. This is to be expected for any older citizen in a country, but the elderly population has not been replaced with younger workers owing to the low birthrates and lack of immigrants. Without further immigration liberalization, it is difficult to arrive at many easy scenarios where Japan dramatically alters its current trajectory.

Japan needs to do better to cultivate an environment where individuals and companies are willing to invest in the country. If you look at a list of Japan's most valuable companies, the collection of businesses is underwhelming for a country that not all that long ago was thought to potentially one day surpass the United States in terms of economic competitiveness. Outside of the carmakers such as Toyota and Honda, there are other quality businesses such as Sony and Nintendo, but the list of top companies clearly points to fundamental problems with innovation happening in the country. At least up until now, the United States has maintained the global business advantage by sustaining the best-in-class higher education system, leveraging dependable business protections, and preserving a capitalist system to cultivate a destination that attracts the best and brightest talent and businesses. If Japan wants to get serious about resuming respectable growth, outside of what I would consider an easy solution tied to immigration, I recommend taking a few pages from how the United States has historically operated.

I would be lying if I did not admit that the parallels between Japan and the modern-day United States were not at least somewhat alarming. Given the U.S.'s stance toward immigrants in recent years, it is entirely possible that it winds up similar to how Japan has been over the past three decades. The reality is that the United States now has a bloated fiscal structure that will weigh on growth in future years. Unless the United States sharply reverses recent immigration policies, the country is going to be required to rely almost solely on productivity growth for GDP growth, which is not an enviable position to be in. The United States does maintain advantages over Japan in the form of a better higher education system along with more innovative and higher quality companies, but the United States must be on guard to maintain these advantages because we are at a precarious time in country history. While not in the same position as Japan in the 1990s, the situation the United States faces today is not all that different. I hope that the United States does not get to a place where it becomes viewed as being not as hospitable to capitalism as it was in the past. As a country, it has certainly been trending in that direction. I remain optimistic, in the sense that the business protections that the United States provides are still unparalleled in the modern day, at least compared to other major economies. Hopefully the United States can learn from Japan's past, and Japan can replicate the U.S.'s historical success.

CHAPTER 8

Germany

Post-World War I (1920–1933)

Background and Market Impact

I wanted to cover Germany after World War I to discuss what impact a major event such as a war could have on an economy. Additionally, I didn't want readers to believe that Zimbabwe was some isolated underdeveloped country example of high inflation. Germany was a major global power that succumbed to the challenges faced by high debt and inflation. What happened with Germany after World War I is an important part of global history and has shaped the world we live in today.

As we now know, what happened after World War I related to Germany paved the way for World War II. Most would argue that the treatment of Germany after World War I was overly harsh. The Treaty of Versailles saddled Germany with the equivalent of $423 billion of debt in today's dollars. The peace treaty effectively said that Germany was solely responsible for World War I and forced the country to pay massive reparations for that being the case. It took Germany 92 years to fulfill the debt obligations tied to World War I. Over the years, Germany defaulted on the debt payments many times, and in 1990, most of the original debt sum was written off, which made it more realistic for Germany to fulfill the obligations.

I won't delve too much into whether Germany's repercussions in light of World War I were justified. I will leave that discussion for someone else and stick to the facts. What we know for certain is that Germany was already heavily indebted prior to the reparations imposed by the Treaty of Versailles owing to costs related to the war that were financed by printing more money. Similar to other cases studied, the root cause of German hyperinflation was attributable to private money printing. As is typical when private commercial banks are incentivized to behave irresponsibly, they printed a massive amount of money until half the money in circulation was private bank money that the Reichsbank readily exchanged for Reichsmarks on demand. You then throw in these new massive costs that were not even productive for the German economy, and it is easy to see how Germany plunged into chaos in the years following World War I. These conditions were at least partially attributable to enabling the rise of Adolf Hitler, who used the fragile domestic conditions to his advantage in terms of clamping down on power, just like we have seen other brutal autocratic leaders do throughout history.

During World War I, up to three million Germans, including 15 percent of the domestic male population (and more than one-third of German men aged 19 to 22), were estimated to have been killed in the war. The Treaty of Versailles reduced Germany's territory by 13 percent, in addition to placing limitations on Germany's armed forces. Included in the 13 percent loss of German territory was 48 percent of Germany's iron production and a sizeable amount of its coal production. As you can see, as a result of the war, Germany was limited in terms of industrial economic potential. Because of the terms of the Treaty of Versailles, the country was pressured economically by the loss of young productive contributors to society, there was a shortage of goods in the country, the domestic currency already pressured from debts taken on to finance the war was put under severe strain from the war reparations and negative affects to the economy, and revolts broke out across Germany.

One of the biggest stories from World War I as it relates to Germany was the debt. Even before the crippling reparations, Germany had printed massive amounts of money to finance the war. Germany had suspended the gold standard so that it could borrow more money to finance the war. This is a topic we will address again later, but there is a loss of monetary accountability when currencies are not tied to hard assets such as gold. It is estimated that Germany increased the Deutschmarks in circulation from 13 to 60 billion with the domestic debt load increasing from five to 100 billion marks. It is starting to become clear as to how hyperinflation took off in Germany after the war. As cited in the Zimbabwe chapter, hyperinflation usually occurs as a result of some combination of war, economic turmoil, high national debt levels, excessive money printing, political instability, and a loss of confidence in the monetary system. All these elements were present in Germany after World War I.

One of the key components of the German inflation story was the shortage of consumer staples, as is often the case when there is high inflation. Germany's problems stemmed from a British naval blockade that continued into 1919 even after the war ended. Germany had not prepared for a war that would last many years and struggled to produce enough food when the country was largely dependent on its domestic farmers. In light of the food shortages, Germany resorted to rationing and price controls. As we know from our case study on the United States, in the 1970s, price controls stimulate inflation instead of decreasing it. When price controls are enacted, this reduces the incentive to create a product or service. You then have a reduction in supply of a particular product or service because there are less individuals and businesses willing to produce that product or service. The United States should have learned from Germany in the early 1900s, because this is exactly what happened then just as it has throughout history related to price controls. When you factor in the loss of productive citizens, a naval blockade that continued after the war, price controls that were kept on some consumer staples, the widespread disarray caused by World War I, along with inflation that was spiraling out of control, it becomes clear as to why consumer staple shortages remained after World War I ended.

By late 1923, it cost more for Germany to print a currency note than it was worth. To give an example of how quickly prices were escalating, a loaf of bread that cost 250 marks in January 1923 soared to 200 million marks in November 1923. Inflation was so out of control it was reported that workers were paid twice per day because the initial payments were often deemed worthless by lunch hour! As referenced in the book *When Money Dies: The Nightmare of Deficit Spending, Devaluation, and Hyperinflation in Weimar Germany*, there are tales of meals at restaurants costing more when the bill arrived compared to when the meal was ordered. By late 1923, 42 billion marks were worth the equivalent of one American cent.

After seeing what was happening in Germany, lenders such as the United States attempted a couple plans to increase the chances that

Germany would pay off their war debts. The Dawes Plan in 1924 called for a reduction in Germany's war debt along with other efforts such as the restructuring of the German national bank that aimed to help stabilize the newly issued German currency. I will further discuss the implications of the new currency and compare how Germany handled this development as compared to Zimbabwe. While the Dawes Plan was considered a success, Germany still had difficulties servicing and paying the war debts. The Young Plan, which was written in 1929, further reduced Germany's war debt. The problem was that the Great Depression occurred shortly after the Young Plan was enacted, which provided another major hurdle for Germany to clear in addition to their other issues. All these developments laid the groundwork for Adolf Hitler to take control of the vulnerable nation. Hitler was named chancellor of Germany in 1933. Germany was looking for a savior from a very difficult period in country history, and Adolf Hitler took advantage by leveraging his gifted public speaking abilities and using then revolutionary technologies, such as the radio, to his advantage. When things go wrong, it is human nature to look for a scapegoat. Unfortunately, for Germany and the world, nobody understood this better than Hitler, and he used the Jewish population as the scapegoats for Germany's problems. Hitler was committed to overturning the entire Treaty of Versailles, and he rallied support from Germans that felt as though the world had turned against them after World War I. Germany did not make any payments on the war debt during Hitler's time in power.

How Businesses Were Affected

As we know from our Zimbabwe hyperinflation case study, these types of economic environments impact every business and citizen. Once inflation unleashes to the degree as to what unfolded in Germany in the 1920s and in Zimbabwe in the 2000s, people and businesses will respond by avoiding the now worthless domestic currency altogether. Some individuals will resort to a form of barter system. It is very difficult to run any kind of business without a reliable medium of exchange. What incentive do workers have to put in the hard labor if they know that their form of payment will be worthless within hours?

It is not practical by any means to have a scenario where businesses are paying their employees with other forms of exchange such as physical goods, and in order for the companies to acquire those goods, they would have to offer some form of payment, which does not solve the problem at hand. The other option is to pay employees in alternative currencies, which happened in Germany in the 1920s. As we studied in the chapter on Zimbabwe, under hyperinflation scenarios, people respond by hoarding physical goods. Citizens stop depositing money into banks and financial institutions because the currency has become worth substantially less or is worthless altogether. Banks dramatically curtail lending or stop lending money because they can't be sure that the interest incurred will compensate for the rise in inflation. At this point, a barter or black-market economy emerges. Citizens spend the paper money where it is accepted as quickly as possible, with the expectation that the money is going to be worth less in the future than today. This is the opposite of the scenario in Japan and the reason that there are diverging impacts on the value of money.

One of the problems facing German businesses in the 1920s was labor unions. The labor unions were demanding dramatic wage increases to compensate for the rampant inflation. The higher wages ultimately led to more domestic currency in circulation, which further exacerbated the inflation problem and in turn every company's ability to operate a business. It then becomes a better business proposition for domestic companies to export their goods or services abroad in exchange for foreign currencies that aren't suffering the same fate as the domestic currency. The relative attractiveness of exports compared to imports for businesses in these scenarios worsens the problem related to the shortage of goods domestically. When all of this happens, you have a situation like what we witnessed in Germany in 1923 where many people spend their currency as quickly as possible in exchange for consumer goods with the expectation that the currency will be worth less tomorrow. Like what we saw in Germany, this is the moment where the economy essentially comes to a complete halt.

What is interesting about the case study with German hyperinflation is that it really wasn't until 1931, over a decade after the hyperinflation episode began, that the German banking system collapsed. Unlike

Zimbabwe, where the country has failed for decades to regain confidence in any domestic currency, in late 1923, Germany issued a new currency called the Rentenmark that gained acceptance and likely staved off a catastrophic banking crisis. The new currency was backed by hard assets such as land and industrial goods (when there is a currency collapse, governments usually turn to hard assets to support paper money). Even though the Rentenmark was marketed as being backed by hard assets such as land, it is highly unlikely that the government would have been able to make good on its promise if a large number of people wanted to convert this new paper money into hard assets. The reality was that the Rentenmark was still an unconvertible paper currency, but the change in name and strategy worked. The money velocity slowed, as people no longer spent their cash as soon as they received it in fear that it would become worthless. I think the most important reason that Germany was able to successfully implement a new currency with public support, as compared to Zimbabwe's decades of trials and tribulations, has everything to do with the credibility of the government. Zimbabwe has a long history of government corruption, and most citizens just haven't trusted the government and in turn have not shown faith in the domestic currency. This was not the case with Germany, as the domestic citizens ultimately bought into the new currency and the overall strategy. After all, a currency is only worth what people think it is. I think this is an important point that is often misunderstood.

While it wasn't until several years after the hyperinflation episode that the German banking system collapsed, the period of hyperinflation set the table for the ultimate banking demise. The German banks saw a decline in the amount of liquid capital on hand during the hyperinflation period, and it was not replenished after conditions stabilized in the mid-1920s. It is estimated that German banks had cash liquidity equal to 3.8 percent of deposits in 1929 compared to 7.3 percent in 1913. Despite the much lower cash liquidity levels, German banks did not curtail their lending after conditions stabilized. Even though overall business was down for German banks leading up to the banking crisis, there were more domestic banks in operation than there were prior to World War I. The high level of competition and lower overall business paired with low cash liquidity and relatively loose oversight set the stage for a classic banking crisis. I think that the German hyperinflation also played a role in the banking collapse from a psychological perspective that impacted risk-taking. When inflation was high, German banks were investing short-term deposits for durations as little as one week in stocks in an attempt to offset inflation. This probably made sense, given the alternatives at the time, but this is an incredibly risky proposition in the event there is a swift collapse in the equity markets. I think that these types of events impacted risk-taking in the banking sector from a psychological perspective that would hasten the impacts of the ultimate banking collapse. As we saw in Iceland, Indonesia, and Chile, foreign capital in the banking sector played a role in the demise. The increase in reliance on foreign capital is at least partially attributable to the hyperinflation developments because, as we discussed, businesses went through a period where it was more attractive to export goods and services abroad owing to issues with the domestic currency. Additionally, Germans were still reluctant to put money into banks even after the new currency adoption out of fear that hyperinflation would return, and their deposits would again become worthless. As we have seen in our other case studies, there was an increasing reliance on foreign capital that was used for short-term deposits matched with long-term loans. Foreign investors were drawn to the German market because of the carry trade the market was offering with relatively high interest rates. In other words, this was mostly speculative capital that fled quickly once market conditions deteriorated, similar to what we studied in Iceland, Indonesia, and Chile. The foreign reserves were not adequate to meet the demands of capital from foreign investors. It is hard to believe that similar scenarios in the banking sector continue to occur even today when this blueprint for disaster could be learned from in the 1930s. The triggers for the demise in the banking systems of Germany, Iceland, Indonesia, and Chile are very similar.

Similar to what the United States would do a few years later in the midst of the Great Depression, Germany declared a banking holiday in 1931, and there were widespread banking failures. In 1931, an organization was created called the Transfer Association, whose goal was to ensure settlements of transfers between German banks. The Transfer Association was only a temporary measure aimed at protecting domestic banks against a bank run initiated by a classic case of mass withdrawals. There was an entity created called Akzeptbank A.G. that assisted banks with making loans accessible by maintaining access to credit from the German central bank. Unlike what we studied in the cases of Iceland, Chile, and Japan, Germany did not resort to nationalizing private banks as a policy response. Government capital was used to support efforts such as the Akzeptbank A.G., but we did not see the massive capital injections like we later saw in banking crisis scenarios in the United States, Iceland, Chile, and Japan. In this book, I have been critical of global central banks essentially concluding that deficits don't matter, resulting in the printing of enormous amounts of currency, but the relatively subdued German policy response likely contributed to the protracted depression conditions (again assuming that fractional-reserve banking will be used without money supply constraints and a gold standard). In fact, it was part of the German chancellor's strategy to implement wage cuts and spending reductions in an effort to lower prices, which would be an unheard-of policy response today in the wake of a major crisis. It is important to strike the proper balance, because as we have seen, piling on too much government debt can be a large contributor to a broken economy that can persist for decades. In the period of hyperinflation following World War I, coupled with the depression conditions in the early 1930s, these events paved the way for the disruptive force by the name of Adolf Hitler to assume power in 1933.

Macroeconomic Impact

As a recap, World War I lasted from 1914 to 1918. World War I set the stage for the hyperinflation years in Germany from 1920 to 1923 owing to massive debts taken on to finance the war, crippling war reparations from the Treaty of Versailles, a shortage of consumer staples that was worsened by the naval blockade that continued even after World War I concluded, a loss of productive citizens during World War I, overall disarray caused by World War I, and disastrous political policies such as price controls that exacerbated inflation. In 1923, Germany adopted a new currency with relative success, and the country went through various debt restructuring programs over the next several years leading up to the Great Depression in 1929. Following the adoption of the new currency in

1923, the German economy experienced an economic boom from 1924 to 1929. As is usually the case, the good economic times masked the underlying issues with the financial system that remained from the hyperinflation years of 1920 to 1923. The Great Depression lasted from 1929 to 1939, and the collapse of the German banking system occurred in 1931. Adolf Hitler took advantage of a vulnerable nation and took power in 1933. This was the beginning of the global collision course for the start of World War II in 1939.

The other major hyperinflation episodes in modern history include Hungary in the 1940s, Yugoslavia in the 1990s, Zimbabwe in the 2000s, and Greece in the 1940s. Most would argue that in a lot of ways this group of countries never really recovered from their hyperinflation periods. We have already studied Zimbabwe at length, and most would agree that Hungary and the current-day countries that once formed Yugoslavia (Slovenia, Croatia, Bosnia and Herzegovina, North Macedonia, Serbia, and Montenegro) are not exactly economic superpowers. Greece has largely been an economic disaster for decades. Greece went on to abandon their domestic currency, the Greek drachma, in 2002, and the country was particularly hard hit during the global financial crisis. Greece had entered the crisis as one of the poorest and most indebted countries. Greece subsequently suffered a debt crisis, and the country has largely been a beacon of economic and political instability.

I don't think it should be surprising that Germany has been a relative (at least compared to other European countries) economic standout in modern times. As of the time of this writing, Germany had the fourth largest economy in the world as measured by GDP. Similar to Chile, Germany learned from its past and has largely eschewed fiscal deficits. Even after the COVID-19 crisis, Germany still had less than 60 percent gross public debt as a percentage of GDP, which was significantly below its peer countries. The fiscal restraint displayed by the likes of Germany and Chile is in stark contrast to the situations we studied in Japan and Zimbabwe. It should be clear by now that there is a correlation between a country's fiscal health and level of economic success. Proponents of the modern monetary theory have likely not spent enough time studying historical case studies, as this trend becomes clear by looking at case studies related to debt in various countries over the years.

This book would not be complete without probably the most signif-icant currency development since 1971 when the United States severed the currency link to gold: the creation of the euro. The European Union (EU) is a political and economic union of 27 member states located in Europe that was created in 1993. The EU enables goods, services, money, and people to move across country borders with few restrictions. The EU includes joint organization planning on a broad range of topics ranging from political policy to climate. The unified currency, the euro, was a product of the EU that began circulation in 2002 (the euro was first launched in 1999, but for the first three years, it was only used for accounting purposes and electronic payments). The euro evolved out of the European Monetary System (EMS) that was created in 1979 to help stabilize exchange rates. We discussed the U.S. decision in 1971 to com-pletely sever the price link to gold that resulted in widespread currency devaluations and played a role in the ultimate creation of the euro. The euro was created with a goal of promoting stability, growth, and economic integration in Europe. The euro is not adopted by all EU members, but most of the countries that do not use the euro as their domestic currency employ some form of currency peg that involves the euro.

The biggest issue with the euro is that a single monetary policy often does not match with the local economic and political conditions of the various constituent nations. Unlike a case such as the United States, where individual states have different economic conditions, the states should, at least in theory, share overall commonalities in terms of political goals, as the individual states are part of one united nation. The political goals of Greece and Germany could be completely different, yet they share the same currency that is governed alike. This does not make any sense. I think the bigger issue with the euro is that the monetary policy that governs the currency does not adapt to fit the local country conditions. A great example of this problem would be Greece. Greece has had many of its own self-inflicted problems with debt levels and overall ineffective political policy over the years, but its issues have been compounded by the fact that the country hasn't been able to dictate its own monetary policy. It would make a lot more sense for Greece to have its own currency that is pegged to a basket of assets such as the U.S. dollar, the euro, the Japanese yen, the Chinese renminbi, the British pound, the Australian dollar, other theoretical individual European country currencies if the euro were disbanded, and gold. At the least, a country like Greece would not be able to blame other countries for the situation it had in 2010, when it resorted to receiving the largest bailout loan in IMF history at that time.

Even though I have discussed some of the problems with the euro and EU more broadly, it has often been believed that the euro has been governed to favor larger constituents such as Germany over the years. Research studies have shown that Germany has been by far the largest beneficiary of the euro, as measured by prosperity per inhabitant since the introduction of the currency. Countries such as Italy, France, and Portugal are shown to have been major losers of the euro since its inception, and a country like Greece that was initially a beneficiary ultimately plunged into disaster and hasn't recovered. It is impossible to say for certain, but one of the biggest questions is if Germany would prosper to the degree that it has without the euro and EU more broadly. Despite Germany's relative economic success over the years, the country does in a lot of ways resemble modern-day Japan with the exception of the situation related to fiscal deficits where Germany is in much better shape. Japan and Germany are the third and fourth largest economies, respectively, in the world based on GDP. Based on 2020 figures, Japan and Germany had the second and fourth highest average median citizen ages, respectively, in the world. Both Japan and Germany, much like the United States, have low birthrates. Both Japan and Germany have had economies relatively reliant on exports driven by strength in manufacturing. Some believe that Germany has benefitted greatly from the free markets offered by the EU and the artificially low currency exchange rate offered by the euro, which has allowed Germany to boost exports, especially to other countries in the EU with few restrictions.

I would have to agree with the assessment that the euro has benefitted Germany, because the currency has provided for artificially low exchange rates that have boosted exports for a country that is reliant on exports for its overall economy. Despite the success, I do not believe that the long-term German economic model is sustainable without some form of domestic consumption encore to the export-driven model. This has been a topic we have covered extensively in this book. In the long term, Germany is in a more challenging situation in a lot of ways than other countries that have traditionally relied on export-driven economic models, such as Indonesia, because Germany is facing an aging population and a population that is expected to decline long term, barring some major shifts. Germany has benefitted greatly from free and open markets and an overall rule of law that would be the envy of most countries in the world. But in the long term, Germany is going to have to do something more to foster innovation because, much like Japan, if you look at the most valuable firms in the country, most are tied to manufacturing, with the bulk being car producers. This is in an era when the world has become a service-oriented economy and the vast majority of the great businesses are not associated with capital-intensive areas such as manufacturing. I think that the citizens of the United States have often taken the domestic innovation environment fueled by a world-class secondary education system for granted, but at least up until now, the United States has been able to foster innovation that other countries with similar long-term demographic challenges such as Germany and Japan have failed to replicate.

In closing, I think the euro has benefitted Germany, but the use of the currency does not make sense for a number of countries in the EU, and I don't think it is sustainable in the long term, even though the currency has lasted almost 20 years as of the time of this writing. There can still be a bloc like the EU that is relatively free of trading restrictions without the use of a common currency that places undue restrictions on participating countries related to monetary policy. While Germany has likely been a beneficiary of the euro and the EU more broadly, I think the country would have done fine if they had kept the Deutschmark. Most people eternally underestimate the power of running a country with good fiscal health and upholding the rule of law to the point where most investors would not worry about scenarios such as the government confiscating their assets. In the long run, Germany is going to have to do more to foster innovation in areas outside of manufacturing. Germany is likely going to have to provide more government incentives to build and maintain businesses in service-oriented industries such as technology.

CHAPTER 9

France

Mississippi Bubble (1716–1720)

Background and Market Impact

An asset bubble is characterized by a rapid increase in the value of an asset or group of assets, followed by a swift and violent collapse often known as the moment when the bubble bursts. During an asset bubble, the quoted prices of the underlying assets far outpace their real intrinsic value (what something is worth according to economic fundamentals). The interesting part about asset bubbles is that there are often what could be argued as being rational and irrational participants in these market events. There will be market participants that do not realize that an asset bubble is taking place. These participants usually see outsized wealth (or at least temporary paper wealth) being created by others in some form of asset and end up piling into an asset at hand in the pursuit of easy gains. Once you have broad-based participation of unknowing market participants, this is often the moment just before the ultimate asset bubble collapse, and the late-stage speculators that came along in the pursuit of easy gains end up with massive financial losses. Perhaps more interesting are the cases when individuals realize that an asset bubble is taking hold, yet these people buy into the asset bubble with the idea that they hope to exit before the bubble ultimately bursts. Some would consider these individuals to be rational asset bubble participants. I personally think it is near-impossible to consistently get the timing correct on market events such as asset bubbles, but many people have tried and continue to try to do it.

Here are some of the most notable asset bubbles in history: the U.S. housing bubble in the mid-2000s leading up to the global financial crisis, the dot-com bubble in the United States in the late 1990s, Japan's real estate and stock market bubble in the late 1980s (which was covered earlier), the U.S. stock bull market in the 1920s leading up to the Great Depression, the British railway mania of the 1840s (covered in the next chapter), the South Sea bubble in Britain in 1720, and the Dutch Tulip Mania in the 1630s. It is up for debate, as of the time of this writing, whether new asset classes, such as cryptocurrencies, are in the midst of an asset bubble.

I want to review the Japanese real estate and stock market bubble before diving into the asset bubble related to the Mississippi Company. As noted in the chapter on Japan, in the late 1980s, we had a wild scenario where the Japanese real estate market was worth four times the U.S. real estate market, even though Japan's total land area is around 4 percent of the size of the United States. How does this happen? Almost every financial crisis and asset bubble in history have been heavily influenced by a period of easy monetary policy where there is too much money chasing too few market opportunities. This concept should be clear from the detailed case studies reviewed in this book, but I will bring in some outside help from one of the greatest investors in history, Stanley Druckenmiller. In an interview, Druckenmiller said:

> I will go to my grave and – often wrong, never in doubt – believing that really loose monetary policy greatly contributed to the financial crisis. There were obviously problems with regulation. But, when we had a 1% Fed Funds Rate in 2003, after, to me it was pretty obvious the economy had turned. [for the better]... I've made some money predicting boom/bust cycles. It's what I do. Sometimes I'm right, sometimes I'm wrong. But, every bust I had ever seen was preceded by an asset bubble generally set up by too loose policy.

There you have it. Druckenmiller's commentary and rationale are consistent with my own research and are supported by thousands of years of financial history.

Now on to the asset bubble tied to the Mississippi Company in France in the early 1700s. The French economy was depressed in the early 1700s, and the French government had accumulated excessive debts. Similar to the period in Germany in the early 1900s when Germany had emerged from World War I heavily indebted and vulnerable, France in the early 1700s had come out of the War of the Spanish Succession with high debt levels and an economy in turmoil. With France in a vulnerable state, a man by the name of John Law proposed a form of new monetary system where precious metals would be replaced with paper money. It is interesting that John Law came to play such an important role in history, as he had essentially zero prior credentials until France allowed Law to try his grand monetary experiment in the country. John Law was born into a wealthy family and ended up gambling away his generous inheritance by the age of 23. It has been written that Law went on to reaccumulate wealth after studying probabilities related to card games. Law had much grander ambitions beyond gambling, as he studied economics and attempted to establish a national bank in Scotland, but Law's proposal was rejected by the Scottish government. With France in a precarious state following a series of wars, Law sensed an opportunity to capitalize on his grand vision of creating a bank on Law's terms. This entire saga with John Law reminded me a lot of when in the 2010s the Malaysian prime minister entrusted billions of dollars and the government's reputation to a con artist by the name of Jho Low. John Law was ultimately granted permission to establish a bank in France where he could test his paper money experiment. Related to paper money and the gold standard, we have come full circle in history. France had previously operated on a monetary system predicated upon precious metals, but now Law had been given permission to issue paper currency through the newly established bank.

It is said that John Law theorized that the underlying issues with the French economy stemmed from the lack of predictability of the supply of gold and silver. Law's solution to this alleged problem was to replace the precious metals with paper money that would allow for more currency in circulation and boost the overall economy. This theory should sound familiar, as this is essentially what the world has been living by since 1971 when the United States severed the link between currency and gold. Since then, global debt levels have exploded, and there has been a proliferation of unsound money policies owing to a lack of accountability in the form of hard assets. It is interesting that global central banks have not heeded the warning of 300 years ago as to what happened in France when John Law attempted this grand monetary experiment that imploded in a spectacular fashion.

In 1716, John Law received permission to test his monetary experiment in France, and Banque Générale was established as a private bank. This new bank was able to issue paper money in the form of banknotes that had not previously existed in France. John Law convinced the public to exchange their precious metals for the banknotes (paper money) that were issued by the newly established private bank. It only took 11 months for it to be possible for the state to collect taxes in this new paper money. This is an early example of many of the topics that have been previously discussed in this book. The government had now monopolized the money supply, which I believe is the single most powerful tool that a government has.

Since Banque Générale had the ability to issue paper money, and this currency could be used to settle taxes, the bank was essentially the equivalent of a modern-day central bank. Other banks used the paper money issued by Banque Générale to extend loans. Pretty similar to what many people argue as a bull case for cryptocurrencies today, John Law's bank convinced the general public to exchange their precious metals for the bank-issued paper money by telling them that the banknotes would protect against future depreciation of the precious metals. The strategy worked probably beyond Law's wildest dreams, with the paper money rising to a 15 percent premium over the precious metals within a year. At least temporarily before inflation got out of control, the newly issued paper money did just as Law said it would: boost money circulation and, in turn, the overall economy.

The banking effort would have been considered an initial success for John Law, but the bank by itself did not help the French royal reduce the massive debts that had been accumulated from the series of wars. This is where the Mississippi Company came in. The Mississippi Company was created and given exclusive trading privileges in a territory stretching from the Mississippi River to Canada for a period of 25 years. John Law financed the operations of the company by selling shares in exchange for paper money, similar to how an initial public offering (IPO) would operate today. There was not a lack of interest in this 1700s' version of an IPO because of interest in the potential gold and silver acquired by the company in their operations. This point is particularly interesting, given that French citizens had spent the previous few years exchanging all their gold and silver for banknotes. The Mississippi Company went on to acquire what would amount to a monopoly on tobacco trading with Africa. The company acquired trading rights with China and the East Indies. The Mississippi Company obtained the rights to produce new precious metals for France, along with the rights to collect taxes on behalf of the French government. Prior to the crash of the Mississippi Company, John Law commanded near-unchecked power. Through his interests in the Mississippi Company, Banque Générale (which was later renamed Bank Royale), and ultimately the controller-general and superintendent general of finance of France, Law was one of the most powerful individuals in the world. Law was essentially granted unilateral power to issue currency on behalf of the French government, control France's foreign trade and international development, and run what would amount to a massive business conglomerate with virtually unlimited financing since Law was in charge of the country's currency issuances.

The broad expansion of operations by the Mississippi Company was being financed by the additional issuance of shares in the company, diluting previous shareholders. If Law wanted to, he could have supported the share price of the Mississippi Company for at least some period of time because he maintained control over the currency issuance and the French government debt. Within a year after Mississippi Company debuted its 1700s version of an IPO, the share price had increased by an astounding 1,900 percent. Like all asset bubbles throughout history, individuals started seeing and hearing about their neighbors getting rich quickly. Because of greed and fear of missing out, more people piled into this financial rocket ship. There may have also been some individuals realizing that an asset bubble was taking place and bought in anyway, but that is unclear and not as likely as later in history because the people at this time didn't have various examples of asset bubbles to study and recognize what was occurring.

The Mississippi Company was initially floated on the public market in January of 1719. After soaring in value throughout 1719, the share price of the company began to slip in January of 1720, as some individuals exchanged their shares in the Mississippi Company for gold. Since John Law essentially maintained unilateral control over the monetary system, he responded to this selling activity by placing restrictions on payment in gold that was above a small threshold (the restrictions on gold were later reversed). What Law did here in the early 1700s was not unlike when the United States passed the Gold Reserve Act 1934. In the 1930s, FDR placed limitations on gold ownership by private citizens of the United States. The goals of John Law in 1720 and FDR in 1934 were the same: monopolize the money supply. Governments have consistently done this throughout history, recognizing that controlling the money supply is the most powerful tool a government has. This reality is particularly relevant and interesting as I write this today, as few are considering the possibility that cryptocurrencies will be outlawed or severely restricted.

The ultimate undoing of the asset bubble tied to the Mississippi Company was triggered when Bank Royale (previously Banque Générale) vowed to exchange banknotes for shares of the Mississippi Company at a quoted market price. The problem was related to the amount of paper money that was issued to make this happen. Almost overnight, the money supply of the country was doubled, and this resulted in soaring inflation. By January of 1720, annual inflation had reached a rate of 276 percent. Because of the inflation that was now out of control, John Law resorted to several devaluations of the Mississippi Company throughout 1720. By September of 1721, less than two years after the shares were made available to the public, the shares of the Mississippi Company were worth the same as they had been when they were initially listed. Despite soaring 1,900 percent in short order, the market crash ended up occurring almost just as swiftly as is often the case with asset bubbles. A combination of the reversal of the restrictions on gold and widespread doubt that was now tied to paper money and the value of the Mississippi Company caused citizens to rush to retrieve gold from the banks as quickly as possible. This series of events was no different than the various bank runs we have seen throughout history. John Law may not have been solely responsible for this disaster (he did receive permission from the head of France after all), but he was forced to flee France in 1720. Law's company and bank were absorbed by the government. It is said that Law later died a poor man, which was once (although briefly) unthinkable.

Macroeconomic Impact

For the remaining chapters, I am going to skip the section *How Businesses Were Affected* owing to a lack of information from the earlier time periods. When you have a situation where inflation spirals out of control like what occurred, it is safe to say that every business and individual is impacted. It wouldn't be until the late 1700s that France would bring back paper currency.

An important event occurred in 1721 (that would drag on for years) after the Mississippi Company meltdown that must be covered here. There were still large debts owed by the king, the Mississippi Company, and the government-controlled bank that was taken over from John Law. These debts amounted to 50 percent of the total GDP, which was a very large figure for this time period. To help resolve this situation, France engaged in a major debt restructuring process. Since France was an absolute monarchy, the government could have opted for outright default on the debt obligations, and all parties would have just had to accept this outcome. This path would have made it more difficult for France to later reintroduce paper currency, because defaults lessen confidence in the domestic monetary system and government overall. A pattern of default also makes it more difficult for governments to access public capital markets, as lenders will either not lend money to a serial defaulter or demand onerous terms. France opted for a debt restructuring where the bank was liquidated, and debts owed by the Mississippi Company were absolved. The restructuring process did not dramatically reduce its debt service levels, and this is important. While this path was positive from the standpoint that it maintained a degree of credibility of the monetary system, it likely led to problems down the line when France entered the Seven Years' War in 1756. France's ongoing debt problems were further compounded by the expenses tied to the Seven Years' War, which played a role in the French Revolution that started in 1789.

Some people don't realize that many of today's developed countries were once emerging countries in terms of the economy. Look no further than France as an example of this concept. The now famous book, *This Time Is Different: Eight Centuries of Financial Folly,* discusses the graduation that some countries make in going from being serial debt defaulters to stable, developed markets. France defaulted on its debt a staggering eight times between 1558 and 1788, with the roots of some of the defaults in the 1700s being discussed in this chapter. Aside from the debatable default on some portion of France's World War I debts, it is often believed that France has not defaulted on its debts since 1812. This is a major turnaround for a country that abandoned paper currency for 80 years in the 1700s and even had a prime minister argue that governments should default at least once every 100 years to *restore equilibrium.* It should be clear from this book that there is a definitive correlation between the overall economic success of a country and the degree to which a country remains fiscally conservative and does not encounter continuous debt problems. As of the time of this writing, countries such as Zimbabwe and Japan have never broken out of their debt cycle problems since the crises that were covered. On the other end of the spectrum, a country such as Chile, which was once a serial debt defaulter and poster child for economic disarray, learned from others' mistakes and went on to manage its finances more conservatively and, coupled with other measures, has evolved into a relative economic success story. At least in comparison to time periods such as the 1700s, France would fall into Chile's camp. As of 2021, France is estimated to have the sixth largest GDP by country in the world, and a lot of this relative success is attributable to France having evolved from an emerging serial defaulting country to a developed and stable economy. While France is far from perfect, they would still be the envy of a great number of emerging markets around the world.

I think now is an appropriate time to review the gold standard and its place in history. What happened during this saga in the early 1700s was a preview of a scenario that would continue to play out time and time again in various countries throughout the world over the next few hundred years. In this situation in France in the early 1700s, the rationale for dropping the gold standard in favor of paper money was that paper money would boost monetary circulation and, in turn, the overall economy. In 1971, the United States severed the link between gold and currency, and the world has really been operating on a global monetary system of fiat currencies not dissimilar from our case study here of France in the early 1700s. While this fiat currency system has been in place for

50 years without completely imploding in contrast to what happened in France, I don't think it is clear this will remain the case in the future. We have entered a new era of monetary policy where modern monetary theory economists have won out and governments have essentially concluded that federal deficits do not matter. The problem with this line of thinking is that history says otherwise. What often happens is that inflation gets out of hand if too much paper money is printed and put into circulation within a given economy. As we saw in our case studies on France, Zimbabwe, and Germany, people ultimately lose confidence in a currency if the limits of monetary and fiscal policy are pushed to the extreme. As I write this chapter today, people are significantly underestimating the chances that history will repeat itself and confidence will again be lost in paper currencies. In fact, I don't think the odds of this happening have ever been higher across a broad number of countries. After the COVID-19 crisis, we have never seen a scenario in modern times where so many countries around the world have used such extreme monetary policies to try and dig themselves out of difficult financial situations.

Let's now review asset bubbles and build on the conversation from earlier in the chapter. Along with Stanley Druckenmiller, I believe that a near-universal characteristic of asset bubbles is that they are facilitated by easy monetary policies. Our 1700s' example in France was an early case study of what happens when a government has little monetary accountability, and the easy monetary and fiscal policies are taken to an extreme. As we have learned from this book, what has always happened throughout history when easy monetary and fiscal policies are taken beyond their outer bounds is that there is ultimately a day of reckoning. This can happen in the form of rampant inflation (France, Germany, and Zimbabwe), an asset bubble and collapse followed by persistent deflation (Japan), or a major financial crisis with asset bubbles as a contributing factor (the United States, Iceland, and Indonesia). Easy monetary policies distort the valuations of various assets. For example, when interest rates are low, a rational individual would be willing to pay a higher price for a stock since the opportunity cost is owning a bond that is earning little in the way of interest. Problems occur when people start to assume that this type of environment is going to continue in perpetuity, and this is usually when asset bubbles get out of control. I would argue that I am seeing that situation play out at this very moment in many asset classes around the world. The trigger for the decline in asset prices is almost always rising interest rates that are used to combat potentially heightened inflation, which is often accelerated by large-scale money printing.

As I write this chapter, many investors and economists are concluding that this time is different, and that easy monetary and fiscal policies can be consistently used without having any unintended consequences. At least to me, it is clear this line of thinking is most certainly not the case, and we have already seen broad-based asset bubbles brought about by valuation distortions due to low interest rates. In a classic sign of an asset bubble, countless prospective homebuyers are coming way over the top on the ask price for houses that are already being listed for prices well above historical rates. Low mortgage rates distort home prices because many people will use the logic that it makes more sense to buy a house and take on a mortgage at a low rate as opposed to paying rent on an apartment. The problem with this line of thinking is that there is an implicit assumption that there won't be a material decline in the equity value on the home, which likely won't be the case if the home is purchased in the midst of an asset bubble. As we have learned from this book, this scenario is the classic setup for a major financial crisis. It will be interesting to see what happens if there were to be a major financial crisis when interest rates are so low (central banks ultimately aggressively raised interest rates in 2022 in response to soaring inflation) and debt levels are so high in many countries around the world. Historically, one of the main tools that governments have used to stimulate economies in the wake of a financial crisis has been to lower interest rates. Even 12 years after the global financial crisis, interest rates remain very low in almost every country around the world. Additionally, after consumer price inflation finally surged in 2021 and 2022 in response to the irresponsible monetary policies from central banks and other factors such as supply disruptions, governments would have a difficult time printing large amounts of additional paper money for bailouts in a financial crisis scenario, as this could further accelerate inflation. A major financial crisis in the near future could provide for a unique scenario in modern history that would test what we think we may know about economics and monetary policy. The canary in the coal mine is likely to be an increase in interest rates. In a recent interview,

Stanley Druckenmiller showed that, if 10-year U.S. interest rates were to go to a more normalized rate around 5 percent, the United States would be spending around 30 percent of the GDP each year just to service the debt (as of late 2022, this scenario was on the path to becoming a reality). Remember that all of this is happening just as we are seeing major demographic shifts in countries such as the United States where older segments of the population are soaking up greater proportions of federal budgets owing to entitlements.

I mentioned cryptocurrencies a few times in this book, and I wanted to briefly touch upon this topic. I do not consider myself to be an expert on cryptocurrencies, but I would like to comment on how they relate to topics such as fiat currencies because that comparison is relevant to many things we have discussed. I have talked about the global financial system having shifted to fiat currencies since 1971 when the United States severed the link between gold and paper money. Even though currencies around the world are not currently backed by hard assets such as gold as they have been at times in the past, I think an argument could still be made that fiat currencies are really being backed by faith in the individual governments themselves. This is interesting to think about because there have recently been arguments that cryptocurrencies have no intrinsic value and aren't backed by anything, and cryptocurrency bulls have countered by saying that the same is true of fiat currencies. I think that an argument could be made that cryptocurrencies are really being backed by faith in the public in contrast to how fiat currencies could be seen as being backed by faith in governments. I am not in any way saying that this is an all-encompassing way to think about cryptocurrencies and fiat currencies, but it is something interesting to think about. The history of countries operating without governments is not good. Ask any citizen of Somalia how it has worked out for them. This is not to say that there are zero practical use cases for a very limited number of cryptocurrencies. Citing a recent example, when Russia invaded Ukraine and Russia was effectively cut off from the global financial system, some individuals in Russia leveraged cryptocurrencies to move financial assets over fears of a classic bank run situation. In a scenario like this, it could be argued that the decentralized components of some cryptocurrencies could be seen as having some practical application.

CHAPTER 10

United States and Europe

The Panic of 1873 (1873–1879)

Background and Market Impact

The Panic of 1873 took place in both the United States and Europe, but my commentary in this chapter will mainly focus on the United States. I had previously referred to the period of 1873 to 1879 that has often been called the Long Depression and was a rare deflationary period in American history. This period originally was referred to as the Great Depression until the unfortunate series of events in the early 1930s took precedence. The Panic of 1873 was a financial crisis that triggered depression conditions in North America and Europe. Many believe that this period marked the first global depression that was the result of industrial capitalism where economies are dominated by trade, industry, and capital (this is the modern-day economic system in the developed world).

As we know by now, virtually every financial crisis in history has followed a period of rapid credit growth. The Panic of 1873 was no different. After the Civil War ended in the United States in 1865, there was a massive railroad boom that was financed by government land grants and subsidies along with speculative capital seeking outsized returns. This was a classic case of too much capital chasing too few opportunities for which an adequate return could be earned. It wasn't known at that time, but these conditions provide the perfect recipe for the bust part of the cycle in an economic cycle. At the time of this U.S. railroad boom, the railroad industry was the largest sector employer in the country after agriculture, which magnified the effects of the bust.

The Civil War played a critical role in the history of the U.S. monetary system. The first coins in America were minted in 1793, but it wasn't until the 1860s in the midst of the Civil War that the United States sought to create a national currency. Two competing currencies were used in the Civil War to finance the war. In the years following the Civil War, the United States government significantly expanded its powers over the monetary system through a series of Supreme Court decisions. In other words, the Civil War laid the groundwork for the monetary system that we have in the United States today. It was only after the Federal Reserve Act of 1913 was passed that the modern-day U.S. central bank was created, but the chips were starting to be put in place in the years following the Civil War.

It is not a coincidence that the first modern global depression occurred not long after the United States authorized the printing of paper money and was happening when governments knew substantially less than we do today about the ripple effects of monetary and fiscal policies. Like virtually all the crisis case studies we have examined, the market was flooded with capital, and then the consensus assumption became that the easy access to capital would continue in perpetuity. The easy money policies were greatly accelerated after the shift to paper money, because this shift reduced monetary accountability. The result was wild market speculation (this should sound similar to the market dynamics in 2021), and over-expansion in areas such as railroads where many projects were not supported by actual business fundamentals.

An important development occurred in 1873 with the passage of the Coinage Act of 1873. Prior to this policy, the United States had backed its currency with a combination of gold and silver. The Coinage Act of 1873, known by some as the *Crime of 1873*, abolished silver dollars from official coinage and paved the way for the gold standard in the United States. An obvious impact of this legislation was that silver prices were hurt, along with the silver mining businesses that referred to the act as the Crime of 1873. More importantly, as it relates to the health of the monetary system at that time, the money supply was reduced with the removal of silver from coinage. This led to an increase in interest rates. The ensuing crisis should not come as a surprise to readers of this book, as we know that periods of excessive credit growth and speculation, followed by a rise in interest rates usually lead to problems with the financial system.

Later in 1873, following the coin legislation, the dominos started to fall following the contraction in the U.S. money supply. This contraction coincided with a stock market crash in Europe. When the European market crashed, European investors that had contributed to the American railroad bubble began selling railroad bonds and were no longer willing to provide capital for the various U.S. railroad projects under construction. In short, capital dried up overnight when there was a boom in construction for one of the most capital-intensive businesses in history. An American firm by the name of Jay Cooke & Company, which was a significant banking entity at that time, had lent millions of dollars to railroad firms just like many other banks. Jay Cooke & Company was even in the process of financing a second transcontinental railroad in 1873 when it was discovered that the firm's credit had become worthless, and the company declared bankruptcy. Following the Jay Cooke bankruptcy, a bank called Henry Clews went under and was followed by a series of U.S. banking failures. When citizens saw Jay Cooke fail, it created a classic bank run scenario where masses of people pulled their money at the same time. All told, over 100 U.S. banks failed during this banking crisis episode. This should be yet another example of why banks and businesses that rely on leverage to earn an adequate return (which I personally still don't believe is adequate) are such horrific businesses. I believe that these types of assets do not possess much intrinsic value, given the guaranteed reliance on leverage as it relates to the standard operating model.

The banking failures in the United States sent shockwaves through the economy, and the New York Stock Exchange was closed for 10 days in 1873 starting September 20. What is amazing is how quickly this rapid series of events developed. Jay Cooke & Company declared bankruptcy on September 18, and the stock exchange closed just two days later, on September 20. The banking failures and contraction in money supply caused roughly a quarter of the United States' railroads to go bankrupt. This had a dramatic impact on the overall U.S. economy, given the economic contribution of railroads at that time. It is estimated that 18,000 businesses in the United States failed in a two-year period. By 1876, the U.S. unemployment rate was estimated to have skyrocketed to 14 percent. The depression would last until 1879, with a contraction in economic productivity leading to wage cuts, which would trigger the Great Railroad Strike of 1877.

I think it is equally important to note what the United States did in response to this crisis as it relates to monetary and fiscal policies. This would be unthinkable in modern times, but President Ulysses S. Grant vetoed a bill in April 1874 that would have added liquidity to financial markets following the banking system collapse in 1873. Grant reasoned that allowing for such a cash infusion would lead to more money printing in the future, which would accelerate inflation. Taking the hard money line even further, the Specie Resumption Act was passed in 1875 that called for the redemption of paper currency and was a step toward the gold standard. While I have lambasted the Federal Reserve for the modern-day view that fiscal deficits don't matter, it is likely that the response by the U.S. government in the 1870s prolonged the depression conditions. Providing some degree of government support to the financial markets in 1873 probably would have been a prudent idea, just like the United States later did in response to the global financial crisis and the COVID-19 crisis. This commentary assumes that countries will continue to disregard limits on money supply growth tied to GDP growth and employ the flawed fractional-reserve banking model. My main issue with the recent monetary and fiscal policy responses has been with the duration for which the Federal Reserve has provided market support. For example, as I write this chapter, the Federal Reserve is still providing market support in response to the COVID-19 crisis well over a year since the start of the crisis and long after most reasonable individuals would conclude that the economy has recovered enough to halt asset purchases and raise interest rates (this costly decision ultimately resulted in soaring consumer price inflation). The Federal Reserve in 2021 has almost solely been focused on the employment figures and disregarded potential negative impacts in the form of inflation and the health of the U.S. dollar. In a span of 150 years, the United States has gone from the extreme of being an uncompromising fiscal hawk to an economic dove with no bounds. There must be some middle ground, because both approaches threaten the lasting health of the U.S. monetary system and the U.S. dollar.

Macroeconomic Impact

What is particularly interesting to note about the boom-and-bust cycle of the U.S. railroads in the 1870s is that Europe experienced a similar ordeal in the 1840s. The major difference between these scenarios was that the irrational exuberance in European railroads was tied to the stock market while the U.S. railroad boom was happening in the private markets. The *British Railway Mania*, as it is referred to by some, of the 1840s was a classic market bubble where the quoted prices of the underlying assets far outpaced their real intrinsic value. This 1840s' bubble is often compared to the dot-com bubble in the United States in the late 1990s owing to the similarities: there was a new innovative technology (railroads and the Internet) that ultimately survived, but the market prices of various assets of little to no value at the time were trading at stratospheric valuations. Like nearly every boom-and-bust cycle I have ever studied, these market bubbles were fueled by easy monetary and fiscal policies, and the inevitable crash coincided with a rise in interest rates. A contributing factor to these bubbles was the rise in the number of railroad and Internet companies going public. At least for a period of time, investors were drawn in by the apparent easy gains offered by these businesses that were built upon the foundation of an innovative technology that appeared to have no limits. This should sound eerily similar to emerging technologies and products such as cryptocurrencies today. While it is likely that there will be a couple players that outlast the current market mania, I can say with almost certainty that the state of the 2021 market in areas such as cryptocurrencies is similar to that of the U.S. Internet companies in the late 1990s and European railroads in the 1840s. Yet again, these bubble conditions have been fueled by easy monetary and fiscal policies, and the bust is likely to coincide with a rise in interest rates and a contraction in the money supply.

A major difference between the U.S. railroad bust in the 1870s and the British Railroad Mania of the 1840s was that the U.S. series of events culminated in a major financial crisis and ensuing depression while the economywide effects in Europe were much less pronounced. The reason for this is that banks and financial institutions making loans to railroads, which were critical components of the U.S. economy in the 1870s, were at the core of what developed in the United States in the 1870s. Given the inherent leverage required to operate a standard bank or financial business that makes loans, these businesses often fail quickly and can take down the entire financial system because the effects are accelerated when consumers rush to retrieve their proceeds at the same time (often referred to as a bank run). The U.S. financial crisis in the 1870s with the financial institutions at the heart of the collapse was similar to our case studies on Iceland, Indonesia, and Chile. On the other hand, the European event of the 1840s was primarily tied to the public markets similar to the U.S. Internet bubble in the 1990s or the Dutch Tulip Mania of the 1630s.

The financial impact in the 1840s was more limited to the individual and institutional investors that had invested in the railroad companies. It is interesting to note that, similar to how modern-day financial crises have repeated for centuries in a resembling manner, market bubbles predicated upon new technologies have done the same. The British Railway Mania, the dot-com bubble, and the ongoing cryptocurrency bubble are all technological market bubbles induced by the same factors. There was a macroeconomic backdrop of easy monetary and fiscal policies that led to an influx of capital and inflated asset valuations. There was a new innovative technology that caused investors to come to believe that almost anything related to this technology must be a good investment regardless of the product or price. On top of these factors, an influx of novice investors inflated the asset bubbles of these investments tied to the new technologies. The number of new investors was accelerated by an increase in the number of ways in which an individual could invest in the new form of technology. During the British Railway Mania, it was the surge in new railroad companies going public similar to the Internet companies during the dot-com bubble and the number of new cryptocurrencies being created seemingly every hour as I write this chapter. There are usually additional new avenues created to invest in the new technologies such as the recent proliferation of exchange traded funds (ETFs) tied to cryptocurrencies. When novice investors start to see easy gains being made in these new innovative technologies, they get a fear of missing out and pile into these types of assets, and this is the point right before the asset bubble bursts. There is nothing more frustrating to many people than seeing their neighbor seemingly get rich quick through some scheme that appears easy. The inevitable crash in the asset bubble is usually accelerated and amplified by a period in which investors are willing and able to take on massive leverage to invest in these new technologies. As an example, I recently read that it is not uncommon for cryptocurrency investors to be leveraged 100 to one! This insane level of risk-taking, from both the investors' and the lenders' points of view, has been enabled by newer trading exchanges. This type of activity is common at or near the peak of a technological asset bubble. Like every other asset bubble in history, this will not end well.

As a review, the 1870s' period was defined by supply-side deflation that was caused by new technological innovations and monopolies that kept prices low. One of the other contributing factors that I had not previously discussed that was at least partially responsible for the 1870s' deflation was how the monetary system was set up at that time. While paper money was being used, the value of the currency was tied to gold and silver up until silver dollars were abolished from official coinage in 1873. The removal of silver from official currency led to a contraction in the money supply, given the link between the value of the paper money and the precious metal. The contraction in the money supply had deflationary effects on the overall U.S. economy, and these trends were exacerbated by other developments such as the technological advancements that were lowering the cost of goods and services.

While I have discussed at length the benefits that the gold standard brings in terms of monetary accountability, one of the main issues with a gold standard system is that it is deflationary in nature. In a pure gold standard system where 100 percent of a currency is backed by an equivalent amount of gold, the only way to increase the money supply is to mine more gold. This can be a serious problem if there is a situation like we had with COVID-19 where the economy effectively is ground to a halt. The Federal Reserve likely would not have been able to provide the temporary market support that it did if we had been operating under a pure gold standard monetary system (assuming the government adhered to the rules of the pure gold standard). While we can't say for certain as to what would have happened if the Federal Reserve didn't step in after the global outbreak of COVID-19, I think that references to historical events such as how the U.S. government responded to the Panic of 1873 and the Great Depression provide some insights. Most would now argue that the contraction in the money supply during the Long Depression and the Great Depression was at least partially responsible for the duration and severity of these economic crises. I would argue that easy monetary and fiscal policies leading up to events such as the Long Depression and the Great Depression (along with virtually every financial crisis in world history) were some of the main reasons that the crashes occurred in the first place. This lack of accountability is why I believe that a form of partial gold standard makes the most sense for a monetary system. A partial gold standard system brings at least some monetary accountability and would prevent a scenario like we have today where governments have made a mockery of the fiat currency systems by effectively concluding that fiscal deficits don't matter. A partial gold standard system allows for central banks to provide for some level of temporary market support within reason during a crisis such as a global pandemic. To be clear, the entire history of money has been one of boom-and-bust cycles where people ultimately lose confidence in paper money and then turn to hard assets such as gold. The only individuals that would believe this is a radical proposition are those looking at the global monetary system through the lens of one portion of a long-term debt cycle (as Ray Dalio discusses in his book *Principles for Dealing with the Changing World Order: Why Nations Succeed and Fail*). Many in the United States today have never thought about a scenario where the U.S. dollar is significantly devalued because in their lifetimes, this has never been an issue. History would tell us that we are on our way to the next global monetary reset.

Proponents of a return to a form of the gold standard, like myself, usually fall into two camps: one proposal that would require at least partial gold backing of a currency without the need for gold convertibility and the alternate proposal that would require currency to be converted to gold in varying degrees. The gold backing proposal without convertibility requires a currency to be supported by an official gold reserve at different rates. For example, it could be required that for every $100 in circulation, the U.S. government stores $20 of this currency value in the form of gold reserves. An obvious issue with this proposal is that the price of gold fluctuates depending on global supply, demand, and other factors, so the gold reserves would have to be periodically rebalanced to take into account the price fluctuations and growth in money supply. This comment assumes that the gold backing is based on the market price of gold, which does not have to be the case. Some proposals prefer to have a portion of the money supply supported by gold reserves that are valued based on a fixed price of gold. I personally don't see how a proposal that includes a fixed price of gold makes sense, as the market price of gold could materially differ from the fixed price set for gold reserve purposes. I think that the fixed gold reserve price undermines one of the key selling points of this proposal because the price of gold would not be representative of real-world gold fundamentals, which weakens the true soundness and stability of the currency. One of the beauties of gold and other commodities is that unlike paper money that can be printed for any number of reasons, miners produce more gold depending on supply and demand dynamics, and the market price responds accordingly. Unlike the gold standard proposal that requires gold convertibility, it would be up to the U.S. government to decide what to do when the money supply gets out of line with the gold reserves that are either represented by the fixed or market prices. In theory, if the U.S. government wants to increase the money supply by 3 percent and there is a constant market price for gold, the U.S. government should purchase 3 percent more gold reserves if the money supply is being fully supported by gold reserves. Unlike the gold convertibility proposal, how the government ultimately responds to the changes in money supply as it relates to gold reserves would be discretionary in nature. Having said that, if the government materially deviates from the gold reserve plans, it will effectively render this plan useless, and the monetary system would not be any different from the fiat currency system in which we operate today. Assuming the government does not abuse its powers and regularly override the gold reserve requirements, the point of this gold standard proposal is to maintain a sound currency and prevent a scenario like we have today with unconstrained growth in the money supply.

The alternate gold standard proposal is predicated upon a requirement for currency to be convertible to gold. This proposal is very different from the proposals seeking to have the government hold gold reserves mainly for the purpose of monetary stability, because citizens could, at any time, retrieve gold for their currency, which would amplify the implications if the Federal Reserve disregarded the gold reserves in relation to the money supply. The proposals based on gold convertibility vary, with some calling for full convertibility to gold, while others advocate for requirements with lesser conversion rates. I don't think the gold convertibility proposals are realistic from a practical perspective, in that it would be expensive and complex to regularly exchange paper currency for gold. Additionally, I don't believe it would be in the interest of a government like the United States to implement a system like this. In doing so, the U.S. government would be greatly limiting its control over the monetary system. It would be easy for U.S. citizens to retrieve gold from the government, and it could be used as currency in place of the U.S. dollar. This would be a serious problem, because as we know from this book, the most powerful tool that a government has is to be able to control the monetary system and money supply and have citizens accept the government-issued currency while paying taxes in that currency. The gold backing proposals would allow for the U.S. government to maintain control over the monetary system while providing for guardrails and stability for the U.S. dollar. A full gold convertibility system would also present a challenge in that the United States could effectively be held hostage by large gold-producing nations such as China, Russia, and Australia that produce the majority of the world's gold supply. These nations could control how much gold goes into circulation with broad implications. The United States would essentially go from having full control over the monetary system to being reliant on other nations that may not always have the same interests as the United States. This would not be an ideal situation.

Building a bit on the last point related to gold supply concentration risk, it would probably make the most sense for this new partial gold standard using gold backing to at least have some degree of diversification in terms of other stores of value involved. Requiring governments to keep a lesser degree of other respected forms of store of value on hand, such as silver and platinum, would help mitigate the concentration risk tied to a small number of nations, effectively controlling the global market for gold. The main problem you run into is that there aren't many reasonable alternatives. Gold has proven to be the best store of value that is near-universally accepted, because while it is used in the form of jewelry, it is not consumed or required as a source of energy on a regular basis. While other commodities such as crude oil, natural gas, coffee, cocoa, and wheat could, in theory, be used by governments to back their currencies, this would not in any way be practical or good for the world because this would be a waste of resources that are used to provide either energy or food and drink consumption. Gold has the additional advantage over most other commodities, in that it does not corrode over time. Gold is arguably the most durable and nonreactive of all the precious metals, which is a contributing factor as to why it has been a near-universally accepted store of value for thousands of years. Other precious metals such as platinum and chromium have proven to be resistant to corrosion, but the number of options is limited. On the other end of the spectrum, commodities such as cocoa and wheat degrade over time. In addition to the fact that these commodities are needed for everyday consumption, the fact that commodities such as cocoa and wheat (and the vast majority of commodities) degrade over time makes them impractical for governments to hold as a store of value in support of their currencies. This is why my gold backing proposal includes partially backing a government's money supply mostly with gold but supplemented with a small collection of other relatively durable commodities that are not required for energy or daily consumption such as platinum and silver. I should note that even silver is prone to tarnishing over time more than is ideal for a scenario where governments could be holding a supply for decades if not centuries.

We don't have to speculate much about how the gold standard proposals would turn out because we have plenty of history to use as a guide. The United States had gold backing for currency from 1879 to 1968 and full gold convertibility for the U.S. dollar from 1879 to 1933. As a brief recap, the world operated under the classical gold standard from 1880 to 1914. The classical gold standard was defined by central banks being willing to buy and sell gold at a fixed price relative to a currency (the second proposal discussed earlier). In 1900, the United States passed the Gold Standard Act that made gold the official standard for redeeming currency. The start of World War I in 1914 marked an end to the classical gold standard era. Major economies around the world suspended the gold standard in response to World War I in order to print more currency to finance war efforts. After World War I, there was a brief restoration of the global gold standard, but this was short-lived owing to the Great Depression that began in 1929. The Great Depression marked a permanent end to the gold standard, with the United States ending the gold standard in 1933 along with gold convertibility in order to expand its monetary policy. FDR signed the Gold Reserve Act of 1934, which ended all private holdings of gold and the use of gold as money, a stunning development considering how the global monetary system had operated up until that point in time. Gold was required to be handed over to the U.S. government for a fixed price of $35 per ounce. This was really the point in time when the United States was well on its way to fully nationalizing the monetary system, and the country would never turn back. The next major development in the history of money would occur toward the end of World War II in 1944. The Bretton Woods Agreement made it so that other currencies were pegged to the U.S. dollar (instead of gold) and the U.S. dollar would, at least for the time, be pegged to gold at a fixed price of $35 per ounce. Despite the fixed price of the U.S. dollar relative to gold, private gold ownership in the United States was still disallowed. The Bretton Woods Agreement was the moment when the U.S. dollar became the world's reserve currency. This form of global monetary system would continue until 1971 when President Richard Nixon completely severed the link between the U.S. dollar and gold and put an end to international dollar conversion to gold. At the end of 1973, Nixon's administration reached deals with oil-producing nations in the Middle East whereby oil was settled exclusively with U.S. dollars. This has unofficially been called the *petrodollar system* and was the preface for the expectation that many other goods and services be settled with unbacked U.S. dollars. Since 1971, the global monetary system has been operating with completely unbacked currencies that are not tied to precious metals. In 1974, President Gerald Ford once again permitted private gold ownership in the United States, but this development was not nearly as significant as it once was considering that gold had been cut out of the global monetary system for all practical purposes.

What is not often discussed is the fact that the downfall of the gold standard was likely due to a lack of adherence to the gold standard as opposed to fundamental problems with the construction of the gold standard. During most of the years the United States had gold backing for currency, the gold reserve requirements were nonbinding in nature. Even when the gold reserve requirements were binding, at least in theory, these requirements were ultimately lowered and removed altogether. Given what has happened since the world went to fiat currencies, I firmly fall into the camp that believes the problem stemmed from a lack of gold standard adherence. It is misguided to say that the gold standard contributed to the cause of events such as the Great Depression. While true that a lack of market support until three years after the start of the Great Depression increased the duration and severity of the depression once it already began, the cause of the start of the Great Depression was not the gold standard. Like nearly every market crisis studied in this book, the Great Depression was caused by excessive debt and speculation fueled by easy monetary and fiscal policies that resulted in a financial system collapse. It is interesting that few people talk about the 61.8 percent increase in the U.S. money supply between 1921 and 1928. Owing to the flawed incentives offered by fractional-reserve banking, there was a large expansion of private credit leading up to the Great Depression. As we know, large increases in the money supply in excess of GDP growth and extended periods of low interest rates lead to inflated asset valuations just as we saw leading up to the Great Depression. During the economic expansion in the 1920s leading up to the Great Depression, money supply growth should have been more subdued so that the response would have been easier when times were tough. This money supply expansion was possible because of a lack of adherence to the gold standard combined with the lack of limits on money supply growth relative to GDP growth (as is still the case today) employed under the fractional-reserve banking system. Countries that have been able to maintain good fiscal health over time have exhibited higher rates of growth and a much lower chance of seeing negative impacts due to financial crises. Adherence to a form of gold standard increases the odds of demonstrating acceptable monetary and fiscal policy.

In the roughly 50-year period since 1971, this has been the only period in modern history when virtually all currencies have been completely unbacked and not tied in some form to hard assets. Is it surprising that since 1971, the world has largely been operating in an environment where we have seen debt levels explode and have had low levels of growth? On June 30, 1971, the year in which the United States completely severed the currency link to gold, the national debt stood at $408 billion. By June 30, 2021, the U.S. national debt had exploded to $28.38 trillion. This means that the U.S. national debt has increased a stunning 69.56 times over a roughly 50-year period with the trend getting worse in recent years. One of the underlying themes of this book has been the correlation between a government's fiscal health and the quality of the economy. With the rise of fiat currencies and a total lack of global monetary accountability, economies have come to rely on monetary supply expansion for growth as opposed to actual productivity. The book, *The Lords of Easy Money: How the Federal Reserve Broke the American Economy*, provides some interesting statistics on this subject. In the 1990s, before the era of ultra-low interest rates and perpetual financial engineering, labor productivity in the United States averaged 2.3 percent. During the ultra-low interest rate era, this figure declined to a 1.1 percent increase. This decline in labor productivity is attributable to the fact that companies have been incentivized by central banks to do things such as take on debt to repurchase shares as opposed to investing in a new factory. Historically, when we have reached this stage of the global monetary cycle, this is the period prior to when countries start to doubt the value of currencies and debt and sell these assets for other perceived store holds of wealth such as gold. This trend is often accelerated because real interest rates at this stage become incommensurate to the risk involved with holding a country's currency and debt due to high levels of debt and declining economic fundamentals. This is when there is a global monetary reset, the last of which occurred toward the end of World War II when the U.S. dollar effectively began its reign as the world's reserve currency.

Since the United States officially went to a fiat currency system in 1971, we have had the stagflationary era of the 1970s, the global financial crisis between 2008 and 2009, which was followed by the slowest economic recovery in U.S. history, and the COVID-19 crisis followed by what has been high inflation that could evolve into a stag-flationary environment akin to the 1970s. While the COVID-19 crisis was a nonfinancial event that brought down the economy, even before the onset of COVID-19, the United States and the global economy had not recovered from the global financial crisis. We have been locked into a recurring cycle where global growth is now controlled by central bankers as opposed to real productivity. In short, the fiat currency experiment is not going well, and few seem to arrive at this realization likely owing to a lack of historical perspective.

The World Bank recently released estimates in 2021 that predict global growth of 1.9 percent per year over the period of 2020 to 2029. One of the major contributing factors to this anemic growth rate is the fact that there have been weaker levels of investment, and this supports my theory that countries have come more to rely on monetary supply expansion for growth as opposed to real productivity. Fiat currencies have encouraged this behavior and are the root cause of the scenario we find ourselves in today due to unchecked monetary and fiscal account-ability. The World Bank projections for the current decade would just fall in line with a long-running trend. A 2011 report showed that, since 1971, when the U.S. dollar link to gold was completely severed, the real GDP growth averaged 2.9 percent per year compared to the 4 percent average growth in the post–World War II gold-linked period. Growth in recent years has only slowed further. The case studies in this book have demonstrated a negative correlation between federal debt levels and growth rates, so this commentary aligns with the rest of the research presented.

During the classical gold standard period in the United States from 1880 to 1914, wholesale prices increased by just 0.1 percent per year compared to the estimated 4 percent average annualized inflation between 1969 and 2022 (although this inflation measure is only using the flawed CPI metric). The classical gold standard in the United States was accompanied by stable money, which coincided with high rates of economic growth. Since the end of the classical gold standard, the United States has had bouts of inflation-ary years in the periods after World War I, World War II, in the 1970s after the link was severed between currencies and gold, and now in the 2020s in wake of the COVID-19 crisis and extraordinary levels of money printing. The country needs a system that encourages stable and trustworthy money and discourages radical monetary and fiscal policies. That system is the gold standard, and it has already been proven.

CHAPTER 11

Rome

Financial Panic of 33 AD (33 AD)

Background and Market Impact

While we have already done a deep dive into the history of the gold standard, I think now would be a prudent time to review the history of money and banking systems. Long before the formulation of fiat currencies and even currencies predicated upon precious metals, there was the barter system. While historical records vary as to the exact timing the barter system originated, the first barter system is believed to have developed between 9000 and 6000 BC. Several historical records cite the tribes in Mesopotamia (a historical region in Western Asia) as being the first known people to use a barter system. The barter system during this period, which is the earliest known medium of exchange, was tied to cattle. People used cows, camels, goats, and other livestock as a form of currency. While not standardized as with currency systems based upon precious metals or fiat currencies, the early barter systems paved the way for what we know today as pricing. For example, back in 6000 BC, a village could arrive at some form of consensus that two camels were worth one goat. Besides the issue of a lack of standardized pricing, the biggest drawback of a barter system is that a seller and a buyer must have access to the specific goods or services that the other party is seeking. For example, if an individual specialized in producing milk from cows, this person would likely then have to go out and find different parties with access to products ranging from corn to rice. This process is not nearly as practical as with a standardized form of currency, and barter can be time-consuming. The barter system later graduated to using other goods beyond cattle such as vegetables and grains, which were considered a relatively standard barter offering.

With the rise of the barter system, the foundation for the modern-day banking system later started to come into focus with the innovation we know today as lending. There may have been lending done on smaller scales in civilizations prior to 2000 BC, but many historians believe that the first evidence of loans in ancient history was in Mesopotamia around 2000 BC. A market for loans arose from the fact that farmers and individuals responsible for cattle would borrow seeds and animals and would repay their lenders later when the plants grew, or new animals were born. Not too different from modern-day finance, there was the introduction of what is now known as collateral, sometime during this period. Depending on the size of the loan, the lenders would sometimes take animals and other assets of value as collateral or would repossess these types of assets if the borrower failed to make the promised payment. In ancient times, what was referred to as a tally stick was used to keep track of loans. An ingenious innovation given the resources present, a tally stick recorded the amount of money owed between parties with notches on the stick. The stick was broken in half and given to the lender and borrower. If there was doubt about whether a borrower owed a lender, they would simply check to see if one half of the tally stick aligned with the other half. There is evidence that the Babylonians (an empire in Mesopotamia) used receipts to record transfers between parties in the form of clay tablets. In a lot of ways, the clay tablets and tally sticks were a prelude to currencies predicated upon precious metals and paper. What some believe to be the first recorded written laws as they relate to banking systems within civilization were conducted by the Babylonians around 1750 BC. Known as the Code of Hammurabi, this legal text consisted of 282 laws and was carved into a stone. The Code of Hammurabi is today known to be one of the earliest and most comprehensive legal codes written, and it focused on rules for commercial interactions that set punishments for failing to abide by the rules. While the Code of Hammurabi did not make specific references to banks, there were rules related to many modern-day banking concepts such as debts owed, loans and trade, and interest incurred. Thinking high level, it makes sense that the foundation of banking systems was put in place prior to standardized mediums of exchange being created. A standardized medium of exchange was the next evolution in allowing for a more seamless transfer of goods and services that began with barter and evolved to include concepts such as lending and interest.

Some believe that the first banks were created in the Mesopotamia region sometime around 2000 BC. There are historical records that indicate modern-day concepts such as letters of credit, deposits, and interest were used at this time. Early formations of banks in Egypt served the purpose of protecting wealth with the banks created in temples to secure precious metals and commodities. For example, a farmer could deposit a certain amount of grain in a bank and would receive an early version of a deposit receipt showing how much grain was stored at the local bank. It is interesting how little has changed with the financial system over the course of thousands of years. The use and storing of grain and commodities at banks would ultimately be displaced with precious metals and later paper money, as it is not practical to use commodities as a form of medium of exchange. The Greek and Roman civilizations would later advance banking systems. For example, there is evidence that, in Rome, bank transactions involving debt were notarized in order to be registered. This shows that banks were starting to become more tightly integrated with a more holistic financial system.

Historical accounts vary on this subject as well, but many historians believe that the first standardized medium of exchange was not a currency based on precious metals but rather cowrie (sea snail) shells. These shells were widely available in the Indian and Pacific Oceans, and it is believed that China was the first to use cowrie shells as a form of currency around 1200 BC. Believe it or not, cowrie shells became a widely adopted currency, and many think it is the currency that lays claim to the longest staying power in history. In fact, some African countries still used cowrie shells as a currency up until the mid-20th century. The harvesting and processing of cowrie shells differed by region. For example, in the Maldives, mats made of coconut leaves would be left on the surface of the water. Cowrie shells would blanket the mats, and then the shells would be taken to the beaches to dry. Once the cowrie shells were dry, they could be used as currency. In other regions such as the Solomon Islands, in order to be used as currency, the cowrie shells would need to be broken into pieces and strung together. So, while the cowrie shells were a widely adopted and long-lasting form of currency that was relatively standardized within civilizations, how the shells were used as a currency could differ between civilizations. The value of the cowrie shells depended on supply and demand just like every other currency, product, or service in history. In locations such as the Maldives where cowrie shells were plentiful, the shells did not carry nearly as much value as in other locations where the shells were relatively scarce. The value placed on the cowrie shells could also vary based on how much work was done to polish and work on them, which could be a time-intensive process.

The next evolution in money came with the first coins consisting of precious metals. Some believe that bronze and copper cowrie shell imitations were made in China around 1000 BC. Others believe that the first coins were created around 600 to 700 BC in Lydia, which was an ancient kingdom in modern-day Turkey. The Lydians created coins using a mix of gold and silver, and some believe that they were the first people to use gold in their monetary system. Other civilizations followed the Lydians in introducing coins into their monetary systems, with the Persian, Greek, and Macedonian empires following suit. These civilizations made coins consisting of gold, silver, and bronze. With the rise of coinage as a medium of exchange, we got our first glimpse at the centralization of monetary systems that we find today with fiat currencies around the world. In fact, the leader of the Persian Empire gave the death penalty to Persian governors who attempted to mint their own coins. Even as far back in time as around 500 or 600 BC, some understood the power of controlling the monetary system. While many historians don't recognize the formal creation of a central bank until 1668 in Sweden (although this point is debated and some historians believe the Bank of Amsterdam in 1609 was the first modern central bank), governments such as the Persian Empire (500 to 600 BC) were effectively acting as central banks, as they were controlling the money supply. Coins continued to spread their way around Europe, and Rome formally introduced gold money into their monetary system around 300 BC.

The next major milestone in the history of currencies occurred around 100 BC when leather money was created in China. This leather money made of white deerskin is often believed to be the first documented form of banknote. The desire for banknotes came from the lack of convenience associated with carrying around coins made of precious metals. It was not until 800 to 900 AD that the first official paper currency was introduced in China. Not unlike when FDR required private ownership of gold to be turned in for paper currency in the United States in the 1930s, with the evolution of paper currency in China around 800 to 900 AD, the Chinese authorities recommended that merchants exchange their precious metal coins for paper money. This is another reference to the early understanding of governments as to the power that can be held by monopolizing the monetary system. The early Chinese paper currency was used for around 500 years, but it was an ominous sign for future paper currencies developed during this time. Like has happened many times throughout history, the Chinese government printed too much paper money, causing hyperinflation. The Ming Empire resorted to abolishing the paper money. Prior to the demise of what is often believed to be the first paper currency, Marco Polo had visited China in the late 13th century and spread the word of paper money to Europe. It would take another several hundred years, but paper money would later arrive in Europe. Perhaps if the Europeans had heard about the hyperinflation associated with the Chinese paper currency, we wouldn't be talking about our global fiat currency experiment today.

When Marco Polo visited China in the late 13th century, China was largely under the control of the Mongolian Empire who, during that period, established what is still the largest contiguous land empire in world history. Marco Polo noted that the Mongols used money made from mulberry bark in a form that would be recognized as paper. The Mongols realized that if they maintained control of the money, merchants could be responsible for the movement of goods and the government would remain in power. It was at this time that a standardized unit of account was established across the sprawling area between China and Persia (although the paper money was later withdrawn in areas such as Persia where there was a revolt against the use of it). According to the book, *Genghis Khan and the Making of the Modern World*, when Marco Polo visited the Mongolian Empire, he wrote, "To refuse it would be to incur the death penalty" in reference to the acceptance of paper money. It is noted that the Mongols established an innovation called bankruptcy, but if an individual declared bankruptcy more than twice, they faced the possibility of execution. While the Mongols employed extreme measures to preserve control and credibility of the paper money system, it is clear they understood the benefits of monopolizing the money supply and having the paper money readily accepted. The Mongols had adopted and refined the Chinese paper money system. Even with the enhancements, inflation was ultimately unleashed, and the Mongolian paper money became effectively worthless in 1356.

The first known formal banknotes in Europe would not be issued until 1661 in Sweden. These Swedish banknotes could later be exchanged for precious metals, so this was not a fiat currency that we have around the world today. This early European paper money was short-lived with the collapse of the issuing bank occurring in 1668. Despite the troubles with the paper money in Sweden (a disturbing trend with paper money should be starting to emerge), banknotes continued to travel around Europe. Between 1661 and 1821, various forms of money were being used across Europe, with most currencies being tied to precious metals in some way. The Dutch guilder and the British pound served as reserve currencies for stretches during this period when their respective countries were global leaders. The next big evolution in money in Europe came with the establishment of the gold standard in the United Kingdom in 1821. The gold standard would continue to be used until many countries suspended and ultimately abandoned the gold standard in the wake of World War I. The next major development in the history of money would occur toward the end of World War II in 1944 when, according to the Bretton Woods Agreement, other currencies were pegged to the U.S. dollar (instead of gold) and the U.S. dollar was pegged to gold at a fixed price, and this form of global monetary system continued until 1971. In 1971, President Richard Nixon completely severed the link between the U.S. dollar and gold and put an end to international dollar conversion to gold. Since 1971, the global monetary system has been operating with completely unbacked currencies that are not tied to precious metals.

The World Bank considers the first *proper* bank to be Goldsmiths of London, which emerged in the 17th century. Similar to banks in Ancient Egypt, people would deposit precious metals into vaults at Goldsmiths and then would be able to collect them. Goldsmiths charged a fee for the services provided and eventually moved on to providing loans. While there were early medieval versions of central banks, many consider the Bank of Sweden to be the first central bank that was formed in 1668. It is not a coincidence that the first central bank coincided with the emerging era of banknotes in Europe. The purpose of a central bank is to help ensure monetary and fiscal stability (which is ironic given the behavior of the Federal Reserve today) by controlling the money supply, influencing interest rates and the cost of borrowing, and acting as a lender of last resort under extreme circumstances. It was the English Free Coinage Act of 1666 that placed control of the money supply into private hands, and the founding of the privately controlled Bank of England in 1694, that first saw a major sovereign relinquishing monetary control. The Bank of England was a central bank that followed the Bank of Sweden, and it issued banknotes and would eventually offer services and products such as checking and modern banking services that would pave the way for the retail banking revolution in the 20th century. It wasn't until the 20th century with the rise of new technologies such as ATMs that retail banking evolved into how most would think of the banking concept today. The Federal Reserve System was not created in the United States until 1913, although Alexander Hamilton laid the groundwork for the U.S. central bank with the creation of the first national bank in 1791.

Now that we have gone over the history of currencies and banking systems, we can proceed to the financial crisis in Ancient Rome in the year 33 AD. At this point in time, Rome had retail banks similar to what we think of today: they distributed loans to individuals to enable the purchase of goods and services. Members of the public often relied on loans granted from wealthy individuals and members of the imperial elite. In the year 33 AD, a law was revived that required creditors to invest two-thirds of their capital in Italian land along with a requirement that two-thirds of all outstanding loan payments be paid off. This would be the modern-day equivalent of the U.S. government requiring J.P. Morgan Chase, Bank of America, Citigroup, and Wells Fargo to use two-thirds of their capital to invest in U.S. real estate. The result was that the wealthy individuals that had lent money to others (and were effectively acting as banks) called in their loans in order to purchase Italian land. In scrambling to come up with the proceeds to invest in the local real estate, the wealthy elite called in their loans and deposits from the bankers. What followed was a series of bank runs and failures, as we have frequently seen throughout history. The result was a credit crunch or decrease in the money supply, which has been one of the triggers of every financial crisis that we have studied in this book. Given the contraction in the money supply, combined with depressed asset prices, some debtors had to resort to turning to money lenders charging exorbitant interest rates. This is not any different than what we saw happen during the global financial crisis or any other period where capital becomes scarce.

When the loans were called in by the wealthy elite and the local banks, the Roman debtors resorted to selling real estate to fulfill their debt obligations, resulting in a collapse of the local real estate market. It is ironic that a policy targeted at investing in local real estate would play a major role in at least temporarily imploding the real estate market. A policy that had the goal of inflating local real estate had the impact of deflating real estate values. It is worth noting the level of financial integration all the way back in the year 33 AD. Some have written that financial integration is a modern phenomenon, but it is really a function of the banking business model more than anything and was present in ancient times as well as today.

What is perhaps most interesting about this early version of a financial crisis was the policy response. The government stepped in and injected liquidity into the financial system with the equivalent of about $2 billion being sent to bankers earmarked for loans to the debtors that were in the most trouble. Interest on the new loans was to be waived for three years. With the goal of stopping the deflationary asset spiral, the new loans were secured against property values that were valued at twice the rate of the now-deflated values. The quick and aggressive policy response was successful, and it prevented prolonged depressed conditions like what we witnessed in the United States in the 1870s and 1930s. The policy response by the Romans in 33 AD was very similar to the United States in the wake of the global financial crisis: inject massive liquidity into the system and keep interest rates very low. As we studied with the United States related to the global financial crisis and COVID-19, quick and aggressive monetary and fiscal policy measures have proven to be the most effective way to prevent protracted depression conditions like what we saw happen in the 1870s and 1930s (again assuming we continue to employ fractional-reserve banking without limits on money supply growth). I think the main difference we see with policy measures today has to do with the length and severity of the monetary and fiscal policy measures (given what ultimately happened in 2022 with the soaring consumer price inflation, it is probably safe to say this assessment proved correct), but only time will tell what the repercussions are, as we are in uncharted territory.

Macroeconomic Impact

Now that we have reviewed the history of banking, I think it is important to ask ourselves if banking is even a net positive for society given the frequent financial crises throughout history that have developed in similar fashion and often had terrible consequences. As much as I dislike banking and lending in terms of it being an investable business, lending and banking functions serve a core role in a prosperous society. My research in this book seems to support Bill Gates's controversial pronouncement in 1994 when he declared, "Banking is necessary, but banks are not." It is not paramount for banks themselves to continue to exist in perpetuity, but we have seen the importance of banking functions such as lending dating all the way back to 2000 BC when farmers and individuals responsible for cattle would borrow seeds and animals and repay their lenders at a later date. Despite the historical risks associated with banks and lending, banking functions benefit society. The book, *Why Nations Fail: The Origins of Power, Prosperity, and Poverty*, does an excellent job of comparing the business environments of the United States and Mexico in the 1800s and 1900s. The book states that in 1818, there were 338 banks in the United States, with total assets of $160 million. By 1914, there were 27,864 banks in the United States, with total assets of $27.3 billion. These figures sharply contrasted with Mexico, where in 1910, there were just 42 banks in total, with two banks accounting for 60 percent of the banking assets. The book describes a banking environment in Mexico that lacked competition, resulting in high interest rates, and borrowing that was more limited to the upper class. *Why Nations Fail: The Origins of Power, Prosperity, and Poverty* argues that the proliferation of the competitive banking system in the United States was critical for the high rates of economic growth and industrialization seen in the country during the 1800s.

It is not a coincidence that the proliferation of ready access to capital in the United States coincided with what some would consider to be the most successful economic period in the country's history. It is also not a coincidence that the Dutch founding of the world's first publicly listed company and the first stock exchange in the early 1600s was at a time when the Dutch Empire ruled the world. With access to capital and business protections that entrepreneurs trust, they can receive the upside of successful ventures and bring a much higher likelihood that the overall economy will be successful. This statement comes with the obvious caveat that prolonged easy monetary and fiscal policies facilitate excessive credit creation that ultimately leads to an unsustainable debt cycle and financial crisis. Ready access to capital is the lifeblood of any economy, and how capital is managed and regulated goes a long way in determining the ultimate success of a given country.

As I mentioned earlier, lending and ready access to capital is critical for an economy, but it is not important that we have traditional banks. While I am not representative of the total market, I use banks for a limited number of functions. I store money in a checking account located at a bank that I know I can safely retrieve from at a nearby ATM at my convenience. I use various credit cards from different banks to take advantage of the increasingly generous perks that banks offer in the form of credit card rewards. While I mostly pay off my credit cards daily and use the credit cards as more of a debit card, I take advantage of bank lending by using the credit cards. While interest rates have remained extremely low in recent years, the money I keep in my checking account at the local bank is taking advantage of bank lending. My local bank can take the proceeds in my checking account, paying me little in the way of interest and lend against that money to a credit card customer and earn a higher rate of interest. You can see how problems arise for banks when large swaths of customers go to retrieve their funds at the same time, given the banking business model and guarantee to give customers their money when they want it. I have used banks less frequently for functions such as ordering foreign currency. Others use banks for core functions such as obtaining mortgages, car loans, and personal loans.

In recent years, we have witnessed a financial technology revolution that is likely only in the early innings. Companies such as SoFi, which only recently cleared final hurdles to be regulated as a bank and claims to be FDIC-insured, now offer traditional banking products such as mortgages, personal loans, and credit cards. We have seen large numbers of nontraditional financial companies enter the fray with firms such as Credit Karma offering checking and savings accounts. Venmo, now a financial technology stalwart, offers debit and credit cards. Even technology giants such as Apple have launched a credit card. How a bank is defined is blurrier than ever, and this trend looks set to accelerate. What is clear is that many companies are now offering financial products that have traditionally been offered by banks. The rapid innovation in this space is mostly a positive for consumers, but new questions should be raised about oversight. I think it is likely that regulation is lagging the innovation (as is usually the case), and we probably do not currently understand the depth and breadth of the shadow banking system. This is something to watch in the coming years, especially when combined with the enormous debt at both the federal and corporate levels.

The vast majority of financial crises that we have studied in history have been facilitated by prolonged periods of easy monetary and fiscal policies that have resulted in excessive credit creation, ultimately leading to an unsustainable debt cycle and financial crisis. As shown from these case studies over the course of thousands of years, the best solution to prevent this scenario is to use a form of partial gold standard supplemented by limits on money supply growth tied to GDP growth and a full-reserve banking model. When we have these guardrails in place to prevent extreme monetary and fiscal policies that inevitably lead to financial crises, responsible lending and other functions of banking such as the storing of assets can exist with less risk to the health of the financial system. Responsibly managing access to capital is one of the most important determinants of whether a country will have a successful economy.

It is critical that we learn from history and do more to prevent a scenario much worse than the global financial crisis, which is certainly possible given the factors we have today.

One of the core issues with the modern fractional-reserve banking system is that the interests of private commercial banks and central banks are not aligned. Private commercial banks care about how much profit they produce, irrespective of how their money creation impacts the health of the domestic currency or financial system. Insurance schemes such as the FDIC and the precedent for massive federal bailouts when the inevitable bank runs occur have only led to an increase in these mis-aligned incentives. Central banks must worry about factors such as how money supply growth will impact inflation and the long-term health of the domestic currency, but under a fractional-reserve banking model the money supply growth often largely occurs at private commercial banks. There must be long-term planning when it comes to money supply growth relative to GDP growth, and the best way to achieve this is by employing a full-reserve banking system paired with limits on money supply growth relative to GDP growth. Under this scenario, the incentives of all parties are aligned, and the odds of having a healthy financial system over the long-term are dramatically higher. I have proposed supplementing a full-reserve banking system with a partial gold standard to provide for further monetary accountability and to decentralize the financial system so that consumer confidence in a currency is less reliant on a central bank. Providing some support for the removal of the power of money creation from private banks, in 1895, American economist Alexander del Mar conducted a study of the English financial system after the passing of the Free Coinage Act of 1666 that inaugurated a series of commercial panics and disasters that were previously completely unknown. Between 1694 and 1890, 25 years never passed without a financial crisis in England.

There were various proposals put forth by economists about what to do in order to fix the banking system, but the economists responsible for the Chicago Plan that was later endorsed by research conducted by the IMF agreed on one concept: to separate the money creation from the lending activity of private commercial banks. This makes perfect sense considering the misaligned incentives discussed earlier coupled with what we know about what always happens throughout history with bank runs, large bailouts, and even the decline of paper currencies. The IMF working paper in support of the Chicago Plan noted:

> The recent empirical evidence of Reinhart and Rogoff (2009) documents the high costs of boom-bust credit cycles and bank runs throughout history. And the recent empirical evidence of Schularick and Taylor (2012) is supportive of Fisher's view that high debt levels are a very important predictor of major crises. The latter finding is also consistent with the theoretical work of Kumhof and Rancière (2010), who show how very high debt levels, such as those observed just prior to the Great Depression and the Great Recession, can lead to a higher probability of financial and real crises.

This statement by the IMF directly supports many of the concepts covered in my book. One of the core issues with a fractional-reserve banking system, as noted by the IMF, is that a nation's money supply usually depends almost entirely on private commercial banks' willingness to create new money, and there is little in the way of recourse for many private commercial banks when things inevitably go awry.

The IMF found support for all four main claims put forth by the Chicago Plan, with the potential for much smoother business cycles, no possibility of bank runs, a large reduction of debt levels across the economy, and a replacement of that debt by debt-free government-issued money. I know there are skeptics asking to what extent eliminating private credit creation would hurt the economy. Remember that central bank experiments such as massive quantitative easing ultimately proved to have done virtually nothing when it comes to increasing societal productivity. In my view, all that ends up happening when there are extended periods of easy monetary policy is that the valuations of assets get distorted, and consumers and businesses overextend themselves. The IMF working paper showed projections for longer-term output gains reaching 10 percent under a full-reserve banking model. The IMF provided support for the long-term output gain projections by noting that the full-reserve banking model:

> Leads to large reductions of real interest rates, as lower net debt levels lead investors to demand lower spreads on government and private debts. It permits much lower distortionary tax rates, due to the beneficial effects of much higher seigniorage income (despite lower inflation) on the government budget. And finally it leads to lower credit monitoring costs, because scarce resources no longer have to be spent on monitoring loans whose sole purpose was to create an adequate money supply that can easily be produced debt-free.

The IMF went on to argue that a full-reserve system would allow for the steady state of inflation to drop to zero. This would be possible because the central bank would operate using a money supply growth rule that would be correlated with economic growth. Private commercial banks would no longer be able to engineer the boom-and-bust cycles that have occurred throughout history as a result of their willingness to lend money, irrespective of factors that are good for the country.

The Bank of Amsterdam was a bank established in 1609 that initially employed full-reserve banking. The Bank of Amsterdam was fully owned by the city of Amsterdam (some historians now argue that it was really the Bank of Amsterdam that was the first modern central bank and not the Bank of Sweden), and its coins were fully backed by gold and silver. In 1683, the Bank of Amsterdam no longer kept full reserves of gold and silver to support the deposits, abandoning the full-reserve banking system in favor of a fractional-reserve system comparable to what we have around the world today. As has been typical throughout history, a series of wars that culminated with the Fourth Anglo-Dutch War in the late 1700s drained the Dutch finances that led to the demise of the Dutch Empire and the Dutch guilder as the world's reserve currency. I don't think it is a coincidence that the abandonment of full-reserve banking at the Bank of Amsterdam closely coincided with the peak of the Dutch Empire around 1680 and set the stage for the debasement of the local currency via irresponsible borrowing. The fractional-reserve banking system paired with the use of a fiat currency encourages monetary excess that ultimately results in the death or substantial debasement of the local fiat currency and the impairment of the country tied to that currency. This has been a recurring cycle throughout history that ultimately results in the home country turning to hard assets such as gold to support the domestic currency.

In response to the global financial crisis, Switzerland attempted to abolish fractional-reserve banking in favor of a sovereign money initiative that would have given the Swiss National Bank the sole authority to create money, but this effort was ultimately voted down in 2018. Iceland entertained a similar initiative in the wake of the global financial crisis, but this plan was never implemented. It will be interesting to see if a country follows through on the abolition of fractional-reserve banking. The odds of this becoming a reality have likely risen with the exploding global debt levels.

Where We Are Now and Heading in the Future

In the chapter on the COVID-19 crisis in the United States, I had cautioned on inflation, even though at that point in time the CPI wasn't indicating a material rise in inflation. For those that have gotten this far in the book, you will know it is clear we were likely to arrive where we are now with soaring consumer price inflation. The Federal Reserve opted to print enormous amounts of paper money, and then consumers went out and spent this money. These actions make paper money less valuable, and consumer price inflation is stimulated. Quoting Ray Dalio, "prices rise when the amount of spending increases by more than the quantities of goods and services sold increase." It is stunning that the Federal Reserve did not realize that they were well behind the curve in that they weren't normalizing interest rates to curtail inflation long after the United States economy had recovered from the shocks tied to COVID-19. Some now believe that the central banks misdiagnosed the problem at the height of the COVID-19 pandemic in 2020. The central banks attempted to stimulate demand through their policy tools, and it now looks like the real problem was the lack of supply in products such as semiconductor chips, fertilizer, and oil. The stimulus provided by the central banks did nothing to resolve the supply shocks, and when economies opened back up there was too much capital chasing too few goods and services that ultimately sent consumer price inflation soaring around the world. Demand–pull inflation is being combined with cost–push inflation, and this trend was greatly accelerated with the outbreak of the war in Ukraine that has sent the price of oil and other commodities such as wheat skyrocketing. It is alarming that Jay Powell has repeatedly denied the existence of a correlation between money supply growth and consumer price inflation, despite historical evidence pointing to the contrary.

Up until recently, most have dismissed comparisons to the stagflationary era of the 1970s, but I am not exactly sure why many have been so quick to dismiss these comparisons. Even before the black swan event in Ukraine that stimulated the cost–push inflation side of the ledger, we already had structural inflationary forces that arose after the onset of the COVID-19 pandemic. For example, we have seen significant wage inflation that is unlikely to abate. The Amazon warehouse workers that saw their pay boosted to $19 per hour are highly unlikely to ever go back to what they were making prior to the pandemic. Even with substantial wage gains seen in many parts of the economy (particularly at the lower end), companies are still having great difficulty hiring enough workers. It is unusual to have large wage gains coupled with a labor shortage, but it seems that some workers that were laid off or quit during the pandemic at least up until now have not rejoined the workforce. This could perhaps be explained by some combination of unemployment benefits (which encourage not working), rising home values (which could help offset a lack of income), and up until recently soaring retirement account values (which were buoyed by increases in assets ranging from equities to cryptocurrencies). Even though we may see more workers attempt to rejoin the workforce with declines in asset valuations such as homes and equities along with a weakening economy, I believe that structural wage inflation is here to stay, and this impacts the costs of goods for consumers over time. Companies usually at least initially take a hit to profits when they are seeing input costs rising owing to factors such as wage inflation, but they will ultimately raise prices to the end consumer if the business is providing products or services that have pricing power. The pricing power a business has is determined by the importance of the product or service to a given end consumer relative to other options available in the marketplace. Put simply, if a given good or service is critical to a consumer, they will pay more for it.

Economist Charles Goodhart makes an interesting argument that low inflation in recent decades was primarily attributable to the inexpensive labor of hundreds of millions of Chinese and Eastern European workers that held down wages and prices as goods from these areas were exported to developed countries. Goodhart believes that inflation will remain high for decades as these trends reverse, with working-age populations shrinking across developed economies for the first time since World War II, coupled with declining birthrates in these countries. This is happening at a time when China's working-age population is projected to decline by 20 percent over the next 30 years. In short, the cheap labor trends that held down prices for the last 30 or 40 years are expected to sharply reverse for the next 20 years, resulting in sustained high prices, at least according to Goodhart. I didn't see Goodhart discuss some deflationary forces that are countering the inflationary forces tied to labor such as technological innovation, but I do agree with some of the assessment on the outlook for labor, and there is a good chance that this will be exacerbated by decreasing levels of globalization. Some of the outlook for global wage inflation could be offset by increasing levels of cheap labor production in countries such as India and Indonesia that have large populations and young workforces. We have operated in a low inflation world for decades, and it could be difficult for many countries to adjust to a new reality where we have sustained levels of elevated inflation.

Where we stand today in the United States draws parallels between a combination of the 1970s energy crisis mixed with some qualities that Japan has had in recent decades. The major difference between the 1970s and today is the bloated fiscal structure that the United States now has that will make it much more difficult to dig itself out of the hole that we are in now. To tame soaring inflation, the classic playbook throughout history has been to raise interest rates. How can the United States significantly increase interest rates when the country has more than $30 trillion of federal debt? As mentioned earlier, Stanley Druckenmiller noted that if 10-year U.S. interest rates were to go to a more normalized rate of around 5 percent, the United States would be spending around 30 percent of its GDP each year just to service the debt (federal deficits have continued to soar since Druckenmiller's interview). As I am editing this chapter, the U.S. federal debt levels stand at $31 trillion with short-term interest rates projected to be well in excess of 4 percent by the end of 2022. If we do have sustained runaway inflation like we witnessed in the 1970s, the United States will likely need to boost interest rates well above Druckenmiller's quoted normalized levels if the goal is to significantly curtail inflation. When combining the amount of money that would be needed annually to service the debt along with the increasing amounts of money required to fund mandatory spending and defense, it is difficult to envision how this ends well. All of this is happening at a time when

U.S. population growth and overall GDP growth are much lower than they were in the 1970s era, and GDP growth is likely to face increasing headwinds in the coming years because of the combination of the federal debt overhang, structural inflationary forces, large mandatory spending requirements, and tepid population growth. It is likely that people will start to question the credibility of United States debt (I don't know why this hasn't already happened) that will ultimately result in the depreciation of the U.S. dollar against hard assets such as gold. Similar stories are playing out across many countries in the developed world.

I tend to agree with Ray Dalio's line of thinking that people generally discount the odds of a particular event happening that has not occurred in their own lifetime but has occurred throughout history. Referencing some concepts from Dalio's *Principles for Dealing with the Changing World Order: Why Nations Succeed and Fail*, people are discounting the odds of the U.S. dollar losing world reserve currency status and there being a long-term decline in the U.S. dollar because this hasn't happened in anyone's lifetime today. Having said that, the loss of reserve currency status has always happened throughout history to dominant empires when they have reached the latter stages of a long-term debt cycle. This is what happened to the Dutch Empire and the British Empire (these countries possessed the two reserve currencies prior to the United States) at the end of their respective long-term debt cycles. Toward the end of a long-term debt cycle, the parties holding the reserve currency and debt ultimately sell them as they lose confidence in these instruments owing to increasing amounts of debt and money being printed by the reserve currency country. Given the recent developments in the United States, there is at least a decent chance we are nearing the end of the long-term debt cycle. This is not a pessimistic analysis of my home country, but a realistic observation of what has been developing. The United States, along with many other countries around the world, has consistently been spending more money than it makes, and this trend was accelerated in the wake of the COVID-19 pandemic. Historically, what has happened when this is done with enough duration and severity is that people lose confidence in a country's currency and debt. That is why the proponents of the modern monetary theory are so misguided.

A potential risk that nobody seems to be discussing is that government debt, even in countries such as the United States, could be significantly devalued or eliminated. Probably the biggest mistake that investors, and people more broadly, tend to make is that they look at what has happened in their lifetime or recent history and assume that is how things always work. This is a dangerous approach that can produce catastrophic results. Citizens of the United States today, along with some other developed countries, have only ever known their government debt to be a reliable place where they have been able to park cash. This recent history coupled with the fact that government debt has low price volatility has lulled investors to sleep. It is insane to me, but I know many individuals that have 80 percent of their net assets tied up in *risk-free* Treasury Bills. The near-term odds of a significant devaluation of U.S. government debt may not be substantial, but history has shown that every currency ultimately dies or is significantly devalued, and when this happens, investors trade out of the local currency and debt in favor of international currencies and hard assets. I don't believe it is ever a good idea to be reliant on any one government to protect your savings.

I am going to elaborate on this topic more in the section, *How This Information Can Be Used*, but I do not want readers to come away with the impression that I believe a host of challenging long-term macroeconomic factors means that an investor should park vast sums of money in cash for perceived protection. I believe the best long-term inflation protection resides in owning businesses that can raise prices over time without having a large impact on demand. While true that sustained high inflation can lower share prices in terms of what investors will be willing to pay for them, the long-term intrinsic value of a business will equal the present value of the discounted cash flows of that entity. The discount factor for equities could be raised to compensate for increased opportunity costs if bonds are paying higher interest rates, but businesses that can raise prices will be a much better choice for the long term than cash. In 2021, it was reported that, in the 50 years since the United States severed the link between the U.S. dollar and gold, the dollar has depreciated by 85 percent. This figure does not capture the recent rise in inflation and includes many years of low inflation after the global financial crisis.

Compared to other currencies, the U.S. dollar has still been a relative safe haven and a beacon of stability up until now, but holding any currency for long periods of time is always a horrible investment because it buys you far less in the future as a result of inflation. According to Ray Dalio's research in *Principles for Dealing with the Changing World Order: Why Nations Succeed and Fail*, only about 20 percent of the approximately 750 currencies that have been in existence since 1700 are still around today, and all these currencies have been devalued. Dalio notes that the average return of interest-bearing cash currency between 1850 and the present day was 1.2 percent, and the real returns of cash since 1912 have been –0.1 percent.

In another repeat of history, I have seen online chatter about possibly implementing price controls to tame the soaring cost of oil and other commodities. Price controls in certain sectors such as food delivery and apartment rentals were initiated in response to the outbreak of COVID-19 in the United States. Have we learned nothing from the past? Perhaps counterintuitive to some, price controls ultimately result in the stimulation of inflation because they remove incentives for businesses to produce a given product or service, and this results in less supply. This much has become clear from our case studies on Zimbabwe, Germany, and the United States in the 1970s. Hopefully those in charge of making these decisions have learned from our past mistakes.

Some of the trends that were accelerated as a result of COVID-19 may have been stickier than initially anticipated. For many white-collar workers, the long-term trend of hybrid work is here to stay. At least partially related, more companies have been moving out of high tax states and relocating to tax-friendly states such as Florida. The same can be said for workers since there has been an increase in the number of employees that can permanently work remotely full-time. If a given individual can make the same salary that they were making while living in San Francisco but move to a rural part of Florida, this is the equivalent of getting a large pay raise. The blending of physical and digital has continued to gather steam. Meetings that previously offered only an in-person option prior to the pandemic now often offer a digital meeting option in case some are unable to physically be there. In general, I think that COVID-19 increased the amount of flexibility that people have for accomplishing tasks. During the pandemic, we had to be flexible about when and where we were doing things, and this trend is sticking around for the long haul, which I view as being one of the positive implications of this period.

Another update as it relates to crisis situations occurred as a result of the war between Russia and Ukraine. While what has developed in Ukraine would be classified as a crisis by every measure, I am going to focus on the impacts to the Russian economy, as that would likely be viewed as more of a standard economic crisis as opposed to the situation in Ukraine where the country has been invaded by foreign troops. As I am writing, the economic crisis in Russia is still playing out. It is highly unlikely that Vladimir Putin envisioned such a staunch resistance from Ukraine militarily and severe sanctions from Western countries at the outset of the war.

Before the onset of the war between Russia and Ukraine, Russia's economy was just $1.5 trillion in size, despite boasting a population of more than 145 million people and having the largest country in the world by land mass. By comparison, much smaller countries such as Germany and the United Kingdom have substantially larger economies.

When Russia was part of the Soviet Union, the economy was largely predicated upon communism where state ownership was widespread and economic activity was managed by central planning from the government. As always happens when there is a system where citizens have no personal incentive to produce anything, the economy collapsed, and the Soviet Union was ultimately dissolved in 1991.

After the collapse of the Soviet Union, the Russian economy had a degree of transformation from a centrally planned economy to one that had some market-based dynamics. Oligarchs that were favored by the government took personal stakes in state-owned firms. Vladimir Putin assumed the role of prime minister in 1999, a role that he has never really relinquished since in terms of domestic influence. Between 1999 and 2008, the Russian economy grew at a compound annual growth rate of 7 percent. Similar to Brazil during this period, Russia was riding a commodity boom that benefitted an economy that had outsized exposure to sectors such as oil and natural gas. In Putin's first years, there were pro-growth initiatives such as tax reform and deregulation, but the booming commodity market covered up what was still a highly flawed economy.

Like Brazil, Russia has never recovered following the global financial crisis and the collapse in commodity prices.

A lot has been talked about the radical transformation that Russia undertook going from communism to a *market-based economy*. However, the Russian economy has never really transformed as much as the Russian government would like others to believe. While some work has been outsourced to a small collection of trusted oligarchs that have garnered outsized wealth, the Russian government has maintained significant influence and ownership over the largest domestic companies such as Gazprom. If you knew that all the economic benefits of a country would ultimately flow to the government and a small group of corrupt individuals with close ties to the government, would you be incentivized to produce anything great? The answer is no. Unsurprisingly, there has been little in the way of domestic innovation despite the puffery during the 2000s that some radical transformation had taken place. As I am writing this chapter, the three largest companies in Russia are oil and gas companies. This might be fine if it were the 1930s, but this is a world that has become increasingly dominated by technology and services. What has made matters worse for Russia is that the country is believed to have the highest inequality of all major economies. Before the recent economic collapse in wake of the war with Ukraine, it was reported that around 500 Russians controlled more wealth than 99.8 percent of the domestic population! This, of course, is attributable to the flawed incentive structure that has at times been deemed to be a market-based economy. In a real version of capitalism, this small collection of individuals would not be gifted portions of state-controlled entities and other people would have more incentive to innovate.

After Russia invaded Ukraine, in short order, we witnessed the most severe economic sanctions against a major economy in modern times. Any Western company that previously operated in Russia has basically been shamed into pulling out of the country, if they did not do so willingly. As I am writing this chapter, over 450 companies have withdrawn from the Russian market. Not only will local consumers be unhappy that they can't purchase their iPhones and McDonald's, but at least in the near term, Russia is going to have difficulties just securing daily essentials, given the reliance on imports. There are reports of consumers waiting in lines for an hour and a half just to acquire daily essentials such as sugar, similar to the days of the Soviet Union. Despite Russian efforts to sanction-proof the economy, Russia is still heavily reliant on imports for components and tools for a wide range of industries such as consumer goods and industrial products. Current projections show the Russian economy shrinking by 10 percent in 2022 as a result of the significant disruptions. In 2021, Russia was the largest global natural gas exporter, the second largest crude oil exporter, and the third largest coal exporter. Given some countries' reliance on Russia for commodity imports such as many located in Western Europe, even with severe economic sanctions it is not as if the Russian economy will come to a full standstill despite the significant components' shortages.

In light of the extreme turmoil economically and politically, Russia closed its domestic stock exchange for a month, a classic response to disruptions of this magnitude to prevent capital flight. Even when the domestic stock exchange opened a month later, there were several caveats. Short selling was banned, foreigners couldn't sell shares, and the Russian sovereign wealth fund would invest $10 billion in stocks to prop up the market.

As should be expected if a country launches a large-scale international war campaign and has severe domestic economic disruptions, the Russian ruble (Russia's currency) plunged to a record low (although it later recovered). In short order, the Russian central bank raised interest rates to 20 percent in an attempt to tame skyrocketing inflation. As almost always happens when there is chaos of this magnitude, there was a dash for hard currency owing to the lack of trust in the domestic currency. Significantly higher interest rates were being charged by banks and exchanges for hard currency. It is difficult to know exactly what has been happening within the Russian borders given the government monopoly on the media, but there were reports of long lines at ATMs around the country. Citizens were fearing cash withdrawal limits, with these fears compounded by the electronic payment's disruptions caused by the Western payment's networks suspending service in Russia. These developments set the stage for yet another bank run in history. As of the time of this writing, it is unclear as to the extent that the domestic banks are holding up.

A significant event developed after Russia invaded Ukraine. As part of the severe Western sanctions that have pummeled the Russian economy and will have various long-lasting effects around the world, the United

States and its allies have moved to effectively cut off Russia from the U.S. dollar-denominated Western financial system. I won't comment on whether I believe this is the right move from the West's perspective, but I can say with almost certainty that this development will push countries such as China to diversify away from the U.S. dollar. Other countries have now seen that the United States and its allies are willing to take such measures, and these actions have significant consequences for a domestic economy overly reliant on the U.S. dollar. We have already discussed several reasons as to why it is likely that we will see a long-term decline in the U.S. dollar unless some of these trends were to sharply reverse, and this development related to Russia will likely only hasten the long-term decline.

We are at an interesting moment in history in the United States and many other countries around the world. The United States has over $30 trillion in federal debt, and the printing presses are rolling faster than ever. Here is a breakdown of what the United States and other countries can do going forward given the large deficits coupled with relatively low levels of GDP growth. The comment on low levels of population growth is specific to the United States, but applicable to some other countries that we covered, such as Japan:

- Grow our way out of the massive deficits. This is highly unlikely, given that population growth will be much lower than after World War II when the United States produced sustained high rates of GDP growth that helped quickly reduce the wartime deficit levels.
- Substantially raise taxes. This will likely happen but raising taxes will hinder economic growth.
- Have sustained cuts to federal expenditures. This is almost never an option because sustained budget cuts are always politically unpopular, and politicians have no incentive to do this because most of the negative effects of running up deficits will happen long after they are gone.
- Print more money. This is almost certain to continue to happen on a large scale.

As you can see, the government is going to continue to print a lot of money. This will lead to high levels of monetary inflation and devalue the currency held. You may be holding the same amount of dollars, but what you can buy with these dollars will be less. This is the same result as losing money and is rarely understood. The U.S. dollar may initially increase in response to rising interest rates as capital flows to the higher rates in what has historically been a very stable market (the U.S. dollar soared in 2022 in response to the rapid interest rate increases), but the long-term trend will likely be down unless there are substantial changes made in terms of fiscal and economic health.

In the chapter on the COVID-19 crisis in the United States, I alluded to the fact that problems from the global financial crisis were never really resolved, and the issues have been covered up by increasingly aggressive monetary policy and central bank bailouts. This entire premise that we can cover up underlying issues related to the economy with actions by the central bank has been contingent upon ongoing confidence in fiat currencies and that consumer price inflation has, up until recently, remained low. As written about at length, if people were to lose confidence in fiat currencies, we would likely resort to a system where hard assets play a role in supporting paper money, as has happened throughout history. Such a scenario would place limitations on money supply growth and not allow for these massive bailout scenarios or large-scale money printing such as what we have witnessed in the last 15 years. The other piece to this puzzle has been that consumer price inflation remained low for a sustained period following the global financial crisis, and central banks largely ignored asset price inflation. The low consumer price inflation allowed central banks to justify increasingly aggressive monetary policy measures. We have even seen increasing levels of support for the misguided modern monetary theory, arguing that currency-issuing governments are essentially monopolists that don't need to worry about rising national deficit levels because taxes and transactions are done with the government-issued currency. The problem now is that, for the first time since before the global financial crisis, we have significant sustained levels of broad-based consumer price inflation. If central banks around the world continue with the ultra-easy monetary policy playbook, consumer price inflation will only get further unshackled. Inflation is effectively a regressive tax and increases income inequality because wealthier individuals can better hedge against inflation through ownership of assets such as stocks and real estate.

Historically, central banks have raised interest rates in response to elevated levels of consumer price inflation. There are factors that will make raising interest rates more difficult this time around. We have had exploding levels of debt at the government, business, and consumer levels since the global financial crisis. For a long time, a large portion of these debts were rolled over at variable rates that were effectively zero. What would happen if, in order to tame rampant consumer price inflation, central banks raised interest rates to 10 percent? We would likely see a brutal unwinding of irresponsible behavior that has been incentivized by central banks around the world since the global financial crisis. If there are sustained levels of elevated consumer price inflation and governments respond with sharply higher interest rates, there will be massive loan defaults and restructurings coupled with lower demand for large purchases that rely on high levels of borrowing. Given the very high levels of global public and private debts coupled with large entitlement programs in countries such as the United States, the base case scenario is likely that governments will choose a middle of the road path that will result in stagflation. The pain would likely be too great to do something akin to Paul Volcker in the 1980s, so governments will likely sacrifice some level of price stability so that they can support the treasury or local government finance department.

One of the major implications of this extended period of ultra-easy monetary policy has been large levels of illusory wealth that has never really existed. For example, if the Federal Reserve prints $100 billion out of thin air and this money is borrowed by consumers at low rates to purchase houses at elevated prices, does this really mean that those individuals owning properties with valuations benefitting from these price increases are richer? Over the long term, they will not be because inflationary effects will erode this perceived wealth creation. The printing of money does not increase wealth. Long-term increases in wealth arise from increases in societal productivity. We will need to get back to a place where productivity increases are center stage instead of the central banks. It would seem the Federal Reserve and other central banks vastly overestimated the positive implications of easy monetary policy measures such as quantitative easing. A large portion of the rationale for conducting these aggressive measures was that these policies were going to boost growth and help lift us out of the prolonged malaise from the global financial crisis. This never happened. Instead of boosting productivity, these policies seem to have mostly benefitted the markets for assets, and this windfall (or perceived windfall in some cases) has mostly flowed to relatively wealthy individuals. Hopefully, we can get back to a place where incentives are more aligned with producing products, services, and jobs that have a positive impact on society more broadly. This process can begin with setting interest rates at levels that do not incentivize reckless behavior. That will be easier said than done given the pain that will be caused by unwinding close to 15 years of irresponsible behavior.

On the topic of housing markets, I think it is possible that many markets around the world have been in bubbles fueled by the extended period of easy monetary policy. With low mortgage rates, the line of thinking was often that a consumer could pay off a mortgage at a rate that was comparable to a rent payment and get equity in a home as the mortgage was being paid down. The difference in terms of monthly payments between a 3 percent mortgage rate and 6 percent is huge, and some have argued that the mortgage rate received is more important than the price of a home. This logic is fine if you assume that home prices will not collapse. But, what if the extended period of monetary policy fueled a housing bubble where it would take perhaps decades for many consumers to see any material price appreciation on their homes? I think this is an entirely possible scenario. As of early 2022, the U.S. housing market was by far the most expensive of the last 65 years in terms of home prices relative to income. Similar dynamics have been in play in many other markets around the world, owing to the low mortgage rates for close to 15 years after the global financial crisis. If economies around the world enter extended periods of economic weakness, it is likely we will see a large amount of home foreclosures. If people lose their jobs, they will ultimately be unable to even make their low mortgage payments that were locked in during the easy money era. We could have a situation where there is a material drawdown in home prices and then central banks respond to the weakness by resorting to the classic playbook: cutting interest rates. There would then be much lower home prices coupled with low mortgage rates. Such a scenario would ease some of the recent demand-side inflation but would not do anything to help with the supply-side inflation we have seen in areas such as commodities and semiconductors. There is a good chance central banks will again have to choose between supporting the economy and maintaining price stability. One of the main problems with real estate as an investment is that unless you are renting the property, where you would receive an ongoing cash flow stream, there is no inherent return on real estate. In this sense, most real estate is purely reliant on the greater fool theory, where in order to make a return someone else must come along and pay a higher price for the same asset. This is very different from an ownership interest in a business that produces cash flows where the future value ultimately converges to some combination of the cash flow production combined with the reinvestment uses for the cash flow.

Something to watch as the U.S. monetary policy progresses will be how overseas markets respond to the tightening in the United States. Remember that, in the past, debt crises were triggered by U.S. tightening cycles similar to what we studied in the chapter on Chile in regard to Latin American countries in the 1980s. Countries with high debt levels that have inadequate foreign exchange reserves can get burned when they see capital flight that can happen when other countries are more aggressive in monetary tightening. This tightening cycle should be particularly interesting because aggregate levels of foreign exchange reserves are likely low because many countries are still recovering from the COVID-19 crisis and never truly recovered from the global financial crisis. As I write this chapter, Sri Lanka has defaulted on its debt for the first time in history. Sri Lanka is suffering from high debt levels, double-digit inflation, and shortages of basic staples such as food and medicine. Make no mistake, various other countries will be following in Sri Lanka's footsteps over the next few years. One of the other differences between the 1980s and today is that debt levels are much higher than they were in the 1980s. Remember, it was reported that half of the world's countries requested a bailout from the IMF in wake of the COVID-19 pandemic. We are just beginning to see the long-term consequences of the unsustainable debt levels come to fruition with rising interest rates. As I am editing this chapter, the United

Kingdom and Japan are mired in currency crises that are related to the soaring U.S. dollar. The British pound plunged in response to a plan for tax cuts that came at a time when the UK has seen soaring deficit levels, economic weakness, and money has been flooding into U.S. dollars in response to the rapid monetary tightening in the United States. Quoting Ray Dalio, the plunge in the UK pound was "due to the recognition that the big supply of debt that will have to be sold by the government is much too much for the demand. That makes people want to get out of the debt and currency." Similar dynamics will likely develop in other markets, if history is any guide. The market response to the proposed UK tax cuts was so severe that the government ultimately opted to scrap the plan to cut the 45 percent top rate of income tax. This disaster in the UK led to Prime Minister Liz Truss resigning after just 45 days in office.

Another development to monitor is the quantitative tightening the Federal Reserve is attempting to accomplish. Quantitative tightening, or QT, is where a central bank seeks to reduce the size of its balance sheet. In the COVID-19 chapter on the United States, I noted that for the first time the Federal Reserve had added securities to its balance sheet such as CLOs in response to the COVID-19 crisis. The Federal Reserve is now trying to draw down its gargantuan $9 trillion balance sheet without a precedent in modern history for a move like this. The last time the Federal Reserve attempted QT was in 2017, and this was on a much smaller scale than we are talking about today, and without exotic instruments such as CLOs. What was the result? Liquidity in the financial system dried up and overnight borrowing costs soared. The Federal Reserve ultimately abandoned quantitative tightening after the liquidity issues. The truth is that nobody knows for certain what will happen this time around. It will be interesting to see if the Federal Reserve follows through on dumping *assets* on the market such as CLOs and mortgage-backed securities (MBS) that they have made the market in since the COVID-19 crisis. Aside from the larger scale of the Federal Reserve balance sheet today and the addition of a lot more exotic and illiquid assets to the Fed balance sheet, the other major difference is that we now have broad-based consumer price inflation. If the Federal Reserve were to renege on its contractionary monetary policies this time around, we would effectively be ensuring sustained consumer price inflation. This was one of the problems discussed about quantitative easing over the years: how do we exit? As I have noted, the quantitative easing experiment really did not accomplish anything other than to stimulate the price growth of assets and in turn widen inequality.

Another update as it pertains to cryptocurrencies. Along with global markets, cryptocurrencies plunged in the first half of 2022. I had previously commented on the extreme leverage being employed in the cryptocurrency markets, and this was likely a contributing factor to some of the problems being seen in the market today. We have witnessed the cryptocurrency equivalent of bank runs, with companies such as Binance halting customer withdrawals. This is interesting considering one of the primary bull cases of many cryptocurrencies has been that they are decentralized in nature. As we have seen, most people in the cryptocurrency market purchase cryptocurrencies from exchanges that suffer from many of the same problems that traditional commercial banks do. The cryptocurrency crash in 2022 appears to have been accelerated when a cryptocurrency called Terra Luna became effectively worthless overnight after having a market capitalization of $40 billion in the previous month. Terra Luna was intertwined with a so-called *stablecoin* named TerraUSD. TerraUSD was allegedly pegged to the U.S. dollar at a 1:1 ratio at all times. When TerraUSD decoupled from the U.S. dollar, Terra Luna became effectively worthless given its reliance on the confidence in TerraUSD maintaining its value (which I am sure was dramatically accelerated with the extreme leverage being employed in the cryptocurrency space). As I am writing now, there is another so-called stablecoin named Tether that is often viewed as the lifeblood of the entire cryptocurrency ecosystem. Tether effectively acts as an unregulated bank, with *investors* estimated to use Tether in over two-thirds of all trades in volatile cryptocurrencies such as Bitcoin. Cryptocurrency traders exchange U.S. dollars or other fiat currency for Tether in a bid to lower fees, and then use Tether to purchase Bitcoin or other cryptocurrencies. What is particularly interesting about Tether is that Tether claims to always be 100 percent backed by liquid assets such as U.S. dollars, but Tether has refused to provide evidence of the reserves. If they didn't have anything to hide, why wouldn't they just come out and show that the stablecoin is in fact fully supported by adequate reserves? It is only a matter of time before this ends badly.

While there were other factors at play, one of the core reasons for the swift and dramatic downfall of the cryptocurrency exchange, FTX, was fractional-reserve banking. A cryptocurrency equivalent of a bank run occurred when investors began to pull money at a rapid pace after the collapse of other cryptocurrency exchanges. I have seen some estimates showing that $6 billion in assets were pulled from FTX over a three-day period shortly before the exchange suspended withdrawals and ultimately filed for bankruptcy. A detailed analysis of this predictable debacle is beyond the scope of this book, but the combination of fractional-reserve banking, a heavy use of leverage, and investors clamoring for their cash at the same time (and likely a lot of fraud but that will ultimately need to be proven through the court systems) was behind the downfall of FTX just like several case studies of fractional-reserve bank runs covered in this book.

As I am finishing the edits on this chapter, my view is that it has become more likely that the war in Ukraine is possibly just the beginning of a new era globally where peace could be more difficult to come by. It may not be the most likely scenario, but I don't believe it would be impossible to imagine a war where the likes of China, Russia, and Iran face off against the United States and the North Atlantic Treaty Organization (NATO) countries. Countries such as China, Russia, Iran, and North Korea have started to challenge the world order that was shaped after World War II. From an investment perspective, it is possible that the relative calm in markets such as the United States in recent decades was the aberration. We could be entering a period unlike any that U.S. investors today have experienced where diversification across countries, currencies, and asset classes could be more important.

How This Information
Can Be Used

I want to make it clear that I wholeheartedly agree with legendary investor Peter Lynch's famous claim: "Far more money has been lost by investors preparing for corrections, or trying to anticipate corrections, than has been lost in corrections themselves." If you have read the detailed country case studies included in this book and believe that you can now accurately predict the next major global financial crisis and decide to withhold all your money from the markets until a crash occurs and plan to pile all your assets in at the market bottom, good luck. The problem with this market timing strategy is that I have never met a single person who has been able to consistently execute it with success. There are two major problems with this market timing strategy. The first is that it is extremely difficult to predict the timing of when a crash is going to occur. You could have been completely right about the analysis of a looming financial crisis in Japan in the 1990s, but it took seven years for the domestic banking crisis to come to fruition after the asset bubble burst. In Germany, in the 1920s and 1930s, it took over a decade for the banking system to collapse after the hyperinflation episode began. The second flaw with the market timing strategy is that, even if you were to consistently make correct predictions about the macroeconomic events and exact timing (which is highly unlikely), when markets are in chaos, everyone believes that they will fall further. I always find it interesting to read about individuals that have claimed to call the timing of a particular market crisis. In the recent COVID-19 crisis, Bill Ackman may have been one of the few people who successfully made a lot of money predicting a market-specific event and the timing with near precision. What usually happens outside of one of these outlier cases is that, when markets start crashing, people tend to put off investing or even sell because they believe that markets will fall further. This behavior becomes catastrophic for long-term returns when investors miss the eventual market rebound. Bank of America released research in 2020 that showed S&P investor returns from 1930 to 2020, which included being invested for all days during that time period, compared to if an investor just missed the 10 best market days per decade. While missing 10 market days per decade doesn't seem consequential, in reality, missing the few best days wipes out almost all market returns. An investor would have earned a cumulative return of 17,715 percent from 1930 to 2020 if they stayed fully invested in an S&P 500 index equivalent. If an investor missed just the best 10 days per decade over that same time period, they would have earned a cumulative 28 percent return! In attempting to execute some form of a market timing strategy, far more often than not, investors wind up with a return looking more like the cumulative 28 percent than the 17,715 percent. I believe it is best to stay mostly invested through all types of markets to avoid the powerful emotional biases that tend to adversely impact long-term returns.

While I don't believe that having an understanding of past market crises is of value in terms of attempting to time the overall market, I believe that studying this history is useful in terms of evaluating various risk factors, many that most people never contemplate. For example, my first rule of investing is to never invest in any business that requires leverage to earn a return. Looking at these case studies throughout history, it is easy to see why risk-averse investors would abide by this rule. The problem with the business models of banks, investment banks, property developers, and other businesses that require leverage to earn a decent return is that a modest loss in value of the assets wipes out all the shareholder equity, and this can happen overnight. This is what happened in several of the banking crisis scenarios covered in this book, and as I am writing this chapter, this is what is happening to overleveraged Chinese property developers. I think it is important to understand past debt cycles because this knowledge is useful in contemplating future risk. Businesses that rely on debt to earn an adequate return inherently assume that abundant credit will always be available, which is not true. Most of the financial crisis scenarios covered in this book happened after a period of rapid credit growth that was followed by a phase of credit contraction. Having studied several scenarios where this happened throughout history, we know it is extremely dangerous to invest in any business that relies on debt because there have been and will be more periods in the future where debt is not readily available. While I have documented the dangers of market timing, understanding where you are in the debt cycle is important in terms of assessing certain risks. As I write this chapter, the world is seeing record levels of debt at the government, corporate, and consumer levels. Seeing this, and having an understanding of debt cycles, we can assume that the world has been in the phase of rapid credit growth that will inevitably be followed by a period of credit contraction most likely triggered by a rise in interest rates (a scenario that has played out in 2022). I don't know the timing of how this will develop, but I do know that, when it happens, it will likely have severe consequences for many businesses that rely on leverage. A rise in interest rates would also make it much more expensive for overleveraged businesses and governments to continue to borrow. More than a decade of ultra-low interest rates has masked these risks that would come roaring back if interest rates were to rise dramatically.

Reviewing these case studies on various market crises in history can provide lessons on the safety of particular investments. In addition to my rule of never investing in a business that requires leverage to earn a return, I prefer to invest mostly in businesses that require little in the way of capital to run the business, and it is ideal if the line of business is a utility. We saw the perils of capital-intensive businesses such as airlines and cruise lines during the COVID-19 crisis. In late March of 2020, Delta Air Lines was burning through $100 million of cash flow per day. This would equate to roughly $36.5 billion per year in lost cash. If it weren't for the combination of government support and excess capital, every airline and cruise line could have gone bankrupt. The problem with businesses that require significant amounts of capital to run their operations is that the companies can't do much to adjust their cost structure when things go wrong. This lack of flexibility can have calamitous consequences when an unforeseen event happens, such as COVID-19 in 2020, where the entire economy was effectively shut down for a period of time. I prefer to invest in businesses that provide products or services that are essentially utilities because, regardless of what is going on in the world, people still need to eat, drink, and use the Internet. We have touched on the COVID-19 crisis and at least briefly discussed Germany during World War I where the economies relied almost exclusively on utilities. During times of war or prolonged unforeseen crises, such an environment can persist for quite some time and could permanently impair businesses that do not provide products or services that are essential. I don't know what the future has in store for us, but an extended period when the entire economy is more or less relegated to utility products or services can't be ruled out. As I am editing this chapter, we are seeing this wartime scenario play out in Ukraine. I am sure that this commentary is relevant for many businesses that operated only in Ukraine.

Having studied various periods in history of high inflation such as post-World War I in Germany, the 1970s energy crisis in the United States, and hyperinflation in Zimbabwe in the 2000s, I have gotten a much better appreciation for businesses with pricing power. A business with pricing power can raise prices without reducing much demand for their products or services. The pricing power a business possesses is somewhat of a referendum on the amount of unique value the product or service is providing to the customer. If a product or service is providing a high amount of unique value to a customer, there is a greater chance that the customer will be willing to pay more for the product or service. Why is pricing power so critical during sustained periods of high inflation such as those that we have witnessed at various points in history? During periods of high cost-push inflation (increase in prices due to a rise in input costs such as wages and materials) such as what we are seeing in the world as I am writing this chapter, businesses with weak pricing power lack the ability to push through price increases to cover the input cost inflation. If the inflationary environment is severe and prolonged, there is a chance that businesses with weak pricing power can become permanently impaired owing to their lack of ability to push through adequate price increases. This is a risk factor that has been largely overlooked until recently because of the recent decades of low inflation. I think it is best to stick with businesses that possess strong pricing power to mitigate inflationary risks.

I want to dispel the myth that holding cash for long periods of time is a safe investment. Particularly during periods of high inflation, currencies get devalued over time. While the nominal amount of money may not decline, what you can purchase with this paper money declines over long stretches of time attributable to inflation. This concept should be reinforced by the various case studies on periods of high inflation in this book. Asset classes such as equities, real estate, and commodities have traditionally performed relatively well compared to other assets during periods of high inflation. Not only does market timing hurt an investor from the standpoint of potentially missing out on the majority of long-term equity returns, but if the alternative is to park large sums of money in cash, this investment is doomed. In general, I believe it is best to have the majority of your savings allocated to productive assets. Examples would include stocks or real estate rental properties that generate cash flow. Ownership of assets that don't produce anything like currencies or a house relies on the greater fool theory to earn an investment return. The only possible way for an investor to earn a return on these types of assets is if someone else comes along and offers a higher price for these assets. This is in stark contrast to a productive asset such as an ownership interest in a business where the company can pay a dividend, repurchase shares, or produce more products or services over time, and the long-term value ultimately converges to the sum of these factors.

Studying the cases included in this book can give an individual a better appreciation for having an element of country diversification in an investment portfolio. If you had decided to put all your retirement savings into Japanese equities in 1989, you would still be waiting to earn a positive return on this investment. This investment decision could have had devastating effects on an individual's well-being, and this is not an isolated event. Getting sucked into any of the market bubbles covered in this book would have been catastrophic for returns if there was a lack of country diversification and investments were done without dollar cost averaging. Dollar cost averaging is when an investor incrementally invests over a period of time to mitigate risks tied to the overall market. Country diversification helps protect an investor against political risks (and in turn currency risks) such as some of those that were discussed in this writing. If you had all or most of your money invested in South African or Zimbabwean property at various points in history, you could have had all your assets confiscated by the government. This is just one of many risks tied to individual countries that could impair an investment portfolio, which would include but are not limited to currency risk, long-lasting effects of financial crises, wars, other political risks such as the nationalization of companies and excessive regulation, and country-specific disasters such as a nuclear reactor meltdown. Just because the United States has been so successful over the last 100 years, this does not mean this will be the case over the next 100 years. What if a future U.S. president decided to nationalize some of the country's most valuable assets? As shown from some examples covered earlier in this book, something like this happening should be considered a nonzero probability. Ray Dalio researched the 10 greatest world powers as of 1900 and found that seven of these 10 countries have seen wealth essentially wiped out at least once since. While Ukraine would not be considered a world power, the recent war between Russia and Ukraine is another reminder of the importance of country diversification, as even in Russia there was a swift decline in wealth overnight as a result. I alluded to the fact that it is possible the war in Ukraine is just the beginning of an era where there are an increasing number of global conflicts. If this were to be the case, investors would want to be increasingly diversified across countries and currencies. For example, if the United States and China were to go to war, every country would be impacted, but a country such as India could disproportionally benefit from an investment perspective because they wouldn't suffer the same relative damage in terms of loss of life, economic impact, and rising debt levels. It is best to hedge your bets when it comes to investing in individual countries.

In addition to country diversification, these case studies can give an investor a better appreciation for having an element of asset class diversification. Asset class diversification can mitigate the risk of extended periods of weak performance within an asset class such as what we have seen at various times throughout history, such as after the Great Depression. During trying times such as a depression, it is true that most assets perform poorly, but I think it helps to have your bets hedged to some degree. Given the historically high debt levels at both the government and corporate levels globally, is the probability really zero for a global financial crisis to happen that would be worse than we have ever seen, one that would weigh on equities for perhaps decades? While this scenario may be a remote possibility, I wouldn't say the probability is zero. With interest rates continuing to run at very low levels as they have for over a decade since the global financial crisis (this was the case up until the surge in global bond yields in 2022), bonds are not going to be investable assets for most people. It is still somewhat of a one-way street in that bond yields in the long term are more likely to rise, thus decreasing the value for current bond holders. Investors can get some asset class diversification by investing in assets such as real estate and commodities.

I believe it is most important for investors to focus on just keeping themselves in the game. As you can see from the list in this chapter and the case studies included in the rest of the book, this goal may not be as easily achievable as it first appears. It is important to learn from history, because while the future won't be exactly the same, we have repeatedly seen similar monetary cycles, business models, currencies, and various other factors over the course of thousands of years of history. It is best to be prepared and have a better understanding of the possible range of outcomes that may be presented the next time we find ourselves in an *unprecedented* situation. It is far too often that these alleged unprecedented scenarios are only unprecedented for those thinking about their own lifetime.

I want to close with an important lesson that legendary investor Chuck Akre reportedly taught his protégés John Neff and Chris Cerrone. Akre taught them to never be so certain about anything. While it is critical to study history in order to better grasp the potential ranges of outcomes that could happen in the future, it is a mistake to assume that the future will look exactly like the past. One of the most common mistakes that investors and people more broadly make is that they assume that the experiences they have had in their lifetime represent how things will be in the future. It is important to study history to understand why this may not be the case. Taking this concept a step further, it would be misguided to assume that we have seen everything over the course of history. From an investment perspective, it is best to be prepared for a world that may not be representative of any that people have come to know in their own lifetimes, or perhaps even in history.

References

United States: COVID-19 (2020–2021)

"Budget Basics: Spending." n.d. *Peter G. Peterson Foundation.* www.pgpf.org/ finding-solutions/understanding-the-budget/spending#:~:text=In%201970 %2C%20only%2031%20percent,spending%20went%20to%20mandatory %20programs (accessed February 2022).

"COVID-19 Impact: Bill Gates Says Over 50% of Business Travel Will 'Go Away'." 2020. *Moneycontrol.* www.moneycontrol.com/news/world/covid-19-impact-bill-gates-says-over-50-of-business-travel-will-go-away-6174071 .html (accessed February 2021).

"Fundsmith Annual Shareholders' Meeting 25th February 2020." 2020. *Fundsmith.* www.fundsmith.co.uk/tv/ (accessed February 2021).

"Some Background How Does the Federal Government Spend Its Money?" Updated 2020. *Tax Policy Center (TPC).* www.taxpolicycenter.org/sites/ default/files/briefing-book/how_does_the_federal_government_spend_its_ money_4.pdf.

"The Black Death." n.d. *Timeline Index.* www.timelineindex.com/content/view/ 589 (accessed February 2021).

"We Have Nothing to Fear, But Fear Itself…or Do We?" 2020. *Wasatch Capital Management of Raymond James.*

Amadeo, K. Updated 2022. "U.S. National Debt by Year." *The Balance.* www .thebalancemoney.com/national-debt-by-year-compared-to-gdp-and-major-events-3306287 (accessed December 2022).

Anderson, R.G., M.D. Bordo, and J.V. Duca. August 2015. "Money and Velocity During Financial Crises: From the Great Depression to the Great Recession." *FRB of Dallas Working Paper*, no. 1503. pp. 1–57.

Asenso, J. and L. Jacobson. 2021. "Fact-Check: Haley's National Debt Blame Is Overly Simplistic." *Statesman.* www.statesman.com/story/news/politics/ politifact/2021/07/08/joe-biden-nikki-haley-national-debt-bigger-economy-fact-check/7900041002/ (accessed January 2022).

Bhansali, V. 2021. "Will the Real Inflation Please Stand Up? Why Paying Attention to Asset Price Inflation Is Important for Investors." *Forbes.* www .forbes.com/sites/vineerbhansali/2021/02/23/why-paying-attention-to-asset-price-inflation-is-important-for-investors/?sh=78f9b2894399 (accessed January 2022).

Board of Governors of the Federal Reserve System. 2022. *Open Market Operations.* www.federalreserve.gov/monetarypolicy/openmarket.htm.

Buffett, W. 2020. *Warren Buffett Berkshire Hathaway Annual Meeting Transcript 2020*. Presented at the Berkshire Hathaway Annual Meeting 2020. www .mybib.com/#/projects/Voo83g/citations/new/speech (accessed February 2021).

Bureau of Economic Analysis U.S. Department of Commerce. 2020. *Gross Domestic Product, 2nd Quarter 2020 (Advance Estimate) and Annual Update.* www.bea.gov/news/2020/gross-domestic-product-2nd-quarter-2020-advance-estimate-and-annual-update.

Carson, J. 2021. "Why 1970s Inflation Numbers Are No More." *The Wall Street Journal.* www.wsj.com/articles/inflation-numbers-1970s-cpi-housing-prices-11626298531 (accessed January 2022).

Cox, J. 2020. "The Fed Is Providing Way More Help for the Markets Now Than It Did During the Financial Crisis." *CNBC.* www.cnbc.com/2020/03/23/fed-is-helping-the-markets-more-than-it-did-during-the-financial-crisis.html (accessed February 2021).

Cox, J. 2020. "The U.S. Entered a Recession in February According to the Official Economic Arbiter." *CNBC.* www.cnbc.com/2020/06/08/the-us-entered-a-recession-in-february-according-to-the-official-economic-arbiter. html (accessed February 2021).

Dalio, R. 2022. "Where We Are in the Big Cycle of Money, Credit, Debt, and Economic Activity and the Changing Value of Money." *LinkedIn.* www .linkedin.com/pulse/where-we-big-cycle-money-credit-debt-economic-activity-ray-dalio/ (accessed March 2022).

Egan, M. 2019. "Americans Now Have a Record $14 Trillion in Debt." *CNN.* www.cnn.com/2019/11/13/business/household-debt-student-loans-fed/index.html (accessed January 2022).

ESPN.com. 2020. "NBA Suspends Season Until Further Notice After Player Tests Positive for the Coronavirus." *ESPN.* www.espn.com/nba/story/_/id/28887560/nba-suspends-season-further-notice-player-tests-positive-coronavirus (accessed February 2021).

Executive Department State of California. March 2020. *Press Release: Governor Gavin Newsom Issues Stay at Home Order.* www.gov.ca.gov/wp-content/uploads/2020/03/3.19.20-attested-EO-N-33-20-COVID-19-HEALTH-ORDER.pdf?emrc=da4ef9.

Fernando, J. 2019. "What Is a Circuit Breaker in Trading? How Is It Triggered?" *Investopedia.* www.investopedia.com/terms/c/circuitbreaker.asp (accessed February 2021).

Franck, T. 2020. "Bill Ackman Warned 'Hell Is Coming' Because of Virus: He Then Pocketed $2B Bets Against Markets." *CNBC.* www.cnbc.com/2020/03/25/bill-ackman-exits-market-hedges-uses-2-billion-he-made-to-buy-more-stocks-including-hilton.html (accessed February 2021).

Frank, S. n.d. "US Debt to GDP—230 Year Chart." *Long Term Trends*. www
.longtermtrends.net/us-debt-to-gdp/ (accessed February 2021).

Franklin, J. and K. Duguid. n.d. "The Decade of Debt: Big Deals, Bigger Risk."
Reuters. www.reuters.com/article/us-global-markets-decade-credit/the-decade-
of-debt-big-deals-bigger-risk-idUSKBN1YY09Y (accessed February 2022).

Ghizoni, S.K. 2013. "Nixon Ends Convertibility of U.S. Dollars to Gold and
Announces Wage/Price Controls." *Federal Reserve History*. www.federalreserve
history.org/essays/gold-convertibility-ends (accessed February 2021).

Griffiths, J., J. Marsh, and T. John. 2020. "February 23 Coronavirus News."
CNN World. www.cnn.com/asia/live-news/coronavirus-outbreak-02-23-20-
hnk-intl/index.html (accessed February 2021).

Grote, D. 2020. "Terry Smith 'Relaxed' Over Coronavirus Impact on Fundsmith."
Citywire South Africa. https://citywire.com/za/news/terry-smith-relaxed-over-
coronavirus-impacton-fundsmith/a1327931?section=wealth-manager (accessed
February 2021).

Hancock, J. 2005. "Greenspan Speaks Out but Markets Ignore Him." *The Baltimore
Sun*. www.baltimoresun.com/news/bs-xpm-2005-06-01-0506010168-story
.html (accessed February 2021).

Horan, P. 2022. "What Would Milton Friedman Say About the Fed's New
Framework?" *Mercatus Center George Mason University*. www.mercatus.org/
research/policy-briefs/what-would-milton-friedman-say-about-feds-new-
framework (accessed July 2022).

Hughes, B. 2020. *The Wandering Investor*. BookBaby.

Imbert, F. 2020. "S&P 500 and Nasdaq Jump to Record Highs, Dow Climbs
More Than 100 Points." *CNBC*. www.cnbc.com/2020/02/19/stock-market-
wall-street-in-focus-amid-coronavirus-outbreak.html (accessed February
2021).

Imbert, F. 2020. "The Dow Lost 12% in One Week. Here's Why and What
Likely Happens Next." *CNBC*. www.cnbc.com/2020/02/28/the-dow-just-
lost-12percent-in-one-week-heres-why-and-what-likely-happens-next.html
(accessed February 2021).

Jacobo, J. 2020. "Federal Reserve Slashes Rates to Near Zero, Announces
$700 Billion Quantitative Easing Program." *ABC News*. https://abcnews
.go.com/US/federal-reserve-slashes-rates-launches-700-billion-quantitative/
story?id=69610447 (accessed January 2022).

Jahan, S., A.S. Mahmud, and C. Papageorgiou. 2014. "What Is Keynesian
Economics?" *International Monetary Fund*. www.imf.org/external/pubs/ft/
fandd/2014/09/basics.htm (accessed January 2022).

Kochhar, R. 2020. "Unemployment Rose Higher in Three Months of COVID-19
Than It Did in Two Years of the Great Recession." *Pew Research Center*. www
.pewresearch.org/fact-tank/2020/06/11/unemployment-rose-higher-in-

three-months-of-covid-19-than-it-did-in-two-years-of-the-great-recession/ (accessed January 2022).

Kumhof, M. and J. Benes. 2012. "The Chicago Plan Revisited." *IMF Working Paper 2012*, no. 202, pp. 1–57.

La Monica, P.R. 2007. "Fed Holds Rates Steady—Again." *CNN*. https://money.cnn .com/2007/01/31/news/economy/fed_rates/index.htm#:~:text=What%20will %20the%20Fed%20do%20with%20interest%20rates%20in%202007% 3F&text=The%20central%20bank%20left%20its,widely%20expected%20on %20Wall%20Street (accessed February 2021).

Laris, M. and L. Aratani, L. 2021. "Taxpayers Spent Billions Bailing Out Airlines. Did the Industry Hold Up Its End of the Deal?" *The Washington Post*. www .washingtonpost.com/transportation/2021/12/14/airline-bailout-covid-flights/ (accessed January 2022).

Leonard, C. 2022. *The Lords of Easy Money: How the Federal Reserve Broke the American Economy*, pp. 102–302. New York, NY: Simon & Schuster.

McKinley, J. 2020. "New York City Region Is Now an Epicenter of the Coronavirus Pandemic." *The New York Times*. www.nytimes.com/2020/03/22/nyregion/ Coronavirus-new-York-epicenter.html (accessed February 2021).

O'Neill, A. 2022. "Annual GDP and Real GDP for the United States 1929-2020." *Statista*. www.statista.com/statistics/1031678/gdp-and-real-gdp-united-states-1930-2019/ (accessed January 2023).

Otani, A. 2020. "Circuit Breaker Halts Stock Trading for First Time Since 1997." *The Wall Street Journal*. www.wsj.com/articles/traders-closely-watching-circuit-breakers-thresholds-11583761223 (accessed February 2021).

Patel, A., D.B. Jernigan, F. Abdirizak, G. Abedi, S. Aggarwal, S.D. Albina, E. Allen, E., et al. December 31, 2019–February 4, 2020. "Initial Public Health Response and Interim Clinical Guidance for the 2019 Novel Coronavirus Outbreak—United States." *Morbidity and Mortality Weekly Report*. www.cdc .gov/mmwr/volumes/69/wr/mm6905e1.htm.

Roos, D. 2020. "How 5 of History's Worst Pandemics Finally Ended." *History*. www.history.com/news/pandemics-end-plague-cholera-black-death-smallpox (accessed February 2021).

Schneider, A. 2020. "The Big Comeback: S&P 500 Closes at Record High 6 Months After Coronavirus Plunge." *NPR*. www.npr.org/sections/coronavirus-live-updates/2020/08/18/903252878/the-big-comeback-s-p-500-closes-at-record-high-6-months-after-coronavirus-plunge (accessed February 2021).

Schneider, H. 2020. "In Pandemic, Fed Showed Its Muscle in Markets Still Matters." *Reuters*. www.reuters.com/article/us-usa-fed-yearend/in-pandemic-fed-showed-its-muscle-in-markets-still-matters-idUSKBN2930VS (accessed February 2021).

Shaban, H. and H. Long. 2020. "The Stock Market Is Ending 2020 at Record Highs, Even as the Virus Surges and Millions Go Hungry." *The Washington Post*.

www.washingtonpost.com/business/2020/12/31/stock-market-record-2020/
(accessed February 2021).

Shipman, P.L. 2020. "The Bright Side of the Black Death." *American Scientist.*
www.americanscientist.org/article/the-bright-side-of-the-black-death (accessed
February 2021).

Staff Writer. 2020. "Delta Announces March Quarter 2020 Financial Results
and COVID-19 Response Actions." *Delta News Hub.* https://news.delta
.com/delta-announces-march-quarter-2020-financial-results-and-covid-19-
response-actions#:~:text=%E2%80%9CWith%20the%20significant%20
impact%20of,Jacobson%2C%20Delta%27s%20chief%20financial%20
officer (accessed February 2021).

The White House. March 2020. *Press Release: Notice on the Continuation of the
National Emergency Concerning the Coronavirus Disease 2019 (COVID-19)
Pandemic.* www.whitehouse.gov/briefing-room/presidential-actions/2022/02/
18/notice-on-the-continuation-of-the-national-emergency-concerning-the-
coronavirus-disease-2019-covid-19-pandemic-2/.

The White House. January 2021. *Press Release: President Biden Announces American
Rescue Plan.* www.whitehouse.gov/briefing-room/legislation/2021/01/20/
president-biden-announces-american-rescue-plan/.

Timiraos, N. 2022. *Trillion Dollar Triage: How Jay Powell and the Fed Battled
a President and a Pandemic—and Prevented Economic Disaster*, p. 190.
New York, NY: Little, Brown & Company

Wade, L. 2020. "From Black Death to Fatal Flu, Past Pandemics Show Why
People on the Margins Suffer Most." *Science.* www.science.org/content/
article/black-death-fatal-flu-past-pandemics-show-why-people-margins-
suffer-most (accessed February 2021).

Wilkie, C. 2020. "Trump Suspends Travel From Europe for 30 Days as Part of
Response to 'Foreign' Coronavirus." *CNBC.* www.cnbc.com/2020/03/11/corona
virus-trump-suspends-all-travel-from-europe.html (accessed February 2021).

World Health Organization. 2020. *Rolling Updates on Coronavirus Disease
(COVID-19).* www.who.int/emergencies/diseases/novel-coronavirus-2019/
events-as-they-happen (accessed February 2021).

Yun, L. 2020. "This Was the Fastest 30% Sell-Off Ever, Exceeding the Pace of
Declines During the Great Depression." www.cnbc.com/2020/03/23/this-
was-the-fastest-30percent-stock-market-decline-ever.html (accessed February
2021).

Iceland: Global Financial Crisis (2008–2009)

"2022 Index of Economic Freedom: Promoting Economic Opportunity and
Prosperity by Country." 2022. *Heritage.* www.heritage.org/index/ (accessed
December 2022).

"About the Federal Deposit Insurance Corporation (FDIC)." n.d. *FDIC.* www
.fdic.gov/about/ (accessed March 2021).

"Economy of Brazil and Business Opportunities." n.d. *Global Tenders.* www
.globaltenders.com/economy-of-brazil.php (accessed March 2021).

"Fitch Revises Iceland's Outlook to Negative; Affirms at 'A'." 2020. *Fitch Ratings.*
www.fitchratings.com/research/sovereigns/fitch-revises-iceland-outlook-to-
negative-affirms-at-a-22-05-2020 (accessed March 2021).

"GDP (Current US$)—Iceland." n.d. *The World Bank.* https://data.worldbank
.org/indicator/NY.GDP.MKTP.CD?locations=IS (accessed March 2021).

"Iceland Population 1950-2023." n.d. *Macrotrends.* www.macrotrends.net/
countries/ISL/iceland/population (accessed March 2021).

"Iceland Weighs Pegging Its Currency to the Euro, Finance Minister Says."
2017. *CNBC Economy.* www.cnbc.com/2017/04/02/iceland-weighs-pegging-
its-currency-to-the-euro-finance-minister-says.html (accessed March 2021).

"Iceland: Spectacular Turnaround From Financial Meltdown." n.d. *International
Monetary Fund.* www.imf.org/en/Countries/ISL/iceland-lending-case-study
(accessed November 2022).

"Iceland's Daring Raid on Fractional Reserve Banks." 2015. *Financial Times.* www
.ft.com/content/6773cec8-deaf-11e4-8a01-00144feab7de (accessed March
2021).

Alderman, L. 2017. "Iceland, Symbol of Financial Crisis, Finally Lifts Capital
Controls." *The New York Times.* www.nytimes.com/2017/03/14/business/
iceland-economy-finance-capital-controls.html (accessed March 2021).

Baudino, P., J. Sturluson, and J. Svorono. 2020. "The Banking Crisis in Iceland."
BIS Media and Public Relations. www.bis.org/fsi/fsicms1.pdf (accessed March
2021).

Benediktsdóttir, S., G. Eggertsson, and E. Þórarinsson. 2017. "The Rise, Fall,
and Resurrection of Iceland: A Postmortem Analysis of the 2008 Financial
Crisis." *NBER Working Paper Series* 24005, pp. 191–308.

Bibler, J. 2021. *Iceland's Secret: The Untold Story of the World's Biggest Con*, p. 229.
United Kingdom: Harriman House Limited.

Bibler, J. 2022. "The Untold Story of Iceland's Financial Meltdown." *World Finance.*
www.worldfinance.com/strategy/the-untold-story-of-icelands-financial-
meltdown (accessed November 2022).

Boyes, R. 2009. "Meltdown Iceland." *The Economist.* www.economist.com/
media/pdf/meltdown-iceland-boyes-e.pdf (accessed March 2021).

Chhabra, H. 2020. "Can Iceland Survive Another Crisis?" *Observer Research
Foundation.* www.orfonline.org/expert-speak/can-iceland-survive-another-crisis/
(accessed March 2021).

Dalrymple, C.A. 2018. "Cruising or Crashing? Iceland's Economy in 2019." *The
Reykjavik Grapevine.* https://grapevine.is/mag/articles/2018/12/18/cruising-
or-crashing-icelands-economy-in-2019/ (accessed March 2021).

Del Valle, G. 2019. "Wow Air's Collapse Has Seriously Affected Iceland's Economy." *Vox.* www.vox.com/the-goods/2019/5/24/18638595/wow-air-bankruptcy-iceland-economy-tourism (accessed March 2021).

Farmbrough, H. 2019. "How Iceland's Banking Collapse Created an Opportunity." *Forbes.* www.forbes.com/sites/heatherfarmbrough/2019/12/23/how-icelands-banking-collapse-created-an-opportunity/?sh=31eab7d95e97 (accessed March 2021).

Guardado, J. and N.F. Desaro. September 2018. "Tourism in Iceland: How Is the Exponentially Increasing Tourism Industry Impacting Iceland's Natural Wonders?" *Embry-Riddle Aeronautical University Scholarly Commons,* pp. 1–17.

Gylfason, T. 2016. "Iceland and Ireland, Eight Years on." *Milken Institute Review.* www.milkenreview.org/articles/iceland-and-ireland-eight-years-on (accessed March 2021).

History.com Editors. 2018. "FDIC." *History.* www.history.com/topics/great-depression/history-of-the-fdic (accessed March 2021).

International Monetary Fund. November 2008. *Press Release: IMF Executive Board Approves US$2.1 Billion Stand-By Arrangement for Iceland.* www.imf.org/en/News/Articles/2015/09/14/01/49/pr08296.

Kollewe, J. 2008. "Iceland Hikes Interest Rates to 18%." *The Guardian.* www.theguardian.com/business/2008/oct/28/creditcrunch-iceland (accessed March 2021).

Kumhof, M. and J. Benes. 2012. "The Chicago Plan Revisited." *IMF Working Paper 2012,* no. 202, pp. 1–57.

López, A.M. 2022. "Inbound Tourism Volume in Iceland 1950–2021." *Statista.* www.statista.com/statistics/694114/number-of-international-tourists-iceland/ (accessed September 2022).

Marcacci, J. 2008. "Kaupthing, Iceland's Largest Bank, Is Nationalized; Lansbanki's Domestic Operations Transferred to Newly Created Bank." *Alston & Bird LLP Financial Markets Crisis Blog.* https://s3.amazonaws.com/documents.lexology.com/14c7eb1d-2f59-44f5-9c46-0beb53d9c208.pdf?AWSAccessKeyId=AKIAVYILUYJ754JTDY6T&Expires=1673125937&Signature=DQAWnX2JhWoasT31xavFWJDMTCQ%3D (accessed March 2021).

Matsangou, E. 2015. "Failing Banks, Winning Economy: The Truth About Iceland's Recovery." *World Finance.* www.worldfinance.com/special-reports/failing-banks-winning-economy-the-truth-about-icelands-recovery (accessed March 2021).

Morris, D.Z. 2021. "What Iceland's Spectacular Banking Collapse Teaches Us About Tether." *Yahoo! Finance.* https://finance.yahoo.com/news/iceland-spectacular-banking-collapse-teaches-164128515.html?guccounter=1 (accessed April 2022).

National Archives Federal Register. n.d. Federal Deposit Insurance Corporation. www.federalregister.gov/agencies/federal-deposit-insurance-corporation.

Nguyen, A. 2017. "Case Study: Iceland's Banking Crisis." *Seven Pillars Institute.* https://sevenpillarsinstitute.org/case-study-icelands-banking-crisis/ (accessed May 2021).

O'Brien, M. 2015. "The Miraculous Story of Iceland." *The Washington Post.* www.washingtonpost.com/news/wonk/wp/2015/06/17/the-miraculous-story-of-iceland/ (accessed March 2021).

Reiss, M. 2012. "What Exactly Is Full Reserve Banking?" *Positive Money.* https://positivemoney.org/2011/07/what-exactly-is-full-reserve-banking-2/#:~:text=Banks%20would%20not%20be%20able,is%20in%20fact%20very%20natural (accessed March 2021).

Reuters Staff. 2008. "IMF Board Approves $2.1 Billion Loan for Iceland." *Reuters.* www.reuters.com/article/us-imf-iceland/imf-board-approves-2-1-billion-loan-for-iceland-idUSTRE4AJ00520081120 (accessed March 2021).

Sheivachman, A. 2019. "The Rise and Fall of Iceland's Tourism Miracle." *Skift.* https://skift.com/2019/09/11/the-rise-and-fall-of-icelands-tourism-miracle/#:~:text=Tourism%20growth%20helped%20the%20country,2013%2C%20according%20to%20Statistics%20Iceland (accessed March 2021).

Sigurjonsson, F. 2015. "Monetary Reform: A Better Monetary System for Iceland." *Government of Iceland.* www.government.is/media/forsaetisraduneyti-media/media/Skyrslur/monetary-reform.pdf (accessed March 2021).

Sigurjónsson, K. 2019. "Iceland Welcomed 2.3 Million International Tourists in 2018." *Túristi.* https://turisti.is/2019/01/iceland-welcomed-2-3-million-international-tourists-in-2018/ (accessed March 2021).

Smith, T. (CEO Fundsmith LLP). Letter to Fellow Investor. 2021. *Annual Letter to Shareholders.* www.fundsmith.co.uk/media/deujnq00/annual-letter-to-shareholders-2020.pdf (accessed March 2021).

Tan, G. 2018. "How Human-Centered Policy Helped Iceland Overcome the Great Financial Crisis." *Asia & The Pacific Policy Society.* www.policyforum.net/10-year-recovery-lessons-iceland/ (accessed March 2021).

Tekelova, M. n.d. "Adair Turner on the Cause of the Financial Crisis." *Economic Reform Australia.* https://era.org.au/adair-turner-on-the-cause-of-the-financial-crisis (accessed March 2021).

Thomsen, P.M. 2011. "How Iceland Recovered From Its Near-Death Experience." *IMF Blog.* www.imf.org/en/Blogs/Articles/2011/10/26/how-iceland-recovered-from-its-near-death-experience (accessed March 2021).

Tranøy, B. and T. Sigurjonsson. 2022. "Back From the Brink Iceland's Successful Economic Recovery." In *Successful Public Policy in the Nordic Countries: Cases, Lessons, Challenges*, eds. C. Porte, G.B. Eydal, J. Kauko, D. Nohrstedt, P. Hart, and B. Tranøy, pp. 388–408. United Kingdom: Oxford University Press.

Valero, J. 2020. "Commission Eyes New Proposal to Unblock Deposit Insurance Scheme." *Euractiv.* www.euractiv.com/section/banking-union/news/commission-eyes-new-proposal-to-unblock-deposit-insurance-scheme/ (accessed March 2021).

Ward, A. 2020. "Growth Returns to Iceland After Two Years." *Financial Times.* www.ft.com/content/d7e615b2-0227-11e0-aa40-00144feabdc0 (accessed March 2021).

Indonesia: Asian Financial Crisis (1997–1998)

"2022 Index of Economic Freedom: Indonesia." n.d. *Heritage.* www.heritage .org/index/country/indonesia#:~:text=Indonesia%27s%20economic%20 freedom%20score%20is,the%20regional%20and%20world%20averages (accessed December 2022).

"Asian Financial Crisis in Indonesia." n.d. *Indonesia Investments.* www.indonesia-investments.com/culture/economy/asian-financial-crisis/item246 (accessed April 2021).

"Asian Financial Crisis: July 1997-December 1998." n.d. *Federal Reserve History.* www.federalreservehistory.org/essays/asian-financial-crisis (accessed April 2021).

"News Brief: Camdessus Says IMF Approval of Indonesian Credit Marks an Important Step in Stabilizing Regional Financial Markets." 1997. *International Monetary Fund.* www.imf.org/en/News/Articles/2015/09/29/18/03/nb9723 (accessed April 2021).

"The Crash Timeline of the Panic." n.d. *PBS Frontline.* www.pbs.org/wgbh/ pages/frontline/shows/crash/etc/cron.html (accessed April 2021).

"The World Bank in Indonesia." n.d. *The World Bank.* www.worldbank.org/en/ country/indonesia/overview (accessed April 2021).

"Timeline of the Crash." 2014. *PBS.* www.pbs.org/wgbh/pages/frontline/shows/ crash/etc/cron.html (accessed April 2021).

Abubakar, A., G.A. Utari, and S. Chen. 2018. "Bank Indonesia Policy in Responding to the Crisis: Economic Liquidity Issue." *Bank Indonesia.* www .bi.go.id/id/publikasi/kajian/Documents/WP_15_2018.pdf (accessed April 2021).

Bennett, M.S. 1999. "Banking Deregulation in Indonesia: An Updated Perspective in Light of the Asian Financial Crisis." *University of Pennsylvania Journal of International Economic Law* 20, no. 1, pp. 1–60.

Bennett, M.S. 2014. "Banking Deregulation in Indonesia." *Penn Law: Legal Scholarship Repository* 16, no. 3. pp. 443–481.

Boorman, J. and A.R. Hume. 2003. "Life With the IMF: Indonesia's Choice for the Future." *International Monetary Fund.* www.imf.org/en/News/Articles/ 2015/09/28/04/53/sp071503 (accessed April 2021).

Bowring, P. 2000. "Economic Scene: Recovery in Thailand Is Slowing, Not Stalling." *The New York Times.* www.nytimes.com/2000/07/19/business/world business/IHT-economic-scene-recovery-in-thailand-is-slowing-not.html (accessed April 2021).

Brownbridge, M. and C. Kirkpatrick. 1999. "Financial Sector Regulation: The Lessons of the Asian Crisis." *Development Policy Review* 17, no. 3, pp. 243–266.

CFI Team. 2022. "Asian Financial Crisis." *CFI.* https://corporatefinanceinstitute.com/resources/economics/asian-financial-crisis/ (accessed January 2023).

Corsetti, G., P. Pesenti, and N. Roubini. 1999. "What Caused the Asian Currency and Financial Crisis?" *Federal Reserve Bank of New York.* www.newyorkfed.org/medialibrary/media/research/economists/pesenti/whatjapwor.pdf (accessed April 2021).

Elias, S. and C. Noone. 2011. "The Growth and Development of the Indonesian Economy." *Reserve Bank of Australia.* www.rba.gov.au/publications/bulletin/2011/dec/pdf/bu-1211-4.pdf (accessed April 2021).

Garnaut, R. 1998. "Exchange Rates in the East Asian Crisis." *ASEAN Economic Bulletin* 15, no. 3, pp. 328–337.

Harvie, C. 1999. "Indonesia: Recovery From Economic and Social Collapse Indonesia: Recovery From Economic and Social Collapse." *Department of Economics, University of Wollongong Australia.* https://ro.uow.edu.au/cgi/viewcontent.cgi?referer=&httpsredir=1&article=1007&context=commwkpapers (accessed April 2021).

Hughes, B. 2020. *The Wandering Investor.* BookBaby.

IMF Staff. June 1998. "The Asian Crisis: Causes and Cures." *Finance & Development* 35, no. 2.

Iriana, R. and F. Sjöholm. 2002. "Indonesia's Economic Crisis: Contagion and Fundamentals." *The Developing Economies* XL, no. 2, pp. 135–151.

Jang, H. and W. Sul. February 2002. "The Asian Financial Crisis and the Co-Movement of Asian Stock Markets." *Journal of Asian Economics* 13, no. 1, pp. 94–104.

Juwana, H. 2005. "Reform of Economic Laws and Its Effects on the Post-Crisis Indonesian Economy." *The Developing Economies* XLIII, no. 1, pp. 72–90.

Kenton, W. 2022. "What Is the International Monetary Fund (IMF)?" *Investopedia.* www.investopedia.com/terms/i/imf.asp (accessed September 2022).

Komatsu, M. 2007. "Lessons From Financial Deregulation Policy, Financial Development and Crisis: Case of Indonesia." *IDE-JETRO.* www.ide.go.jp/library/English/Publish/Reports/InterimReport/2006/pdf/2006_04_18_05.pdf (accessed April 2021).

Kovanen, A., O.M. Frecaut, B.E. Baldwin, and C. Enoch. 2001. "Indonesia: Anatomy of a Banking Crisis Two Years of Living Dangerously 1997–99." *IMF Working Paper,* no. 052.

Lee, J. and W. Mckibbin. 2007. "Domestic Investment and External Imbalances in East Asia." *OECD.* www.oecd.org/economy/growth/38728451.pdf (accessed April 2021).

Mandala, S. 2006. "Indonesian Bankruptcy Law: An Update." *OECD*. www
.oecd.org/indonesia/38184160.pdf (accessed April 2021).

Mishkin, F.S. 1999. "Lessons From the Asian Crisis." *Journal of International Money and Finance* 18, no. 4, pp. 709–723.

Mydans, S. 1998. "Indonesia Agrees to I.M.F.'s Tough Medicine." *The New York Times*. www.nytimes.com/1998/01/16/business/indonesia-agrees-to-imf-s-tough-medicine.html (accessed April 2021).

Pham, S. 2020. "IMF Says Half the World Has Asked for a Bailout." *CNN*. www
.cnn.com/2020/04/16/economy/imf-global-bailout/index.html (accessed April 2021).

Reuters Staff. 2017. "Iceland Ends Capital Control After More Than Eight Years of Restrictions." *Reuters*. www.reuters.com/article/us-iceland-capital-controls-fin-min/iceland-ends-capital-controls-after-more-than-eight-years-of-restrictions-idUSKBN16J0S0 (accessed April 2021).

Sarel, M. 1996. "Growth in East Asia: What We Can and What We Cannot Infer." *Economic Issues 1*. www.imf.org/external/pubs/ft/issues1/ (accessed April 2021).

Staff, IMF. 2000. "Recovery From the Asian Crisis and the Role of the IMF." *International Monetary Fund*. www.imf.org/external/np/exr/ib/2000/062300. HTM (accessed April 2021).

Steele, S. 1999. "The New Law on Bankruptcy in Indonesia: Towards a Modern Corporate Bankruptcy Regime?" *Melbourne University Law Review* 23, no. 1.

Tan, W. 2018. "Indonesia's Rupiah Falls to Its Weakest Level in More Than 20 Years." *CNBC*. www.cnbc.com/2018/09/03/indonesia-rupiah-falls-to-weakest-level-in-more-than-20-years.html (accessed April 2021).

World Bank. 2021. "GDP per Capita (Current US$)—Indonesia: Data." *Worldbank
.org*. https://data.worldbank.org/indicator/NY.GDP.PCAP.CD?locations=ID (accessed February 2022).

Zimbabwe: Hyperinflation (2007–2009)

"An Assessment of Arrears Clearance and Sustainable Debt Options for Zimbabwe." 2018. *Zimbabwe Economic Policy Analysis and Research Unit*. www.zeparu.co.zw/sites/default/files/2019-03/An%20assesment%20of%20 arrears%20clearance%20web%20%281%29.pdf (accessed May 2021).

"Analysis: Was Zimbabwe Ever the Breadbasket of Africa?" 2017. *Africa Check*. https://africacheck.org/fact-checks/blog/analysis-was-zimbabwe-ever-breadbasket-africa (accessed May 2021).

"The Native Land Act Is passed." n.d. *South African History Online*. www.sahistory.org
.za/dated-event/native-land-act-passed#:~:text=The%20Natives%20Land%20 Act%20(No,time%20since%20Union%20in%201910 (accessed May 2021).

"The World Bank in Zimbabwe." 2022. *The World Bank.* www.worldbank.org/
en/country/zimbabwe/overview (accessed January 2023).

"Zim's Banking Execs in Custody." 2004. *News 24.* www.news24.com/fin24/
zims-banking-execs-in-custody-20041005 (accessed May 2021).

"Zimbabwe." n.d. *Debt Justice.* https://debtjustice.org.uk/countries/zimbabwe
(accessed May 2021).

"Zimbabwe Net Migration Rate 1950-2023." n.d. *Macrotrends.* www.macro
trends.net/countries/ZWE/zimbabwe/net-migration (accessed May 2021).

"Zimbabwe: Unjust Debt Undermines Democracy." 2012. *Progressio.* www
.progressio.org.uk/blog/poverty-bites/zimbabwe-unjust-debt-undermines-
democracy (accessed May 2021).

"Zimbabwe's Elections Turn Violent." 2018. *The Economist.* www.economist
.com/middle-east-and-africa/2018/08/02/zimbabwes-elections-turn-violent
(accessed May 2021).

"Zimbabwean Independence Day." n.d. *South African History Online.* www
.sahistory.org.za/dated-event/zimbabawean-independence-day (accessed May
2021).

Acemoglu, D. and J.A. Robinson. 2012. *Why Nations Fail: The Origins of Power,
Prosperity and Poverty,* p. 368. London: Profile Books, Cop.

Banya, N. 2007. "Zimbabweans Hunt for Food in Price Control crisis." *Reuters.*
www.reuters.com/article/zimbabwe-prices/zimbabweans-hunt-for-food-in-
price-control-crisis-idUKNOA53023120070705 (accessed May 2021).

Batiz-Lazo, B. 2015. "Zimbabwe Ditches Its Dollar, Ending an Economic Era."
The Conversation. https://theconversation.com/zimbabwe-ditches-its-dollar-
ending-an-economic-era-43263 (accessed May 2021).

Chidziva, B. 2016. *The Role of Corporate Governance in Preventing Bank Failures
in Zimbabwe [dissertation].* Minneapolis, MN: Walden University.

Cropley, E. and M. Dzirutwe. 2017. "Mugabe's Zimbabwe Gets Busy Creating
'Friction Money'." *Reuters.* www.reuters.com/article/us-zimbabwe-dollars/
mugabes-zimbabwe-gets-busy-creating-fiction-money-idUSKBN16Y1NO
(accessed May 2021).

Dzirutwe, M. 2015. "As Currency Dies, Zimbabweans Will Get $5 for 175
Quadrillion Local Dollars." *Reuters.* www.reuters.com/article/us-zimbabwe-
currency/as-currency-dies-zimbabweans-will-get-5-for-175-quadrillion-
local-dollars-idUSKBN0OR23Y20150611 (accessed May 2021).

Dzirutwe, M. 2018. "Zimbabwe's Inflation at Highest in a Decade as Dollar
Shortage Bites." *Reuters.* www.reuters.com/article/ozabs-us-zimbabwe-inflation-
idAFKCN1NI1H9-OZABS (accessed May 2021).

Haslam, P. and R. Lamberti. 2015. *When Money Destroys Nations: How Hyperinflation Ruined Zimbabwe, How Ordinary People Survived, and Warnings for
Nations That Print Money,* pp. 104–105, 251.

Herald, T. 2014. "Black Friday 17th Anniversary." *The Herald*. www.herald .co.zw/black-friday-17th-anniversary/ (accessed May 2021).

Herbert, M. (M.P. Minister of Finance). 1999. Letter to Mr. Michel Camdessus (Managing Director International Monetary Fund). *Memorandum on the Economic Policies of the Government of Zimbabwe for 1999*.

Hughes, B. 2020. *The Wandering Investor*. BookBaby.

International Monetary Fund. 2022. "International Monetary Fund—Homepage." *IMF*. www.imf.org/en/Home (accessed January 2023).

International Trade Association. 2022. *Country Commercial Guides: Zimbabwe— Mining and Minerals*. www.trade.gov/country-commercial-guides/zimbabwe-mining-and-minerals#:~:text=Zimbabwe%27s%20mining%20sector%20is%20highly,gold%2C%20coal%2C%20and%20diamonds.

Kairiza, T. n.d. "Unbundling Zimbabwe's Journey to Hyperinflation and Official Dollarization." *National Graduate Institute for Policy Studies (GRIPS)*. www .grips.ac.jp/r-center/wp-content/uploads/09-12.pdf (accessed May 2021).

Kuyedzwa, C. 2021. "Foreign Entities Can Now Fully Own Mines in Zimbabwe Following Outcry." *News 24*. www.news24.com/fin24/economy/africa/foreign-entities-can-now-fully-own-mines-in-zimbabwe-following-outcry-20210203-2 (accessed February 2022).

Matloff, J. 1995. "Latest Drought Hits Zimbabwe Farms Hard." *The Christian Science Monitor*. www.csmonitor.com/1995/0424/24071.html (accessed May 2021).

Maunganidze, F., D. Bonnin, and S. Ruggunan. January 2021. "Economic Crisis and Professions: Chartered Accountants in Zimbabwe." *SAGE Open* 11, no. 1.

Mhlanga, P. 2020. "Zim Sitting on Debt Time Bomb." *Business Times*. https:// businesstimes.co.zw/zim-sitting-on-debt-time-bomb/ (accessed May 2021).

Moyo, J. and N. Onishi. 2017. "Robert Mugabe Under House Arrest as Rule Over Zimbabwe Teeters." *The New York Times*. www.nytimes.com/2017/11/15/ world/africa/zimbabwe-coup-mugabe.html (accessed May 2021).

Muronzi, C. 2019. "IMF: Zimbabwe Has the Highest Inflation Rate in the World." *Aljazeera*. www.aljazeera.com/economy/2019/9/27/imf-zimbabwe-has-the-highest-inflation-rate-in-the-world (accessed May 2021).

Muyeche, D. and C. Chikeya. January–February 2014. "Zimbabwe's Debt Problem: Lessons for the Future." *Global Journal of Commerce & Management Perspective* 3, no. 1, pp. 15–19.

Noko, J. 2011. "Dollarization: The Case of Zimbabwe." *Cato Journal* 31, no. 2, pp. 339–365.

Reuters Staff. 1998. "Zimbabwe Troops Might Help Congo Fight Rebels." *The New York Times*. www.nytimes.com/1998/10/15/world/zimbabwe-troops-might-help-congo-fight-rebels.html (accessed May 2021).

Reuters Staff. 2007. "Timeline—Chronology of Zimbabwe's Economic Crisis." *Reuters*. www.reuters.com/article/uk-zimbabwe-inflation/timeline-chronology-of-zimbabwes-economic-crisis-idUKL2714678920070627 (accessed May 2021).

Reuters Staff. 2019. "Zimbabwe Declares Interim RTGS Dollar Its Sole Legal Currency." *Reuters*. www.reuters.com/article/uk-zimbabwe-economy/zimbabwe-declares-interim-rtgs-dollar-its-sole-legal-currency-idUKKCN1TP13W (accessed May 2021).

Reuters Staff. 2020. "Zimbabwe Agrees to Pay $3.5 Billion Compensation to White Farmers." *Reuters*. www.reuters.com/article/us-zimbabwe-farmers/zimbabwe-agrees-to-pay-3-5-billion-compensation-to-white-farmers-idUSKCN24U1OM (accessed May 2021).

Reuters Staff. 2020. "Zimbabwe Says Foreign White Farmers Can Apply to Get Back Seized Land." *Reuters*. www.reuters.com/article/us-zimbabwe-farmers/zimbabwe-says-foreign-white-farmers-can-apply-to-get-back-seized-land-idUSKBN25R2GO (accessed May 2021).

Sithole, S.T.M. and G. Mtetwa. 2009. "Bank Failures in Zimbabwe: Lessons From the 2003-2004 Bank-Wide Liquidity Crisis." *UNISWA Research Journal* 24, pp. 44–56.

Staff Reporter. 2007. "Zim's Return to a Barter Economy." *Mail & Guardian* (accessed May 2021).

Staff Representatives for the 2004 Consultation with Zimbabwe. 2004. "Zimbabwe: 2004 Article IV Consultation—Staff Report; Staff Statement; and Public Information Notice on the Executive Board Discussion." *International Monetary Fund*. www.imf.org/external/pubs/ft/scr/2004/cr04297.pdf (accessed May 2021).

Swarns, R.L. 2002. "After Zimbabwe's Land Revolution, New Farmers Struggle and Starve." *The New York Times*. www.nytimes.com/2002/12/26/world/after-zimbabwe-s-land-revolution-new-farmers-struggle-and-starve.html (accessed May 2021).

The Street Staff. 2022. "What Is Hyperinflation? Definition & Examples." *The Street*. www.thestreet.com/dictionary/h/hyperinflation (accessed January 2023).

Toscano, P. 2011. "The Worst Hyperinflation Situations of All Time." *CNBC*. www.cnbc.com/2011/02/14/The-Worst-Hyperinflation-Situations-of-All-Time.html (accessed May 2021).

Zeldin, W. 2008. "Zimbabwe: Indigenization and Empowerment Act." *Library of Congress*. www.loc.gov/item/global-legal-monitor/2008-04-02/zimbabwe-indigenization-and-empowerment-act/ (accessed May 2021).

United States: Energy Crisis (1973–1980)

"1850-2022: Oil Dependence and U.S. Foreign Policy." n.d. *Council on Foreign Relation*. www.cfr.org/timeline/oil-dependence-and-us-foreign-policy (accessed January 2023).

"Brief History." n.d. *Organization of Petroleum Exporting Countries*. www.opec
.org/opec_web/en/about_us/24.htm#:~:text=The%20Organization%20
of%20the%20Petroleum,Kuwait%2C%20Saudi%20Arabia%20and%20
Venezuela (accessed June 2021).

"How the U.S. Oil and Gas Industry Works." n.d. *Council on Foreign Relations*.
www.cfr.org/backgrounder/how-us-oil-and-gas-industry-works (accessed June
2021).

"Nixon Ends Convertibility of U.S. Dollars to Gold and Announces Wage/
Price Controls." 2013. *Federal Reserve History*. www.federalreservehistory.org/
essays/gold-convertibility-ends (accessed June 2021).

"Shadow of '70s Bear Looms, But Was It Really as Bad as We Think?" 1996.
L.A. Times. www.latimes.com/archives/la-xpm-1996-11-03-fi-60777-story.html
(accessed June 2021).

"The End of the Bretton Woods System (1972-81)." n.d. *International Monetary
Fund*. www.imf.org/external/about/histend.htm (accessed June 2021).

"The Gold Standard: Revisited." 2011. *CBC*. www.cbc.ca/news/business/the-
gold-standard-revisited-1.1069604 (accessed June 2021).

"Timeline of Events: 1971 to 1980." n.d. *Energy.gov*. www.energy.gov/lm/doe-
history/doe-history-timeline/timeline-events-1971-1980#:~:text=November
%207%2C%201973,from%20dependence%20on%20foreign%20oil
(accessed June 2021).

"U.S. Becomes World's Largest Crude Oil Producer and Department of Energy
Authorizes Short Term Natural Gas Exports." 2018. *Energy.gov*. www
.energy.gov/articles/us-becomes-world-s-largest-crude-oil-producer-and-
department-energy-authorizes-short-term (accessed June 2021).

Authers, J. 2021. "Nixon Broke With Gold 50 Years Ago. What Comes Next?"
Bloomberg. www.bloomberg.com/opinion/articles/2021-08-15/nixon-broke-
with-gold-50-years-ago-what-comes-next (accessed February 2022).

Black, B.C. 2018. "How an Energy Crisis Pushed the Government Into Creating
National Fuel Efficiency Standards." *Pacific Standard*. https://psmag.com/
environment/the-origin-of-fuel-efficiency-standards (accessed June 2021).

Bordo, M. 2017. "The Operation and Demise of the Bretton Woods system:
1958 to 1971." *VoxEU CEPR*. https://cepr.org/voxeu/columns/operation-and-
demise-bretton-woods-system-1958-1971#:~:text=The%20compromise%20
created%20an%20adjustable,authorities%20to%20maintain%20full%20emp
loyment (accessed June 2021).

Bordo, M.D. n.d. "Gold Standard." *Library of Economics and Liberty*. www
.econlib.org/library/Enc1/GoldStandard.html (accessed June 2021).

Bryan, M. 2013. "The Great Inflation." *Federal Reserve History*. www
.federalreservehistory.org/essays/great-inflation (accessed June 2021).

Comstock, O. and M. Hamilton. 2019. "Monthly U.S. Crude Oil Imports
From OPEC Fall to a 30-Year Low." *EIA*. www.eia.gov/todayinenergy/detail
.php?id=39852 (accessed June 2021).

Goldstein, J., D. Karlan, S. Douglis, K. Malone, R. Palmer, J. Simon, J. Judd, and C. Kasell. 2019. "When Reagan Broke the Unions." *Npr.* Planet Money Podcast. www.npr.org/transcripts/788002965.

Graefe, L. 2013. "Oil Shock of 1978-79." *Federal Reserve History.* www.federal reservehistory.org/essays/oil-shock-of-1978-79#:~:text=Oil%20prices%20began %20to%20rise,of%20oil%20during%20the%20crisis (accessed June 2021).

Gross, S. 2017. "The 1967 War and the 'Oil Weapon." *Brookings.* www.brookings.edu/ blog/markaz/2017/06/05/the-1967-war-and-the-oil-weapon/ (accessed June 2021).

Haluga, M. 2017. "The Oil Crisis of 1973: President Nixon's Actions to Maintain American Prosperity." *American Studies Forum.* Final Research Paper, Provi- dence College. https://digitalcommons.providence.edu/cgi/viewcontent.cgi? article=1002&context=american_studies_forum (accessed June 2021).

Hershey, R.D. 1981. "President Abolishes Last Price Controls on U.S.-Produced Oil." *The New York Times.* www.nytimes.com/1981/01/29/us/president- abolishes-last-price-controls-on-us-produced-oil.html (accessed June 2021).

Hiller, J. 2020. "Few U.S. Shale Firms Can Withstand Prolonged Oil Price War." *Reuters.* www.reuters.com/article/us-global-oil-shale-costs-analysis/few-u-s-shale- firms-can-withstand-prolonged-oil-price-war-idUSKBN2130HL (accessed June 2021).

History.com Editors. 2009a. "Jimmy Carter Shuts Down Oil Imports From Iran." *History.* www.history.com/this-day-in-history/carter-shuts-down-oil- imports-from-iran (accessed June 2021).

History.com Editors. 2009b. "This Day in History: June 05." *History.* www .history.com/this-day-in-history/fdr-takes-united-states-off-gold-standard (accessed June 2021).

History.com Editors. 2009c. "Yom Kippur War." *History.* www.history.com/ topics/middle-east/yom-kippur-war (accessed May 2022).

Konish, L. 2022. "Millions of Calif. Families to Get 'Inflation Relief' Stimulus Checks of up to $1,050: What We Know About Whether Other States Will Follow." *CNBC.* www.cnbc.com/2022/06/28/california-plans-inflation-relief- checks-will-other-states-follow.html (accessed December 2022).

Lock, C. 2022. "Demand-Pull Inflation." *Forbes.* www.forbes.com/advisor/ investing/demand-pull-inflation/#:~:text=Demand%2Dpull%20inflation %20is%20when%20there%20is%20an%20increase%20in,and%20services %20are%20pulled%20higher (accessed June 2021).

Maloney, S. and K. Razipour. "Order From Chaos: The Iranian revolution— A Timeline of Events." *Brookings.* www.brookings.edu/blog/order-from-chaos/ 2019/01/24/the-iranian-revolution-a-timeline-of-events/ (accessed June 2021).

Manly, R. 2021. "British Requests for $3 Billion in US Treasury Gold—The Trigger That Closed the Gold Window." *Bullionstar.* www.bullionstar.com/ blogs/ronan-manly/british-requests-for-3-billion-in-us-treasury-gold-the- trigger-that-closed-the-gold-window/ (accessed February 2022).

McTeer, R. 2011. "A Brief History of the Gold Standard." *National Center for Policy Analysis*. www.ncpathinktank.org/pub/ba746#:~:text=In%201834%2C %20the%20dollar%20was,an%20ounce%20a%20century%20later (accessed June 2021).

Rafuse, J. 2007. "History 101: Price Controls Don't Work." *Chicago Tribune*. www.chicagotribune.com/news/ct-xpm-2007-06-07-0706061080-story.html (accessed June 2021).

Reuters Staff. 2008. "Timeline: Half a Century of Oil Price Volatility." *Reuters*. www.reuters.com/article/us-oil-prices/timeline-half-a-century-of-oil-price-volatility-idUKTRE4AJ3ZR20081120 (accessed June 2021).

Romer, C.D. n.d. "Business Cycles." *Econlib*. www.econlib.org/library/Enc/Business Cycles.html (accessed June 2021).

Sawyers, A. 2013. "1979 Oil Shock Meant Recession for U.S., Depression for Autos." *Automotive News*. www.autonews.com/article/20131013/GLOBAL/310 139997/1979-oil-shock-meant-recession-for-u-s-depression-for-autos (accessed June 2021).

Skarbek, E. 2016. "Nixon's Wage and Price Controls." *Econlib*. www.econlib.org/ archives/2016/12/nixons_wage_and.html (accessed June 2021).

Winck, B. 2022. "A Fracking Boom Made the US the World's Biggest Oil Producer. Now Its End Pushing Gas Prices Much Higher." *Business Insider*. www .businessinsider.com/why-gas-prices-rising-energy-fracking-boom-ending-oil-shortage-2022-6 (accessed November 2022).

Yeboah, Y. n.d. "The Prize Chapter 26: OPEC and the Surge Pot | EGEE 120: Oil: International Evolution." *Penn State College of Earth and Mineral Sciences*. www.e-education.psu.edu/egee120/node/257 (accessed June 2021).

Yergin, D. and J. Stanislaw. 1997. "Nixon, Price Controls, and the Gold Standard (Excerpt From the Commanding Heights)." *The Commanding Heights*, pp. 60–64. www.pbs.org/wgbh/commandingheights/shared/minitext/ess_ nixongold.html (accessed June 2021).

Zycher, B. n.d. "OPEC." *Econlib*. www.econlib.org/library/Enc/OPEC.html (accessed June 2021).

Chile: Latin American Debt Crisis (1982–1989)

"Chile—Agriculture." n.d. *Nations Encyclopedia*. www.nationsencyclopedia.com/ Americas/Chile-AGRICULTURE.html (accessed July 2021).

"Copper Prices—45 Year Historical Chart." n.d. *Macrotrends*. www.macrotrends. net/1476/copper-prices-historical-chart-data (accessed July 2021).

"Entrepreneurship and Business Statistic." n.d. *GEDI The Global Entrepreneurship and Development Institute*. http://thegedi.org/global-entrepreneurship-and-development-index/ (accessed January 2023).

"Iowa Pathways." n.d. *IOWA PBS*. www.iowapbs.org/iowapathways/mypath/
2422/farm-crisis-1980s (accessed July 2021).

"The Debt Crisis: Further Reforms and Recovery." n.d. *Country Studies*. http://
countrystudies.us/chile/67.htm (accessed July 2021).

"The U.S. Financial Crisis: Lessons From Chile." 2008. *EveryCRSReport.com*.
www.everycrsreport.com/reports/RS22961.html (accessed July 2021).

Alves, B. 2022. "Mining Sector as Share of GDP in Chile 2010-2021." *Statista*.
www.statista.com/statistics/1056760/chile-mining-sector-contribution-gdp/
(accessed January 2023).

Arias, M.A. and P.R. Echavarria. 2015. "Sovereign Debt Crisis in Europe Recalls
the Lost Decade in Latin America." *Federal Reserve Bank of St. Louis*. www
.stlouisfed.org/publications/regional-economist/january-2015/sovereign-
debt-crisis (accessed July 2021).

Boughton, J. 2001. "The Crisis Erupts." *In Silent Revolution the International
Monetary Fund 1979–1989*. International Monetary Fund. www.imf.org/
external/pubs/ft/history/2001/ch08.pdf.

Caputo, R. and D. Saravia. January 2019. "The Case of Chile." *Becker Friedman
Institute*, pp. 1–53.

Caputo, R. and D. Saravia. n.d. "The Case of Chile." *Manifold*. https://manifold
.bfi.uchicago.edu/read/case-of-chile/section/322342e4-f2fa-49f0-8998-
ecc92fa065e4 (accessed July 2021).

Caputo, R. and D. Saravia. n.d. "The History of Chile." *Manifold*. https://manifold
.bfi.uchicago.edu/read/a-monetary-and-fiscal-history-of-latin-america-1960-
2017/section/71c11e3e-491d-48e8-a1b5-28f54da11951 (accessed July 2021).

Chan-Lau, J.A. 2010. "The Global Financial Crisis and Its Impact on the
Chilean Banking System." *International Monetary Fund*. www.imf.org/en/
Publications/WP/Issues/2016/12/31/The-Global-Financial-Crisis-and-its-
Impact-on-the-Chilean-Banking-System-23781 (accessed May 2022).

Cowen, T. 2019. "Paul Volcker's Complicated Latin American Legacy." *Bloomberg*.
www.bloomberg.com/opinion/articles/2019-12-10/paul-volcker-death-he-
left-a-complicated-legacy-in-latin-america#xj4y7vzkg (accessed July 2021).

Dicken, E. 2015. "An Assessment of the Pinochet Regime in Chile."
E-International Relations. www.e-ir.info/2015/05/14/an-assessment-of-the-
pinochet-regime-in-chile/ (accessed July 2021).

Dornbusch, R., I. Goldfajn, R.O. Valdes, S. Edwards, and M. Bruno. 1995.
"Currency Crises and Collapses." *Brookings Papers on Economic Activity*, no. 2,
pp. 219–293.

Epstein, J. 1994. "Chile's Economy Still Bustling." *The Christian Science Monitor*.
www.csmonitor.com/1994/1208/08082.html (accessed July 2021).

History.com Editors. 2020. "Chilean President Salvador Allende Dies in Coup."
History. www.history.com/this-day-in-history/allende-dies-in-coup (accessed
July 2021).

International Trade Association. 2022. *Country Commercial Guides: Chile—Important Tariffs.* www.trade.gov/country-commercial-guides/chile-import-tariffs#:~:text=The%20U.S.%2DChile%20Free%20Trade,(i.e.%2C%20zero%20tariff).

Margitich, M. 1999. "The 1982 Debt Crisis and Recovery in Chile." *Lehigh Preserve,* pp. 35–45.

Montaldo, I. 2020. "Torres Suspendidas O La Puesta En Crisis de La Compresión." *Arquisur Revista* 10, no. 7, pp. 18–31.

Rowe J.L., Jr. 1985. "The Rise and Fall of Chile." *The Washington Post.* www.washingtonpost.com/archive/business/1985/08/18/the-rise and fall-of-chile/0d3c8fc8-fb82-441a-b215-84b39156c5c2 (accessed July 2021).

Ruiz-Tagle, J.V. and F. Castro. 2001. "The Chilean Pension System." *OECD Journal on Budgeting,* pp. 117–127.

Sachs, J. 1985. "External Debt and Macroeconomic Performance in Latin America and East Asia." *Brookings Papers on Economic Activity* 2, pp. 523–583.

Sims, J. and J. Romero. 2013. "Latin American Debt Crisis of the 1980s." *Federal Reserve History.* www.federalreservehistory.org/essays/latin-american-debt-crisis (accessed July 2021).

Vásquez, I. 2019. "Chile's Success Story Is Difficult to Deny." *CATO Institute.* www.cato.org/blog/chiles-success-story-difficult-deny (accessed July 2021).

Velasco, A. 1991. "3 Liberalization, Crisis, Intervention: The Chilean Financial System, 1975–85." *Banking Crises.* United States: International Monetary Fund.

Venditti, B. 2022. "Ranked: The World's Largest Copper Producers." *Visual Capitalist.* www.visualcapitalist.com/visualizing-the-worlds-largest-copper-producers/ (accessed January 2023).

Japan: Lost Decade (1991–2001)

"Dodd-Frank Act: Minimum Capital Requirements." n.d. *Moody's Analytics.* www.moodysanalytics.com/-/media/article/2011/11-01-03-Dodd-Frank-Act-regulations-minimum-capital-requirements.pdf (accessed May 2022).

"Global Prospects and Policies." April 2011. *International Monetary Fund,* pp. 53–58.

"Historical Experiences of Deflation and Policy Lessons." n.d. *International Monetary Fund.* www.google.com/url?sa=t&rct=j&q=&esrc=s&source=web&cd=&ved=2ahUKEwij0cqW0bL8AhWik2oFHWauD10QFnoECC8QAQ&url=https%3A%2F%2Fwww.elibrary.imf.org%2Fdownloadpdf%2Fbook%2F9781589062276%2FC3.pdf&usg=AOvVaw1SfcSWR2RmFgrKkFelRMsD.

"Japan GDP Growth Rate 1961-2023." n.d. *Macrotrends.* www.macrotrends.net/countries/JPN/japan/gdp-growth-rate (accessed December 2022).

"Japan General Government Gross Debt to GDP." n.d. *Trading Economics.* https:// tradingeconomics.com/japan/government-debt-to-gdp#:~:text=Govern ment%20Debt%20to%20GDP%20in,percent%20of%20GDP%20in%20 1980 (accessed December 2022).

"Nikkei 225 Index—67 Year Historical Chart." n.d. *Macrotrends.* www.macro trends.net/2593/nikkei-225-index-historical-chart-data (accessed September 2022).

"S&P 500 PE Ratio—90 Year History Chart." n.d. *Macrotrends.* www.macrotrends .net/2577/sp-500-pe-ratio-price-to-earnings-chart (accessed August 2021).

Akimoto, D. 2021. "Japan's Changing Immigration and Refugee Policy." *The Diplomat.* https://thediplomat.com/2021/03/japans-changing-immigration-and-refugee-policy (accessed May 2022).

Capital, V. 2021. "Roaring Eighties: The Japanese Bubble During the 1980s." *Voss Capital.* https://vosscapital.substack.com/p/roaring-eighties (accessed May 2022).

Carmel, U. 2017. "This Is What a Bubble Looks Like: Japan 1989 Edition." *Investing.com.* www.investing.com/analysis/this-is-what-a-bubble-looks-like:-japan-1989-edition-200197309 (accessed August 2021).

Chira, S. 1986. "International Report: A Year After Plaza Accord, Currency Issues Remain Divisive; Impact on Japanese Is Wide; American Hopes Unfulfilled." *The New York Times.* www.nytimes.com/1986/09/22/business/international-report-year-after-plaza-accord-currency-issues-remain-divisive.html (accessed August 2021).

Chung, F. 2022. "Australian Residential Land Value to GDP Ratio Now Higher Than Japan at Height of 1989 Bubble." *news.com.au.* www.news.com.au/ finance/economy/australian-economy/australian-residential-land-value-to-gdp-ratio-now-higher-than-japan-at-height-of-1989-bubble/news-story/ 140872e9ed0fffb9e9a544d3ed68d1fd (accessed September 2022).

Das, D.K. September 1993. "The Yen Appreciation and the Japanese Economy." *Japan and the World Economy* 5, no. 3, pp. 243–264.

Demetriou, D. April 11, 2017. "Japan's Population to Shrink by a Third by 2065." *The Telegraph.* www.telegraph.co.uk/news/2017/04/11/japans-population-shrink-third-2065/#:~:text=Japan%27s%20population%20is%20expected %20to.

Dulaney, C. and J. Zweig. 2022. "How the 1985 Plaza Accord Ended an Earlier Bout of Dollar Strength." *The Wall Street Journal.* www.wsj.com/livecoverage/ stock-market-news-today-09-22-2022/card/plaza-accord-1985-deal-to-weaken-the-u-s-dollar-turns-37-w0HJRmBna5PQXWxgUh0Q (accessed June 2022).

Epstein, E.J. 2009. "What Was Lost (And Found) in Japan's Lost Decade." *Vanity Fair.* www.vanityfair.com/news/2009/02/what-was-lost-and-found-in-japans-lost-decade (accessed August 2021).

Fujii, M. and M. Kawai. 2010. "Lessons From Japan's Banking Crisis, 1991–2005." *ADBI Working Paper Series* 222, pp. 1–22.

Fujita, Y. 2022. "Japan's National Debt Tops 10m Yen Per Capita for First Time." *Nikkei Asia*. https://asia.nikkei.com/Economy/Japan-s-national-debt-tops-10m-yen-per-capita-for-first-time (accessed December 2022).

Kanaya, A. and D. Woo. 2000. "The Japanese Banking Crisis of the 1990s: Sources and Lessons." *IMF Working Paper*, pp. 1–47.

Kawanami, T., Y. Saito, and T. Minami. 2021. "After 20 years, Japan Still Stuck in Deflationary Mindset: Kuroda." *Nikkei Asia*. https://asia.nikkei.com/Economy/After-20-years-Japan-still-stuck-in-deflationary-mindset-Kuroda2 (accessed September 2022).

Komiya, R. n.d. "12. Economic Maturity and Slowdown: 1970s-80s." *Grips*. www.grips.ac.jp/teacher/oono/hp/lecture_J/lec12.htm (accessed August 2021).

Makkar, V. 2022. "Japan's Bubble Economy Is About to Burst Again, and It May Never Recover From It." *TFIGlobal*. https://tfiglobalnews.com/2022/09/14/japans-bubble-economy-is-about-to-burst-again-and-it-may-never-recover-from-it/ (accessed January 2023).

Parkes, D. 2020. "Japan in the 1980s: When Tokyo's Imperial Palace Was Worth More Than California and Golf Club Membership Could Cost US$3 Million—5 Crazy Facts About the Bubble Economy." *SCMP*. www.scmp.com/magazines/style/news-trends/article/3091222/japan-1980s-when-tokyos-imperial-palace-was-worth-more (accessed August 2021).

Penouilh, G. n.d. "The Japanese Economy: The Bubble Economy and the aftermath." *Rincon del Vago*. https://html.rincondelvago.com/japanese-economy.html (accessed August 2021).

Powell, B. 2009. "Japan, After The Bubble." *Time*. https://content.time.com/time/specials/packages/article/0,28804,1902809_1902810_1905192,00.html (accessed August 2021).

Reuters Staff. 2017. "Japan Tries to Take Heart From Slightly Slower Population Fall." *Reuters*. www.reuters.com/article/us-japan-population-decline/japan-tries-to-take-heart-from-slightly-slower-population-fall-idUSKBN17C11L (accessed August 2021).

Scaggs, A. 2019. "After 20 Years, Has Japan Redefined Monetary Policy Success." *Barron's*. www.barrons.com/articles/japan-dropped-interest-rates-to-zero-20-years-ago-theyre-still-there-51549994899 (accessed August 2021).

Shiratsuka, S. n.d. "The Asset Price Bubble in Japan in the 1980s: Lessons for Financial and Macroeconomic Stability." *BIS* 21, pp. 42–62. www.bis.org/publ/bppdf/bispap21e.pdf.

Smith, T. (CEO Fundsmith LLP). Letter to Fellow Investor. 2021. "Annual Letter to Shareholders." www.fundsmith.eu/media/a5zly520/2020-fefs-annual-letter-to-shareholders.pdf (accessed August 2021).

Statista Research Department. 2022. "Percentage of Population Aged 65 Years and Older Japan 1960-2020." *Statista*. www.statista.com/statistics/1149301/japan-share-of-population-aged-65-and-above/ (accessed January 2023).

Stone, D. and W.T. Ziemba. 1993. "Land and Stock Prices in Japan." *The Journal of Economic Perspectives* 7, no. 3, pp. 149–165.

The Investopedia Team. 2022. "Were There Any Periods of Major Deflation in U.S. History?" *Investopedia*. www.investopedia.com/ask/answers/040715/were-there-any-periods-major-deflation-us-history.asp#:~:text=During%20the%20period%20between%201873,of%20the%20presence%20of%20deflation (accessed November 2022).

Wada, T. and L. Kihara. 2022. "Consumer Inflation in Japan's Capital Hits 33-Year High." *Reuters*. www.reuters.com/markets/asia/consumer-inflation-japans-capital-hits-33-year-high-2022-10-28/ (accessed December 2022).

Germany: Post-World War I (1920–1933)

"20 Key Effects of World War I." n.d. *Museum Facts*. https://museumfacts.co.uk/effects-of-world-war-i/ (accessed September 2021).

"About: General German Trade Union Federation." n.d. *DBpedia*. https://dbpedia.org/page/General_German_Trade_Union_Federation (accessed September 2021).

"Aftermath of World War I and the Rise of Nazism, 1918–1933." n.d. *History*. www.ushmm.org/learn/holocaust/path-to-nazi-genocide/chapter-1/aftermath-of-world-war-i-and-the-rise-of-nazism-1918-1933 (accessed September 2021).

"Average Age by Country 2023." n.d. *World Population Review*. https://worldpopulationreview.com/country-rankings/median-age (accessed September 2021).

"Countries in the EU and EEA." n.d. *GOV.UK*. www.gov.uk/eu-eea#:~:text=The%20EU%20countries%20are%3A,%2C%20Slovenia%2C%20Spain%20and%20Sweden. (accessed September 2021).

"GDP by Country." n.d. *Worldometer*. www.worldometers.info/gdp/gdp-by-country/ (accessed September 2021).

"Germany." n.d. *PBS*. www.pbs.org/wgbh/commandingheights/lo/countries/de/de_money.html#:~:text=1915%2D1918%3A%20Like%20most%20countries,make%20honoring%20the%20bonds%20impossible (accessed September 2021).

"Rationing and Food Shortages During the First World War." n.d. *IWM*. www.iwm.org.uk/history/rationing-and-food-shortages-during-the-first-world-war (accessed September 2021).

"Spotlights on History: The Blockade of Germany." n.d. *National Archives*. www.nationalarchives.gov.uk/pathways/firstworldwar/spotlights/blockade.htm (accessed September 2021).

"The Dawes Plan of 1924." 2012. *History Learning Site.* www.historylearningsite .co.uk/modern-world-history-1918-to-1980/weimar-germany/the-dawes-plan-of-1924/ (accessed September 2021).

"The Dawes Plan, the Young Plan, German Reparations, and Inter-Allied War Debts." n.d. *Office of the Historian.* https://history.state.gov/milestones/1921-1936/ dawes (accessed September 2021).

"The Weimar Republic 1918-1929." n.d. *BBC.* www.bbc.co.uk/bitesize/guides/ z9y64j6/revision/5#:~:text=This%20flood%20of%20money%20led,than %20the%20note%20was%20worth (accessed September 2021).

"Why a Common Currency." n.d. *EU.* https://european union.europa.eu/ institutions-law-budget/euro/history-and-purpose_en#:~:text=After%20 a%20decade%20of%20preparations,changeover%20in%20history%20 took%20place (accessed September 2021).

"Yugoslavia Countries 2023." n.d. *World Population Review.* https://worldpopu lationreview.com/country-rankings/yugoslavia-countries (accessed September 2021).

Army Service Forces Manual M356-5 Revised. 1945. *Military Government Handbook Germany.* Section 5: Money and Banking. www.google.com/url? sa=t&rct=j&q=&esrc=s&source=web&cd=&ved=2ahUKEwj88eahiLj8Ah WyMzQIHVTsAGUQFnoECCAQAQ&url=https%3A%2F%2Fcgsc.con tentdm.oclc.org%2Fdigital%2Fapi%2Fcollection%2Fp4013coll8%2Fid %2F2581%2Fdownload&usg=AOvVaw0UN_DbKP5fxUXvTh7Mu3Tu.

Blakemore, E. 2019. "Germany's World War I Debt Was so Crushing It Took 92 Years to Pay Off." *History.* www.history.com/news/germany-world-war-i-debt-treaty-versailles (accessed May 2022).

Blakemore, E. 2019. "How the Treaty of Versailles ended WWI and Started WWII." *National Geographic.* www.nationalgeographic.com/culture/article/ treatyversailles-ended-wwi-started-wwii#:~:text=The%20document%20 stripped%20Germany%20of,was%20forbidden%20to%20draft%20soldiers (accessed September 2021).

Blakemore, E. n.d. "After the Treaty of Versailles Germany's World War I Debt Was so Crushing It Took 92 Years to Pay Off." *World War 1 Centennial.* www.worldwar1centennial.org/index.php/communicate/press-media/wwi-centennial-news/6436-germany-s-world-war-i-debt-was-so-crushing-it-took-92-years-to-pay-off.html (accessed September 2021).

CFI Team. Updated 2023. "European Monetary System (EMS)." *CFI.* https:// corporatefinanceinstitute.com/resources/economics/european-monetary-system-ems (accessed September 2021).

Fergusson, A. 2010. *When Money Dies: The Nightmare of Deficit Spending, Devaluation, and Hyperinflation in Weimar Germany,* p. 140. London: Kimber.

Gasparotti, A. and M. Kullas. 2019. "20 Years of the Euro: Winners and Losers." *Centers for European Policy Network.* cepStudy. www.cep.eu/Studien/20_Jahre_ Euro_-_Gewinner_und_Verlierer/cepStudy_20_years_Euro_-_Winners_and_ Losers.pdf.

Goodman, G.J.W. 1981. "The German Hyperinflation, 1923, Excerpt From Paper Money by Adam Smith." *PBS.* www.pbs.org/wgbh/commanding heights/shared/minitext/ess_germanhyperinflation.html (accessed September 2021).

Graham, F.D. 1932. "Review of Exchange, Prices and Production in Hyper- inflation: Germany, 1920-1923." *The American Economic Review* 22, no. 1, pp. 146–149.

Hardach, G. 1995. "Banking in Germany, 1918–1939." *Banking, Currency, and Finance in Europe Between the Wars,* pp. 269–295. Oxford, United Kingdom: Oxford University Press.

Harris, M. 2019. "Book Review: 1931: Debt, Crisis, and the Rise of Hitler by Tobias Straumann." *LSE.* https://blogs.lse.ac.uk/lsereviewofbooks/2019/11/ 21/book-review-1931-debt-crisis-and-the-rise-of-hitler-by-tobias-straumann/ (accessed September 2021).

Hetzel, R. 2002. "German Monetary History in the First Half of the Twentieth Century." *Federal Reserve Bank of Richmond Economic Quarterly* 8, no. 1, pp. 1–35.

History.com Editors. 2009. "Adolf Hitler Is Named Chancellor of Germany." *History.* www.history.com/this-day-in-history/adolf-hitler-is-named-chancellor- of-germany (accessed September 2021).

History.com Editors. 2009. "Great Depression History." *History.* www.history.com/ topics/great-depression/great-depression-history (accessed September 2021).

History.com Editors. 2009. "World War I." *History.* www.history.com/topics/ world-war-i/world-war-i-history (accessed September 2021).

History.com Editors. 2009. "World War II." *History.* www.history.com/topics/ world-war-ii/world-war-ii-history (accessed September 2021).

History.com Editors. 2020. "European Union Goes Into Effect." *History.* www .history.com/this-day-in-history/european-union-goes-into-effect (accessed September 2021).

Hughes, R.A. 2022. "As Croatia Joins the Euro, Which 7 EU Countries Still Use Their Own currency?" *euronews.travel.* www.euronews.com/travel/2022/12/08/ as-croatia-joins-the-euro-which-7-eu-countries-still-use-their-own-currency (accessed September 2021).

James, H. 1984. "The Causes of the German Banking Crisis of 1931." *The Economic History Review* 37, no. 1, pp. 68–87.

Kalovyrna, G. and I. Melander. 2015. "Nostalgia for Drachma Grows in Greece." *Reuters.* www.reuters.com/article/uk-eurozone-greece-drachma-idAFKBN0P42 4820150624 (accessed September 2021).

Kiger, P.J. 2019. "The Treaty of Versailles Punished Defeated Germany With These Provisions." *History*. www.history.com/news/treaty-of-versailles-provisions (accessed September 2021).

Kumhof, M. and J. Benes. 2012. "The Chicago Plan Revisited." *IMF Working Paper*, no. 202, pp. 1–57.

Lang, O. 2010. "Why Has Germany Taken so Long to Pay Off Its WWI Debt?" *BBC*. www.bbc.com/news/world-europe-11442892 (accessed September 2021).

O'Neill, A. 2022. "German Territorial and Resource Losses as a Result of the Treaty of Versailles." *Statista*. www.statista.com/statistics/1086370/territorial-resource-loss-treaty-of-versailles (accessed January 2023).

Polleit, T. 2013. "90 Years Ago: The End of German Hyperinflation." *Mises Daily Articles*. https://mises.org/library/90-years-ago-end-german-hyperinflation (accessed September 2021).

Pontzen, M. and D. Bundesbank. n.d. "Banking Crisis in Germany and the First Step Towards Recovery." *National Bank of Serbia*. www.nbs.rs/export/sites/NBS_site/documents/publikacije/konferencije/seemhn_conf/SEEMHN_13_Martin_Pontzen.pdf (accessed September 2021).

Richardson, G. 2013. "The Great Depression." *Federal Reserve History*. www.federalreservehistory.org/essays/great-depression#:~:text=The%20Great%20Depression-,1929%E2%80%931941,World%20War%20II%20in%201941 (accessed September 2021).

Salemi, M.K. n.d. "Hyperinflation." *Econlib*. www.econlib.org/library/Enc/Hyperinflation.html (accessed September 2021).

Suddath, C. 2010. "Why Did World War I Just End?" *Time*. https://content.time.com/time/world/article/0,8599,2023140,00.html (accessed September 2021).

Toscano, P. 2011. "The Worst Hyperinflation Situations of All Time." *CNBC*. www.cnbc.com/2011/02/14/The-Worst-Hyperinflation-Situations-of-All-Time.html (accessed September 2021).

Wohlgemuth, M. 2020. "Germany's 'Fat Years' Are Over." *GIS Reports Online*. www.gisreportsonline.com/r/covid-germany/ (accessed September 2021).

Wroughton, L., H. Schneider, and D. Kyriakidou. 2015. "How the IMF's Misadventure in Greece Is Changing the Fund." *Reuters*. www.reuters.com/investigates/special-report/imf-greece/ (accessed September 2021).

France: Mississippi Bubble (1716–1720)

"Ch. 1, Money Mania—The Mississippi Scheme." n.d. *Econlib*. www.econlib.org/book-chapters/chapter-ch-1-money-mania-the-mississippi-scheme/ (accessed October 2021).

"Famous Bubbles from Tulipmania to Japan's 'Bubble Economy'." n.d. *PBS.* www.pbs.org/wgbh/pages/frontline/shows/dotcon/historical/bubbles.html (accessed October 2021).

"GDP Ranked by Country 2023." n.d. *World Population Review.* https://worldpopulationreview.com/countries/by-gdp (accessed January 2023).

"John Law (economist)." Updated 2022. *New World Encyclopedia.* www.newworld encyclopedia.org/entry/John_Law_(economist) (accessed October 2021).

"John Law." n.d. *Undiscovered Scotland.* www.undiscoveredscotland.co.uk/usbiography/l/johnlaw.html (accessed October 2021).

"The HIPC Initiative: Background and Critiques." n.d. *Peterson Institute for International Economics*, pp. 13–40. www.piie.com/publications/chapters_preview/337/2iie3314.pdf.

"The Long and Short Reasons for Why Revolution Broke Out in France in 1789." n.d. *Swansea University.* www.swansea.ac.uk/history/history-study-guides/the-long-and-short-reasons-for-why-revolution-broke-out-in-france-in-1789/#:~:text=French%20involvement%20in%20the%20Seven,12%20billion%20livres%20by%201789 (accessed October 2021).

Adams, J.W. 2005. "Medals Concerning John Law and the Mississippi System." *Numismatics.* http://numismatics.org/digitallibrary/ark:/53695/nnan152775 (accessed October 2021).

Anderson, D. 2022. "Nearly 6,000 U.S. Homes Have Sold For $100,000+ Above Asking Price This Year." *Redfin.* www.redfin.com/news/homes-sold-above-asking-price-2022/ (accessed December 2022).

Bojesen, L. 2012. "History of Defaults: Greece Did It First; Spain Most Often." *CNBC.* www.cnbc.com/id/47814564 (accessed October 2021).

Buchan, J. 2019. "John Law: A Scottish Adventurer of the Eighteenth Century." *The New York Review.* www.nybooks.com/articles/2019/04/18/john-law-man-who-invented-money/ (accessed October 2021).

Carlos, A., L. Neal, and K. Wandschneider. 2005. "The Origins of National Debt: The Financing and Re-Financing of the War of the Spanish Succession." *National Bureau of Economic Research*, pp. 1–36. https://conference.nber.org/confer/2005/si2005/dae/neal.pdf.

Daley, B. 2022. "How the Russia-Ukraine Conflict Has Put Cryptocurrencies in the Spotlight." *The Conversation.* https://theconversation.com/how-the-russia-ukraine-conflict-has-put-cryptocurrencies-in-the-spotlight-180527 (accessed December 2022).

Druckenmiller, S. 2019. "112th Year 507th Meeting." Presented at The Economic Club of New York. www.econclubny.org/documents/10184/109144/2019 DruckenmillerTranscript.pdf.

Forsyth, R.W. 2021. "50 Years After Nixon Ended the Gold Standard, Dollar's Dominance Faces Threat." *Barron's.* www.barrons.com/articles/gold-standard-dollar-dominance-bretton-woods-51628890861 (accessed June 2022).

History.com Editors. "Seven Years' Warm." *History*. www.history.com/topics/european-history/seven-years-war (accessed October 2021).

Lebowitz, M. 2015. "Money Printing Lessons From the French Revolution." *VettaFi Advisor Perspectives*. www.advisorperspectives.com/articles/2015/10/12/money-printing-lessons-from-the-french-revolution (accessed October 2021).

Macdonald, L. 2020. "John Law's Mississippi Bubble and the Plague of 1720." *The Globe and Mail*. www.theglobeandmail.com/investing/investment-ideas/article-john-laws-mississippi-bubble-and-the-plague-of-1720/ (accessed October 2021).

Moen, J. 2001. "John Law and the Mississippi Bubble: 1718-1720." *Mississippi History Now*. www.mshistorynow.mdah.ms.gov/issue/john-law-and-the-mississippi-bubble-1718-1720 (accessed October 2021).

Parkes, D. 2020. "Japan in the 1980s: When Tokyo's Imperial Palace Was Worth More Than California and Golf Club Membership Could Cost US$3 Million—5 Crazy Facts About the Bubble Economy." *SCMP*. www.scmp.com/magazines/style/news-trends/article/3091222/japan-1980s-when-tokyos-imperial-palace-was-worth-more (accessed October 2021).

Ponciano, J. 2021. "Billionaire Investor Druckenmiller Blasts Fed's 'Radical' Stimulus Policy, Warns It Risks Stock 'Bubble Blowing Up'." *Forbes*. www.forbes.com/sites/jonathanponciano/2021/05/11/billionaire-investor-druckenmiller-blasts-feds-radical-stimulus-policy-warns-it-risks-stock-bubble-blowing-up/?sh=7c904f442fe8 (accessed June 2022).

Reinhart, C.M. and K.S. Rogoff. 2011. *This Time Is Different: Eight Centuries of Financial Folly*. Princeton, NJ: Princeton University Press.

Schuler, K. 2009. "This Time Is Different: Eight Centuries of Financial Folly." *Center for Financial Stability Book Reviews*. https://centerforfinancialstability.org/oped/ReviewofReinhartandRogoff.pdf.

Velde, F. 2016. "What We Learn From a Sovereign Debt Restructuring in France in 1721." *Federal Reserve Bank of Chicago*. www.chicagofed.org/publications/economic-perspectives/2016/5-velde (accessed October 2021).

Velde, F.R. 2014. "Government Equity and Money: John Law's System in 1720 France." *SSRN Electronic Journal*, pp. 1–241.

United States and Europe: The Panic of 1873 (1873–1879)

"Banking and the Civil War." n.d. *The Historic New Orleans Collection*. www.hnoc.org/virtual/money-money-money/banking-and-civil-war (accessed November 2021).

"Banking Panics of the Gilded Age." n.d. *Federal Reserve History*. www.federalreservehistory.org/essays/banking-panics-of-the-gilded-age (accessed November 2021).

"Bill Signed to Allow Owning Gold in U.S." n.d. *The New York Times*. www
.nytimes.com/1974/08/15/archives/bill-signed-to-allow-owning-gold-in-us-
gold-ownership-in-u-s.html (accessed January 2022).

"Chromium." Updated 2018. *Corrosionpedia*. www.corrosionpedia.com/definition/
274/chromium#:~:text=Chromium%20metal%20has%20proven%20
of,resistance%20and%20a%20shiny%20finish (accessed December 2021).

"Creation of the Bretton Woods System." 2013. *Federal Reserve History*. www
.federalreservehistory.org/essays/brettonwoods-created (accessed January 2022).

"Ever Wondered—Why Does Silver Tarnish?" 2020. *Assay Office*. www.assayoffice
.co.uk/news/ever-wondered-why-does-silver-tarnish (accessed December 2021).

"Federal Reserve Act." n.d. *Board of Governors of the Federal Reserve System*. www
.federalreserve.gov/aboutthefed/fract.htm (accessed November 2021).

"Financial Panic of 1873." n.d. *U.S. Department of the Treasury*. https://home
.treasury.gov/about/history/freedmans-bank-building/financial-panic-of-
1873#:~:text=The%20Panic%20of%201873&text=One%20of%20the%20
worst%20happened,in%20American%20projects%2C%20particularly%20
railroads (accessed November 2021).

"Founding of the OCC & the National Banking System." n.d. *Office of the
Comptroller of the Currency*. www.occ.treas.gov/about/who-we-are/history/
founding-occ-national-bank-system/index-founding-occ-national-banking-
system.html#:~:text=On%20February%2025%2C%201863%2C
%20President,National%20Currency%20Act%20into%20law (accessed
November 2021).

"FreightWaves Classics/Leaders: J.P. Morgan Controlled US Railroads and Industry
Policies." 2021. *FreightWaves*. www.freightwaves.com/news/freightwaves-
classicsleaders-jp-morgan-greatly-influenced-us-railroads-in-the-late-19th-
century (accessed May 2022).

"From the Collected Works of Milton Friedman Compiled and Edited by Robert
Leeson and Charles G. Palm: Statement and Testimony on the Gold Cover."
1968. *Hoover Institute Library and Archives*. https://miltonfriedman.hoover.org/
internal/media/dispatcher/215154/full (accessed February 2022).

"Historical Timeline: 1850-1899." n.d. *FDIC*. www.fdic.gov/about/history/
timeline/1850-1899.html (accessed November 2021).

"Panic of 1873." n.d. *teachinghistory.org*. https://teachinghistory.org/history-content/
beyond-the-textbook/24579 (accessed November 2021).

"Platinum." n.d. *Berkeley Rausser College of Natural Resources*. https://nature
.berkeley.edu/classes/eps2/wisc/pt.html (accessed December 2021).

"The Classical Gold Standard." n.d. *World Gold Council*. www.gold.org/history-
gold/the-classical-gold-standard (accessed December 2021).

"The Great Depression." n.d. *Federal Reserve History*. www.federalreservehistory
.org/essays/great-depression (accessed January 2022).

"The Heyday of the Gold Standard, 1820-1930." 1873. *World Gold Council*. www .gold.org/sites/default/files/documents/1873feb12.pdf (accessed November 2021).

"The History of U.S. Circulating Coins." Updated 2021. *United States Mint*. www.usmint.gov/learn/history/us-circulating-coins#:~:text=The%20 Mint%20delivered%20the%20nation%27s,bulky%20size%20for%20 small%20chanch (accessed May 2022).

"The Panic of 1873." n.d. *Library of Congress Research Guides*. https://guides.loc.gov/ this-month-in-business-history/september/panic-of-1873#:~:text=The%20 Panic%20of%201873%20triggered,stock%20market%20crash%20of%20 1929 (accessed November 2021).

"The Panic of 1874." n.d. *PBS*. www.pbs.org/wgbh/americanexperience/features/ grant-panic/ (accessed November 2021).

"The Very Beginning of the Financial Panic of 1873…." n.d. Timothy Hughes Rare & Early Newspapers. www.rarenewspapers.com/view/672650 (accessed November 2021).

"Value of $2.13 From 2022 to 1969." n.d. *Official Data*. www.officialdata.org/us/ inflation/2022?endYear=1969&amount=2.13#:~:text=The%20dollar%20 had%20an%20average,Labor%20Statistics%20consumer%20price%20 index (accessed January 2023).

"Victoria Railways." n.d. *The National Archives*. www.nationalarchives.gov.uk/ education/resources/victorian-railways/ (accessed November 2021).

Anderson, N.F. and S. Kaufman. 2021. *Vision: Our Strategic Infrastructure Roadmap Forward*. Strategic Infrastructure Performance Institute.

Andrews, E. 2015. "6 Disastrous Economic Bubbles." *History*. www.history.com/ news/6-disastrous-economic-bubbles (accessed November 2021).

Ashworth, W. Updated 2022. "18 Bitcoin ETFs and Cryptocurrency Funds You Should Know." *Kiplinger*. www.kiplinger.com/investing/cryptocurrency/ 603600/bitcoin-etfs-cryptocurrency-funds (accessed November 2021).

Bordo, M.D. n.d. "Gold Standard." *Econlib*. www.econlib.org/library/Enc/ GoldStandard.html (accessed January 2022).

Brown, B. 2017. *A Tale of Two "Deflationary" Booms—The Gilded Age vs. Today*. Hudson Institute. www.hudson.org/economics/a-tale-of-two-deflationary- booms-the-gildedage-vs-today (accessed November 2021).

Cooper, R. n.d. "The Gold Standard: Historical Facts and Future Prospects." *Brookings*. www.brookings.edu/wp-content/uploads/1982/01/1982a_bpea_ cooper_dornbusch_hall.pdf (accessed January 2022).

Crabbe, L. 1989. "The International Gold Standard and U.S. Monetary Policy From World War I to the New Deal." *Fraser*. Federal Reserve Bank of St. Louis. https://fraser.stlouisfed.org/files/docs/meltzer/craint89.pdf.

Dalio, R. 2021. *Principles for Dealing With the Changing World Order*, pp. 8–51. New York, NY: Avid Reader Press.

Elwell, C.K. 2011. "Brief History of the Gold Standard in the United States." *CRS Report for Congress.* https://sgp.fas.org/crs/misc/R41887.pdf.

Fender, A.H. 2006. *Jay Cooke's Gamble: The Northern Pacific Railroad, the Sioux, and the Panic of 1873.* Review of Https://Eh.net/Book_reviews/ Jay-Cookes-Gamble-The-Northern-Pacific-Railroad-The-Sioux-And-The-Panic-of-1873/, by J. Lubetkin. https://eh.net/book_reviews/jay-cookes-gamble-the-northern-pacific-railroad-the-sioux-and-the-panic-of-1873/.

Forsyth, R.W. 2021. "50 Years After Nixon Ended the Gold Standard, Dollar's Dominance Faces Threat." *Barron's.* www.barrons.com/articles/gold-standard-dollar-dominance-bretton-woods-51628890861#:~:text=President%20 Richard%20Nixon%20announcing%20the,15%2C%201971 (accessed January 2022).

Fulmer, S. 2022. "United States: New York Clearing House Association, the Panic of 1873." *Journal of Financial Crises* 4, no. 2, pp. 1258–1277.

Garside, M. 2022. "Gold Production Ranked by Major Countries 2021." *Statista.* www.statista.com/statistics/264628/world-mine-production-of-gold/ #:~:text=The%20leading%20gold%20mining%20countries,3%2C000%20 metric%20tons%20in%202021 (accessed January 2023).

Gillham, S. 2018. "4 Reasons Why Gold Is an Amazing Metal and How to Recognize Fake Gold." *Medium.* https://medium.com/@allwastematters/4-reasons-why-gold-is-an-amazing-metal-and-how-to-recognize-fake-gold-bebb5be41f5f (accessed December 2021).

Glass, A. 2013. "President McKinley signs Gold Standard Act, March 14, 1900." *Politico.* www.politico.com/story/2013/03/this-day-in-politics-088821 (accessed December 2021).

Gordon, J. 2022. "Great Depression—Explained." *The Business Professor.* https:// thebusinessprofessor.com/en_US/economic-analysis-monetary-policy/great-depression-definition (accessed July 2022).

Gourinchas, P. 2022. "Global Economic Growth Slows amid Gloomy and More Uncertain Outlook." *IMF Blog.* www.imf.org/en/Blogs/Articles/2022/07/26/ blog-weo-update-july-2022 (accessed October 2022).

Grant, U.S. Address Senate of the United States. April 22, 1874. *Presidential Speeches.* Charlottesville, VA: UVA Miller Center.

Harrison, E. 2011. "The Age of Fiat Currency: A 38-Year Experiment in Inflation." *Business Insider.* www.businessinsider.com/the-age-of-fiat-currency-2011-7 (accessed January 2022).

History.com Editors. 2009. "FDR Takes United States Off Gold Standard." *History.* www.history.com/this-day-in-history/fdr-takes-united-states-off-gold-standard#:~:text=On%20June%205%2C%201933%2C%20the,to%20 demand%20payment%20in%20gold (accessed January 2022).

Juglar, C. 1916. *A Brief History of Panics in the United States,* eds. D.W. Thom. New York, NY and London: G. P. Putnam's Sons.

Kadlec, C. 2011. "Nixon's Colossal Monetary Error: The Verdict 40 Years Later." *Forbes*. www.forbes.com/sites/charleskadlec/2011/08/15/nixons-colossal-mone taryerror-the-verdict-40-years-later/?sh=3a6a0fc69f77 (accessed January 2022).

Leonard, C. 2023. *The Lords of Easy Money: How the Federal Reserve Broke the American Economy*, p. 302. New York, NY: Simon & Schuster.

Little, B. 2022. "The 1877 Strike That Brought US Railroads to a Standstill." *History*. www.history.com/news/1877-railroad-strike-trains (accessed November 2021).

Long, H. and T. Luhby. 2016. "Yes, This Is the Slowest U.S. Recovery Since WWII." *CNN*. https://money.cnn.com/2016/10/05/news/economy/us-recovery-slowest since-wwii/index.html (accessed January 2022).

Nast, T. n.d. "Keeping the Money Where It Will Do Most Good." *New York Times Archives*. https://archive.nytimes.com/www.nytimes.com/learning/general/on thisday/harp/1011.html (accessed November 2021).

Office of Corporate Communications. 2017. "U.S. Mint History: The 'Crime of 1873'." *United States Mint*. www.usmint.gov/news/inside-the-mint/mint-history-crime-of-1873 (accessed November 2021).

Pruitt, S. 2018. "Why the Civil War Actually Ended 16 Months After Lee Surren-dered." *History*. www.history.com/news/why-the-civil-war-actually-ended-16-months-afterlee-surrendered (accessed November 2021).

Reynolds, O. 2018. "Railway Mania: The Largest Speculative Bubble You've Never Heard of." *Focus Economics*. www.focus-economics.com/blog/railway-mania-the-largest-speculative-bubble-you-never-heard-of (accessed November 2021).

Rooney, K. and M. Fitzgerald. 2021. "Bitcoin Traders Using Up to 100-to-1 Leverage Are Driving the Wild Swings in Cryptocurrencies." *CNBC*. www. cnbc.com/2021/05/25/bitcoin-crashes-driven-by-big-margin-bets-new-crypto-banking.html, (Accessed November 2021).

Salameh, M.G. 2015. "Has the Petrodollar Had Its Day?" *USAEE Working Paper*, no. 15–216, pp. 1–23.

Salter, A.W. 2018. "The Economics of the Classical Gold Standard." *American Institute for Economic Research*. www.aier.org/article/the-economics-of-the-classical-gold-standard/ (accessed January 2022).

Siripurapu, A. Updated 2020. "The Dollar: The World's Currency." *Council on Foreign Relations*. www.cfr.org/backgrounder/dollar-worlds-currency (accessed January 2022).

The White House Historical Tables. n.d. "Introduction to the Historical Tables Structure, Coverage, and Concepts." www.whitehouse.gov/omb/budget/historical-tables/.

Thornton, M., R.H. Timberlake, Jr., and T.J. Thompson. 1999. "Gold Policy in the 1930s." *Independent Institute*. www.independent.org/publications/article .asp?id=165 (accessed January 2022).

U.S. Congress. 1871, 1873. *U.S. Statutes at Large, Volume 17-1873, 42nd Congress*. United States. Periodical. www.loc.gov/item/llsl-v17/.

U.S. Department of Treasury. 2009. *Appendix 1: An Historical Perspective on the Reserve Currency Status of the U.S. Dollar.* https://home.treasury.gov/system/files/206/Appendix1FinalOctober152009.pdf.

Rome: Financial Panic of 33 AD (33 AD)

"1661—First Banknotes in Europe." n.d. *Sveriges Riksbank.* www.riksbank.se/en-gb/about-the-riksbank/history/historical-timeline/1600-1699/first-bank notes-in-europe/ (accessed February 2022).

"1914—The Gold Standard Collapses." n.d. *Sveriges Riksbank.* www.riksbank.se/en-gb/about-the-riksbank/history/historical-timeline/1900-1999/the-gold-standard-collapses/ (accessed February 2022).

"A History of The Notary—Ancient Rome." 2013. *Malaysian Notary Public.* https://malaysiannotarypublic.wordpress.com/2013/06/04/history-part-1-ancient-rome/ (accessed February 2022).

"Anglo-Dutch Wars." n.d. *Heritage History.* www.heritage-history.com/index.php?c=resources&s=war-dir&f=wars_anglodutch (accessed March 2022).

"Apple Card." n.d. *WalletHub.* https://wallethub.com/d/apple-credit-card-417c (accessed September 2022).

"Development of Banking in Mesopotamia." n.d. *Computer Smiths.* www.computersmiths.com/chineseinvention/coins.html#:~:text=Bronze%20and%20Copper%20and%20iron,also%20first%20used%20in%20China (accessed February 2022).

"Dutch Empire." 2020. *New World Encyclopedia.* www.newworldencyclopedia.org/entry/Dutch_Empire#:~:text=The%20Dutch%20held%20territory%20in,Southern%20Iran%20by%20the%201680s (accessed March 2022).

"Fourth Anglo-Dutch War." n.d. *DBpedia.* https://dbpedia.org/page/Fourth_Anglo-Dutch_War (accessed March 2022).

"Get Your Money Right." n.d. *SoFi.* www.sofi.com/products/ (accessed December 2022).

"History of Banking." n.d. *History World.* www.historyworld.net/wrldhis/plaintexthistories.asp?historyid=ac19 (accessed February 2022).

"History of Money." n.d. *History World.* www.historyworld.net/wrldhis/plaintexthistories.asp?historyid=ab14 (accessed February 2022).

"Iceland's Daring Raid on Fractional Reserve Banks." 2015. *Financial Times.* www.ft.com/content/6773cec8-deaf-11e4-8a01-00144feab7de (accessed March 2021).

"Is My Money Safe/FDIC Insured?" 2022. *SoFi.* https://support.sofi.com/hc/en-us/articles/11378818269709-Is-my-money-safe-FDIC-insured (accessed January 2023).

"The First Paper Money." 2009. *Time.* https://content.time.com/time/specials/packages/article/0,28804,1914560_1914558_1914593,00.html#:~:text=

Paper%20bills%20were%20first%20used,Europe%20in%20the%2017th%20 century (accessed February 2022).

"The History of Banks." n.d. *Worldbank.org.ro.* www.worldbank.org.ro/about-banks-history (accessed February 2022).

"The History of Currency: From Bartering to the Credit Card." n.d. *Host Merchant Services.* www.hostmerchantservices.com/articles/the-history-of-currency-from bartering-to-the-credit-card/#:~:text=1%2C200%20BC%3A%20The%20 Widespread%20Use,almost%20impossible%20to%20forge%20them (accessed February 2022).

"The History of Gold as Money." 2019. *GLINT.* https://glintpay.com/en_us/ blog/gold-diversify-portfolio-2/ (accessed February 2022).

"The History of Money." Updated 2002. *PBS.* www.pbs.org/wgbh/nova/moolah/ history.html (accessed February 2022).

"Throwback Thursday: The History of Paper Money." 2018. *PaySpaceMagazine.* https://payspacemagazine.com/banks/throwback-thursday-the-history-ofpaper-money/#:~:text=Sweden%20%E2%80%94%201661&text=These %20banknotes%20were%20backed%20by,carry%20than%20large %20copper%20daler (accessed February 2022).

Acemoglu, D. and J.A. Robinson. 2012. *Why Nations Fail: The Origins of Power, Prosperity and Poverty,* pp. 33–34. London: Profile Books, Cop.

Agrawal, A. 2022. "Digital Lending | RBI Must Crystallise Its Guidelines Towards a Digital Banking Regulation Act." *Money Control.* www.moneycontrol.com/ news/opinion/digital-lending-rbi-must-crystallise-its-guidelines-towards-a-digital-banking-regulation-act-9147491.html (accessed February 2022).

Amery, A. 2018. "A Brief History of Loans: Business Lending Through the Ages." *Become.* www.become.co/blog/a-brief-history-of-loans-business-lending-through-the-ages/ (accessed February 2022).

Askari, H. and N. Krichene. 2018. "The Bank of Amsterdam Through the Lens of Monetary Competition." *Mises.* https://mises.org/library/100-percent-reserve-banking-and-path-single-country-gold-standard (accessed March 2022).

Atkins, R. "Swiss Voters Reject 'Sovereign Money' Initiative." *Financial Times.* www.ft .com/content/686e0342-6c97-11e8-852d-d8b934ff5ffa (accessed March 2022).

Bartlett, C. 2018. "The Financial Crisis, Then and Now: Ancient Rome and 2008 CE." *Harvard University.* https://epicenter.wcfia.harvard.edu/blog/ financial-crisis-then-and-now#:~:text=In%2033%20CE%2C%20the%20 Roman,enforcement%20of%20it%20had%20lapsed (accessed February 2022).

Carl, B.M. 2012. "The Laws of Genghis Khan." *Law and Business Review of the Americas* 18, no. 2, pp. 147–170.

Cohen, D. 2020. *How Hamilton Laid the Foundation for the Fed.* Federal Reserve Bank of St. Louis. www.stlouisfed.org/open-vault/2020/july/how-hamilton-laid-foundationfor-federal-reserve#:~:text=Hamilton%20was%20 persistent%2C%20and%20in,25%2C%201791 (accessed February 2022).

Davies, R. and G. Davies. 1996. *A Comparative Chronology of Money*. University of Exeter. https://projects.exeter.ac.uk/RDavies/arian/amser/chrono1.html (accessed February 2022).

Daychopan, D. 2016. "From Barter To Bitcoin." *Tech Crunch*. https://techcrunch .com/2016/01/21/barter-to-bitcoin-a-story-of-money-and-blockchain/#:~:text= Bartering%20was%20first%20recorded%20in,of%20exchange%20 became%20more%20sophisticated (accessed February 2022).

Etonomics. 2022. "The Roman Financial Crisis of AD 33." *Etonomics*. https:// etonomics.com/2022/09/09/the-roman-financial-crisis-of-ad-33/ (accessed February 2022).

Gershon, L. 2021. "Babylonians Used Applied Geometry 1,000 Years Before Pythagoras." *Smithsonian Magazine*. www.smithsonianmag.com/smart-news/ ancient-tablet-shows-babylonians-used-pythagorean-geometry-1000-years-pythagoras-180978376/ (accessed February 2022).

Ghizoni, S. K. 2013. "Creation of the Bretton Woods System." *Federal Reserve History*. www.federalreservehistory.org/essays/bretton-woods-created (accessed February 2022).

Guan, H., N. Palma, and M. Wu. 2022. *The Rise and Fall of Paper Money in Yuan China, 1260–1368 [discussion paper]*. Manchester M13 9PL: The University of Manchester.

Hanson, M. 2022. "Roman Currency." *English History*. https://englishhistory .net/romans/roman-currency/ (accessed September 2022).

Harford, T. 2017. "How Chinese Mulberry Bark Paved the Way for Paper Money." *BBC*. www.bbc.com/news/business-40879028 (accessed February 2022).

Harford, T. 2017. "What Tally Sticks Tell Us About How Money Works." *BBC*. www.bbc.com/news/business-40189959 (accessed February 2022).

Harris, J. 2016. "The World's First Banks Were Religious Temples." *Dealstruck*. https://dealstruck.com/resources/first-banks-religious-temples/ (accessed February 2022).

History.com Editors. 2009. "Code of Hammurabi." *History*. www.history.com/ topics/ancient-middle-east/Hammurabi (accessed February 2022).

History.com Editors. n.d. "FDR Takes United States Off Gold Standard." *History*. www.history.com/this-day-in-history/fdr-takes-united-states-off-goldstandard (accessed February 2022).

Holt, F.L. 2021. "The Invention of the First Coinage in Ancient Lydia." *World History Encyclopedia*. www.worldhistory.org/article/1793/the-invention-of-the-first-coinage-in-ancient-lydi/ (accessed February 2022).

Hudson, M. 2019. "How Did Ancient Bureaucrats Set Their Interest Rates?" *Biblical Archaeology Society*. www.biblicalarchaeology.org/daily/ancient-cultures/daily-life-and-practice/ancient-interest-rates/ (accessed February 2022).

Hundley, A., Y. Yang, and A. Nguyen. n.d. "The Babylonian Empire." *Sutori*. www
.sutori.com/en/story/the-babylonian-empire--sjAV2NDKowHrSwxgb65cYwJz
(accessed February 2022).

Jones, C. 2020. "Was the Bank of Amsterdam the World's First Central Bank?"
Financial Times. www.ft.com/content/54201866-0f27-41a6-8c58-368a4eb
47d41 (accessed March 2022).

Kumhof, M. and J. Benes. 2012. "The Chicago Plan Revisited." *IMF Working
Paper*, no. 202, pp. 1–57.

Lazarony, L. 2022. "Should You Bank With Credit Karma Money?" *USA Today*.
https://reviewed.usatoday.com/money/content/pros-and-cons-banking-
credit-karma-money (accessed December 2022).

Marie, M. 2022. "The First Currency in History: Kingdom of Lydia Minted Gold,
Silver Coins." *Egypt Today*. www.egypttoday.com/Article/4/113533/The-first-
currency-in-history-Kingdom-of-Lydia-minted-gold (accessed May 2022).

Martin, K. 2015. "Shell Money Tradition Lives on in the Solomon Islands."
Medium. https://medium.com/@Kiva/shell-money-tradition-lives-on-in-the-
solomon-islands-3ffc1e812c35 (accessed February 2022).

Maxwell, T. 2022. "What You Need to Know About the Venmo Card?" *creditcards
.com*. www.creditcards.com/card-advice/venmo-debit-card/ (accessed May 2022).

McCarthy, N. 2020. "The Biggest Empires in Human History." *Statista*. www.statista.
com/chart/20342/peak-land-area-of-the-largest-empires/#:~:text=The%20
Mongol%20Empire%20existed%20during,contiguous%20land%20
empire%20in%20history (accessed February 2022).

Mingren, W. Updated 2019. "Paying With Shells: Cowrie Shell Money Is
One of the Oldest Currencies Still Collected Today." *Ancient Origins*. www
.ancient-origins.net/history-ancient-traditions/shell-money-0011793
(accessed February 2022).

Mint. 2021. "Guide to the Barter Economy & the Barter System History." *Intuit*.
https://mint.intuit.com/blog/personal-finance/guide-to-the-barter-economy-
the-barter-system-history/ (accessed February 2022).

Muchlis, D. and A. Suganda. January 2021. "Restructuring of Banking Credit
as a Safety Efforts to Improve Credits That Are Made in Notary." *European
Scholar Journal* 2, no. 1, pp. 33–41.

Mundell, R.A. February 2002. "The Birth of Coinage." *Columbia University
Department of Economics Discussion Paper Series*, pp. 1–43.

Norman, J. Updated 2022. "Marco Polo Describes the Issue of Paper Money
in the Mongol Empire." *Jeremy Norman's History of Information*. www
.historyofinformation.com/detail.php?entryid=287 (accessed January 2023).

Pearce, L.E. 1992. *The Cowrie Shell in Virginia: A Critical Evaluation of Potential
Archaeological Significance [Dissertations, Theses, and Masters Projects]*. Williams-
burg, VA: William & Mary.

Pethokoukis, J. 2016. *What the Story of ATMs and Bank Tellers Reveals About the 'Rise of the Robots' and Jobs*. American Enterprise Institute. www.aei.org/economics/what-atms-bank-tellers-rise-robots-and-jobs/ (accessed February 2022).

Petram, L. 2014. *The World's First Stock Exchange*. Columbia University Press. http://cup.columbia.edu/book/the-worlds-first-stock-exchange/9780231163781 (accessed February 2022).

Petram, L. 2020. "The World's First IPO." *Worlds First Stock Exchange*. www.worlds firststockexchange.com/2020/10/15/the-worlds-first-ipo/ (accessed February 2022).

Polkinghorne, K. 2020. *Mesopotamian Interest Rates: 3000–400 BC*. BTCM Research. https://btcm.co/mesopotamian-interest-rates/ (accessed February 2022).

Quinn, S. and W. Roberds. 2006. "An Economic Explanation of the Early Bank of Amsterdam, Debasement, Bills of Exchange, and the Emergence of the First Central Bank." *Federal Reserve Bank of Atlanta Working Paper Series*, pp. 1–50.

Quinn, S. and W. Roberds. 2014. "Death of a Reserve Currency." *Federal Reserve Bank of Atlanta Working Paper Series*, pp. 1–31, 1–55.

Revill, J. 2018. "Swiss Voters Reject Campaign to Radically Alter Banking System." *Reuters*. www.reuters.com/article/us-swiss-vote-sovereign/swiss-voters-reject-campaign-to-radically-alter-banking-system-idUSKBN1J60C0 (accessed March 2022).

Rodney, E., J. Tor, and D. Waldenström. 2018. *Sveriges Riksbank and the History of Central Banking*. Online: Cambridge University Press.

Rooney, K. 2022. "SoFi Stock Soars After Clearing Final Regulatory Hurdle to Become a Bank." *CNBC*. www.cnbc.com/2022/01/18/sofi-stock-soars-after-clearing-final-regulatory-hurdle-to-become-bank.html (accessed February 2022).

Rosyth, R.W. 2021. "50 Years After Nixon Ended the Gold Standard, Dollar's Dominance Faces Threat." *Barron's*. www.barrons.com/articles/gold-standard-dollar-dominance-bretton-woods-51628890861 (accessed February 2022).

Schwartz, A.J. 1984. "Introduction to a Retrospective on the Classical Gold Standard, 1821–1931." *A Retrospective on the Classical Gold Standard, 1821–1931*, pp. 1–22. Chicago, Illinois, IL: University of Chicago Press.

Smith, S.V., C. Garcia, and C. Elliott. 2019. "The Roman Financial Crisis of A.D. 33." Podcast: The Indicator from Planet Money, npr. www.npr.org/transcripts/792386687.

Square. 2000. "The History of the Trade and Barter System." *Square*. https://square up.com/us/en/townsquare/a-history-of-the-trade-and-bartersystem#:~:text=Mesopotamia%20tribes%20were%20likely%20the,weapons%2C%20and%20spices%20they%20needed (accessed February 2022).

Staff of Federal Reserve Bank of Kansas City. 2013. "Federal Reserve Act Signed Into Law." *Federal Reserve History*. www.federalreservehistory.org/essays/federal-reserve-act-signed#:~:text=December%2023%2C%201913,development%20of%20a%20central%20bank (accessed February 2022).

Swanson, D.L. 2018. "An Ancient Bankruptcy Law in China." *Mediatbankry*. https://mediatbankry.com/2018/09/13/an-ancient-bankruptcy-law-in-china/ (accessed February 2022).

Walker, B. 2023. "Venmo Has Its Own Credit Card: 5 Things to Know Before You Apply." *Finance Buzz*. https://financebuzz.com/venmo-credit-card (accessed January 2023).

Weatherford, J. 2005. *Genghis Khan and the Making of the Modern World*, pp. 204–250. New York City, NY: Crown.

Where We Are Now and Heading in the Future

"Chapter 1 Who Is Mr. Putin?" n.d. *Brookings*. www.brookings.edu/wp-content/uploads/2016/07/Chapter-One-1.pdf (accessed August 2022).

"Energy Fact Sheet: Why Does Russian Oil and Gas Matter?" 2022. *IEA*. www.iea.org/articles/energy-fact-sheet-why-does-russian-oil-and-gas-matter (accessed September 2022).

"Foreigners Banned From Selling Russian Stocks as Market Set for Limited Reopening." 2022. *Reuters*. www.reuters.com/business/finance/limited-russian-stock-market-trading-resume-march-24-central-bank-says-2022-03-23/ (accessed September 2022).

"GDP by Country." n.d. *Worldometer*. www.worldometers.info/gdp/gdp-by-country/ (accessed August 2022).

"GDP Growth (Annual %)—United States." n.d. *The World Bank*. https://data.worldbank.org/indicator/NY.GDP.MKTP.KD.ZG?locations=US (accessed August 2022).

"Home Price to Income Ratio (US & UK)." n.d. *Longtermtrends*. www.longtermtrends.net/home-price-median-annual-income-ratio/ (accessed October 2022).

"Kremlin Gets Control of Gazprom." 2005. *The New York Times*. www.nytimes.com/2005/06/17/business/worldbusiness/kremlin-gets-control-of-gazprom.html (accessed September 2022).

"Largest Countries in the World (By Area)." n.d. *Worldometer*. www.worldometers.info/geography/largest-countries-in-the-world/#:~:text=The%20largest%20country%20in%20the,Most%20Populous%20Countries (accessed August 2022).

"Russia Is Second-Biggest Oil Producer Only To U.S." 2021. *Warsaw Institute*. https://warsawinstitute.org/russia-second-biggest-oil-producer-u-s/ (accessed September 2022).

"Russia's 500 Super Rich Wealthier Than Poorest 99.8%—Report." Updated 2021. *The Moscow Times*. www.themoscowtimes.com/2021/06/10/russias-500-super-rich-wealthier-than-poorest-998-report-a74180 (accessed September 2022).

"The U.S. Population Is Growing at the Slowest Rate Since the 1930s." *PRB*. www .prb.org/resources/u-s-population-growing-at-slowest-rate-since-the-1930s/ (accessed January 2023).

"Visa and Mastercard Suspend Russian Operations." 2022. *BBC*. www.bbc.com/ news/business-60637429 (accessed September 2022).

Amery, P. 2021. "Tether Dominates Bitcoin Trading." *New Money Review*. https:// newmoneyreview.com/index.php/2021/10/11/tether-dominates-bitcoin-trading/ (accessed December 2022).

Åslund, A. 2008. "An Assessment of Putin's Economic Policy." *PIIE*. www .piie.com/commentary/speeches-papers/assessment-putins-economic-policy (accessed September 2022).

Åslund, A. 2020. "The Russian Economy in Health, Oil, and Economic Crisis." *Atlantic Council*. www.atlanticcouncil.org/commentary/long-take/the-russian-economy-inhealth-oil-and-economic-crisis/ (accessed August 2022).

Baltrusaitis, J. 2021. "Inflation Erodes the Value of the U.S. Dollar by 85% in 50 Years." *Finbold*. https://finbold.com/inflation-erodes-the-value-of-the-u-s-dollar-by-85-in-50-years/#:~:text=The%20United%20States%20dollar%20 value,over%20the%20last%2050%20years (accessed November 2022).

Barnato, K. 2016. "Russia Is the Most Unequal Major Country in the World: Study." *CNBC*. www.cnbc.com/2016/09/01/russia-is-the-most-unequal-major-country-in-the-world-study.html (accessed September 2022).

Barncaccio, D. and R. Conlon. 2022. "Why Over 450 Companies Have With-drawn From Russia, and Why Some Haven't." *Marketplace*. www.marketplace .org/2022/03/29/why-over-450-companies-have-withdrawn-from-russia-and-why-some-havent/ (accessed September 2022).

Bird, L. 2022. *'A Major Problem': The US Surpasses $31 Trillion in Debt, Made Worse by Rising Interest Rates—and This Is Who Holds the IOUs*. yahoo! www.yahoo.com/now/us-national-debt-now-tops-210000112.html (accessed January 2023).

Bloomberg. 2022. "Russia's Population Is in a Historic Decline as Emigration, War and a Plunging Birth Rate Form a 'Perfect Storm'." *Fortune*. https://fortune .com/2022/10/18/russia-population-historic-decline-emigration-war-plunging-birth-rate-form-perfect-storm/ (accessed November 2022).

Brown, J. 2022. "Billionaire Ray Dalio Disapproves of UK Government Fiscal Plan, Says It 'Suggests Incompetence'." *CEO Weekly*. https://ceoweekly.com/ billionaire-ray-dalio-disapproves-of-uk-governmenfiscal-plan-says-it-suggests-incompetence/ (accessed January 2023).

Browne, R. 2022. "Tether Claims Its Stablecoin Is Now Partially Backed by Non-U.S. Government Bonds." *CNBC*. www.cnbc.com/2022/05/19/tether-claims-usdt-stablecoin-is-backed-by-non-us-bonds.html (accessed December 2022).

CFI Team. 2022. "Intrinsic Value." *CFI*. https://corporatefinanceinstitute.com/resources/valuation/intrinsic-value-guide/ (accessed December 2022).

Chappell, B. 2022. "Russia's Central Bank Doubles a Key Interest Rate as Sanctions Spark Economic Turmoil." *NPR*. www.npr.org/2022/02/28/1083478065/russias-central-bank-doubles-a-key-interest-rate-as-sanctions-spark-economic-tur (accessed September 2022).

Connolly, R. 2020. "The Soviet Planned Economy." *The Russian Economy: A Very Short Introduction*. Oxford: Oxford Academic.

Cuthbertson, A. 2022. *'I Lost My Life Savings': Terra Luna Cryptocurrency Collapses 98% Overnight*. yahoo! https://finance.yahoo.com/news/lost-life-savings-terra-luna-160848651.html?guccounter=1&guce_referrer=aHR0c HM6Ly93d3cuZ29vZ2xlLmNvbS8&guce_referrer_sig=AQAAALXw1w5 snK5tRcdS2h3tM4AJLofILZ8zRCyFIVpYLIZg4qp5PZ-PMXA7y2WIM ANJnsNk8lyyDEIbH9W8JHz80Irj4F-REPaTPMRjPbhYlat7T2hbBkxF jnez0zdCWorcJ5SD3zbPuXOIekzdb9JhBRS5vjnH1dlNH8TY3pjztpEK (accessed December 2022).

Dalio, R. 2021. *Principles for Dealing With the Changing World Order*, pp. 56–132, 141–142. New York, NY: Avid Reader Press.

Fairless, T. 2022. "Will Inflation Stay High for Decades? One Influential Economist Says Yes." *The Wall Street Journal*. www.wsj.com/articles/inflation-high-forecast-economist-goodhart-cpi-11646837755 (accessed August 2022).

Fortune Editors. 2022. *Ray Dalio Believes a Strong Middle Can Balance Out a Polarized America*. yahoo! www.yahoo.com/video/ray-dalio-believes-strong-middle-221500278.html (accessed November 2022).

Fowers, A. and A.D. Van. 2021. "The Most Unusual Job Market in Modern American History, Explained." *The Washington Post*. www.washingtonpost.com/business/2021/12/29/job-market-2021/ (accessed August 2022).

Gopinath, G. and P. Gourinchas. 2022. "How Countries Should Respond to the Strong Dollar." *IMF*. www.imf.org/en/Blogs/Articles/2022/10/14/how-countries-should-respond-to-the-strong-dollar (accessed November 2022).

Greene, R. 2022. "How Sanctions on Russia Will Alter Global Payments Flows." *Carnegie Endowment for International Peace*. https://carnegieendowment.org/2022/03/04/how-sanctions-on-russia-will-alter-global-payments-flows-pub-86575 (accessed September 2022).

Hanke, S.H. and N. Hanlon. 2022. "Jerome Powell Is Wrong. Printing Money Causes Inflation." *The Wall Street Journal*. www.wsj.com/articles/powell-printing-money-supply-m2-raises-prices-level-inflation-demand-prediction-wage-stagnation-stagflation-federal-reserve-monetary-policy-11645630424 (accessed June 2022).

Harris, A. 2022. "Fed's QT to Hit 'Full Stride' With Central Bank Shrinking $9 Trillion Portfolio." *Bloomberg.* www.bloomberg.com/news/articles/2022-08-29/qt-to-hit-full-stride-with-fed-shrinking-9-trillion-portfolio (accessed December 2022).

Hjelmgaard, K. 2022. "British Prime Minister Liz Truss Resigns Amid Economic Turmoil After Six Weeks in Office." *USA Today.* www.usatoday.com/story/news/world/2022/10/20/liz-truss-british-prime-minister-resigns/104949 16002/ (accessed January 2023).

Hoskins, P. n.d. "Sri Lanka Defaults on Debt for First Time in Its History." *BBC.* www.bbc.com/news/business-61505842 (accessed October 2022).

Iacurci, G. 2022. "Why Labor Economists Say the Remote Work 'Revolution' Is Here to Stay." *CNBC.* www.cnbc.com/2022/12/01/why-labor-economists-say-the-remote-work-revolution-is-here-to-stay.html (accessed December 2022).

Ivanoa, P. and M. Seddon. 2022. "Russia's Wartime Economy: Learning to Live Without Imports." *Financial Times.* www.ft.com/content/6c01e84b-5333-4024-aaf1-521cf1207eb4 (accessed January 2023).

Kharpal, A. and R. Browne. 2022. "Cryptocurrency Luna Crashes to $0 as UST Falls Further From Dollar Peg." *CNBC.* www.cnbc.com/2022/05/13/cryptocurrency-luna-crashes-to-0-as-ust-falls-from-peg-bitcoin-rises.html (accessed December 2022).

Lawless, J. 2022. "UK Scraps Tax Cut for Wealthy That Sparked Market Turmoil." *PBS.* www.pbs.org/newshour/world/uk-scraps-tax-cut-for-wealthy-that-sparked-market-turmoil (accessed November 2022).

Levanon, G. and F. Steemers. 2021. "Why Wages Are Growing Rapidly Now—And Will Continue to in the Future." *The Conference Board.* www.conference-board.org/pdfdownload.cfm?masterProductID=34781 (accessed November 2022).

Levy, A. and M. Sigalos. 2022. "Crypto Peaked a Year Ago—Investors Have Lost More Than $2 Trillion Since." *CNBC.* www.cnbc.com/2022/11/11/crypto-peaked-in-nov-2021-investors-lost-more-than-2-trillion-since.html (accessed December 2022).

Ludden, J. 2022. "Rent Control Expands as Tenants Struggle With the Record High Cost of Housing." *NPR.* www.npr.org/2022/11/28/1138633419/rent-control-economists-tenants-affordable-housing-ballot-measures (accessed January 2023).

Martin, K. and C. Smith. 2022. "The Mystery of How Quantitative Tightening Will Affect Markets." *Financial Times.* www.ft.com/content/435a5e35-bf30-4518-a4fc-a6d5c2d66076 (accessed December 2022).

Monteiro, A. 2022. "World Debt-GDP Ratio Plummets But Remains Above Pre-Covid Level." *Bloomberg.* www.bloomberg.com/news/articles/2022-12-12/world-debt-gdp-ratio-plummets-but-remains-above-pre-covid-level?leadSource=uverify%20wall (accessed January 2023).

Nelson, E. and P. Cohen. 2022. "Russian Economy Contracts Sharply as War and Sanctions Take Hold." *The New York Times.* www.nytimes.com/2022/08/12/business/russia-economy-gdp.html (accessed September 2022).

Nguyen, J. 2022. "Companies Still Say They Can't Find Enough Workers. What's Going On?" *Market Place.* www.marketplace.org/2022/03/23/companies-still-say-they-cant-find-enough-workers-whats-going-on/ (accessed November 2022).

Ostroff, C. 2022. "Russia Central Bank Bans Short Selling as Stocks Plunge." *The Wall Street Journal.* www.wsj.com/livecoverage/russia-ukraine-latest-news/card/russia-central-bank-bans-short-selling-as-stocks-plunge-SjQFvNNXoXUKE4lkESfe#:~:text=Russia%27s%20central%20bank%20said%20Thursday,practice%20known%20as%20short%2Dselling (accessed September 2022).

Palmer, A. 2022. "Amazon Hikes Pay for Warehouse and Delivery Workers." *CNBC.* www.cnbc.com/2022/09/28/amazon-hikes-pay-for-warehouse-and-delivery-workers.html (accessed November 2022).

Pham, S. 2020. "IMF Says Half the World Has Asked for a Bailout." *CNN.* www.cnn.com/2020/04/16/economy/imf-global-bailout/index.html (accessed October 2022).

Ponciano, J. 2021. "Billionaire Investor Druckenmiller Blasts Fed's 'Radical' Stimulus Policy, Warns It Risks Stock 'Bubble Blowing Up'." *Forbes.* www.forbes.com/sites/jonathanponciano/2021/05/11/billionaire-investor-druckenmiller-blasts-feds-radical-stimulus-policy-warns-it-risks-stock-bubble-blowing-up/?sh=21ad96a02fe8 (accessed August 2022).

Reid, J. 2022. "British Pound Plunges, Bonds Sink After Government Announces Tax Cuts." *CNBC.* www.cnbc.com/2022/09/23/british-pound-plunges-to-fresh-37-year-low-of-1point10-.html#:~:text=British%20pound%20plunges%2C%20bonds%20sink%20after%20government%20announces%20tax%20cuts,-Published%20Fri%2C%20Sep&text=Sterling%20dropped%20as%20low%20as,month%20not%20seen%20since%201985 (accessed October 2022).

Reuters. 2022. "Isolated Russians Scramble for Hard Currency, Fear Worse Is Yet to Come." *Reuters.* www.reuters.com/markets/asia/isolated-russians-scramble-hard-currency-fear-worse-is-yet-come-2022-03-01/ (accessed September 2022).

Reuters. 2022. "Rouble Hits Record Low in Moscow, Remains Volatile Outside Russia." *Reuters.* www.reuters.com/markets/europe/russian-rouble-slips-past-100-vs-dollar-banks-hunt-fx-2022-03-02/ (accessed May 2022).

Reuters. 2022. "Russian Central Bank Hikes Rate to 20% in Emergency Move, Tells Firms to Sell FX." *Reuters.* www.reuters.com/business/finance/russia-hikes-key-rate-20-tells-companies-sell-fx-2022-02-28/ (accessed September 2022).

Rexaline, S. 2022. "Billionaire Ray Dalio Warns of Stagflation, Calls Fed 'Naïve and Inconsistent' for Raising Interest Rates." *Markets Insider.* https://markets .businessinsider.com/news/stocks/billionaire-ray-dalio-warns-of-stagflation-calls-fed-na%C3%AFve-and-inconsistent-for-raising-interest-rates-10315 43652 (accessed August 2022).

Riley, C. 2022. "Should the Government Control the Price of Food and Gas?" *CNN.* www.cnn.com/2022/01/18/economy/price-controls-inflation/index .html (accessed August 2022).

Robertson, H. 2022. "Russia Shuts Its Stock Market for a 3rd Day as Its Government Readies $10 Billion to Buy Up Plunging Assets." *Markets Insider.* https://markets.businessinsider.com/news/stocks/russia-stock-market-closed-government-buying-assets-ukraine-sanctions-crisis-2022-3#:~:text= Russia%20has%20ordered%20its%20sovereign,stock%20market%20 once%20it%20reopens (accessed January 2023).

Rosalsky, G. 2022. "How 'Shock Therapy' Created Russian Oligarchs and Paved the Path for Putin." *NPR.* www.npr.org/sections/money/2022/03/22/10876 54279/how-shock-therapy-created-russian-oligarchs-and-paved-the-path-for-putin (accessed August 2022).

Roth, A. 2022. "'We're Going Back to a USSR': Long Queues Return for Russian Shoppers as Sanctions Bite." *The Guardian.* www.theguardian.com/ world/2022/mar/23/were-going-back-to-a-ussr-long-queues-return-for-russian-shoppers-as-sanctions-bite (accessed September 2022).

Sheets, N. 2012. "Back to the Future: Lessons From U.S. Fiscal Deleveraging After World War II." *CITI Group.* www.citivelocity.com/citigps/back-future-lessons-u-s-fiscal-deleveraging-world-war-ii/ (accessed September 2022).

Smith, E. 2022. "Russia's Economy Is Beginning to Crack as Economists Forecast Sharp Contractions." *CNBC.* www.cnbc.com/2022/04/04/russias-economy-is-beginning-to-crack-as-economists-forecast-sharp-contractions.html (accessed September 2022).

Smith, T. (CEO Fundsmith LLP). Letter to Fellow Investor. 2022. "Fundsmith Equity Fund ("Fund") Performance." www.fundsmith.co.uk/media/deujnq00/ annual-letter-to-shareholders-2020.pdf (accessed September 2022).

Smolentseva, A., J. Huisman, and I. Froumin. 2018. "Transformation of Higher Education Institutional Landscape in Post-Soviet Countries: From Soviet Model to Where?" *25 Years of Transformations of Higher Education Systems in Post-Soviet Countries,* pp. 1–43. Cham: Palgrave Studies in Global Higher Education, Palgrave Macmillan.

Stapp, A. 2021. "Price Controls Won't Fix What's Ailing the Restaurant Industry." *Innovation Frontier.* https://innovationfrontier.org/wp-content/uploads/2021/02/IFP-Price-Controls.pdf (accessed August 2022).

Statista Research Department. 2022. "Coal Export Volume in Russia 2021, by Destination." *Statista.* www.statista.com/statistics/1066718/russian-coal-export-volume-by-destination/#:~:text=Coal%20exports%20from%20Russia%20were,were%20to%20Asia%2DPacific%20markets (accessed January 2023).

Statista Research Department. 2022. "Largest Public Companies in Russia 2022, by Market Value." *Statista.* www.statista.com/statistics/1206622/market capitalization-of-leading-russian-companies/ (accessed December 2022).

The Editorial Board. 2022. "How Inflation Taxes the Poor." *The Wall Street Journal.* www.wsj.com/articles/how-inflation-taxes-the-poor-britain-consumer-prices-boris-johnson-economy-11652897954 (accessed October 2022).

Tremayne-Pengelly, A. 2022. "Binance Pauses Customer Withdrawals Amid Heightened Crypto Scrutiny." *Observer.* https://observer.com/2022/12/binance-pauses-customer-withdrawals-amid-heightened-crypto-scrutiny/#:~:text=Binance%27s%20halting%20of%20withdrawals%20comes,its%20rival%20crypto%20exchange%20FTX (accessed December 2022).

Turak, N. 2022. "Long Lines at Russia's ATMs as Bank Run Begins—With More Pain to Come." *CNBC.* www.cnbc.com/2022/02/28/long-lines-at-russias-atms-as-bank-run-begins-ruble-hit-by-sanctions.html (accessed September 2022).

Walker, N. and J. Curtis. 2022. "UK Response to the Human Rights and Economic Situation in Sri Lanka." *UK Parliament.* https://commonslibrary.parliament.uk/research-briefings/cdp-2022-0194/ (accessed December 2022).

Westfall, C. 2022. "If Wall Street Is so Smart, Why Is It Moving to Florida?" *Risk Market News.* www.riskmarketnews.com/if-wall-street-is-so-smart-why-is-it-moving-to-florida-2/ (accessed August 2022).

Wilson, T. and A. Berwick. 2022. "Crypto Exchange FTX Saw $6 Bln in Withdrawals in 72 Hours." *Reuters.* www.reuters.com/business/finance/crypto-exchange-ftx-saw-6-bln-withdrawals-72-hours-ceo-message-staff-2022-11-08/ (accessed December 2022).

Woelfel, J. and B. Levisohn. 2022. "Russian Stock Market Rises After Closing for a Month." *Barron's.* www.barrons.com/articles/russian-stock-market-moex-index-51648063294 (accessed September 2022).

How This Information Can Be Used

"Semi-Annual Investor Call." 2022. AKRE Focus Fund. www.akrefund.com/semiannual-investor-call-replay/ (accessed 2022).

"What Is Dollar Cost Averaging?" 2017. *Charles Schwab*. https://intelligent.schwab
.com/article/dollar-cost-averaging#:~:text=Dollar%20cost%20averaging%20
is%20the,as%20well%20as%20your%20costs (accessed January 2023).

Campbell, P. 2020. "What Is Pricing Power and How Does Price Power Affect
Business Success?" *ProfitWell*. www.profitwell.com/recur/all/pricing-power#
:~:text=Pricing%20power%20refers%20to%20a,it%20is%20to%20raise
%20prices (accessed December 2022).

Chen, L. 2022. "China Builders Have $292 Billion of Debt Coming Due
Through 2023." *Bloomberg*. www.bloomberg.com/news/articles/2022-10-31/
china-builders-have-292-billion-of-debt-coming-due-through-2023 (accessed
December 2022).

Dalio, R. 2022. "The Changing World Order Is Approaching Stage 6 (The War
Stage)." *LinkedIn*. www.linkedin.com/pulse/changing-world-order-approaching-
stage-6-warray-dalio/ (accessed January 2023).

Goldman, M.C. 2020. "Delta Is Burning Through $100 Million a Day." *The
Street*. www.thestreet.com/video/delta-is-burning-through-100-million-a-day
(accessed December 2022).

Goodkind, N. 2023. "The World Has a Major Debt Problem. Is a Reset Coming?"
CNN. www.cnn.com/2023/01/17/investing/premarket-stocks-trading/index
.html (accessed January 2023).

Groves, J. 2022. "How to Invest in Japan." *Forbes*. www.forbes.com/uk/advisor/
investing/how-to-invest-in-japan/ (accessed January 2023).

Hoffman, L. 2022. "Bill Ackman Scored on Pandemic Shutdown and Bounceback."
The Wall Street Journal. www.wsj.com/articles/bill-ackman-scored-on-pandemic-
shutdown-andbounceback-11643634004 (accessed December 2022).

Holodny, E. 2014. *Investors Lose More Money Anticipating Corrections Than From
Corrections Themselves*. yahoo! https://news.yahoo.com/investors-lose-more-
money-anticipating-201900159.html (accessed December 2022).

James, H. 1984. "The Causes of the German Banking Crisis of 1931." *The
Economic History Review* 37, no. 1, pp. 68–87.

Kanaya, A. and D. Woo. 2000. "The Japanese Banking Crisis of the 1990s:
Sources and Lessons." *IMF Working Paper*, pp. 4–35.

Schmidt, J. Updated 2022. "How Inflation Erodes the Value of Your Money." *Forbes*.
www.forbes.com/advisor/investing/what-is-inflation/ (accessed December 2022).

Shen, W. 2022. "Asset Allocation in the Era of High Inflation." *T. Rowe Price*.
www.troweprice.com/institutional/us/en/insights/articles/2022/q2/asset-
allocation-in-the-era-of-high-inflation-na.html (accessed December 2022).

Smith, E. 2022. "Global Government Debt Set to Soar to Record $71 Trillion
This Year, New Research Says." *CNBC*. www.cnbc.com/2022/04/06/global-
government-debt-set-to-soar-to-record-71-trillion-this-year-research.html
(accessed December 2022).

Stevens, P. 2021. "This Chart Shows Why Investors Should Never Try to Time the Stock Market." *CNBC*. www.cnbc.com/2021/03/24/this-chart-shows-why-investors-should-nevertry-to-time-the-stock-market.html (accessed December 2022).

Weidenhammer, R. 1932. "Review of Reviewed Work: Exchange, Prices and Production in Hyperinflation: Germany, 1920–1923, by F.D. Graham." *The American Economic Review* 22, no. 1, pp. 146–149.

About the Author

Brendan has more than a decade of industry experience in investments and public finance since graduating from James Madison University with a Bachelor of Business Administration degree in Finance and Accounting. For the last several years, Brendan has worked as a Registered Investment Advisor for Lafayette Investments. For Lafayette, Brendan manages a portion of the $800 million in assets under management, primarily for high-net-worth individuals. Brendan assists in the investment decision-making process for equity portfolios and advises clients on topics such as asset allocation, long-term saving strategies, and tax efficiency. Brendan formerly worked as a Senior Analyst for Primatics Financial where he served as a consultant primarily for large banks, advising them on matters such as credit risk.

Brendan is a Chartered Financial Analyst (CFA) charterholder. He has served on various boards and committees, including the James Madison University College of Business Board of Advisors (Associate Board Member), Cystic Fibrosis Foundation's Maryland Chapter (Board Member), CanEducate (Board Member for a charitable organization that helps schools in developing countries such as Haiti), ZERV Inc. (former Board Member for a Canadian technology startup that was acquired), and the Member Engagement Committee for CFA Society Washington D.C. (Committee Member). Brendan is a two-time winner of the Tomorrow's Leader Award for his contributions to the Cystic Fibrosis Foundation.

Brendan is the author of a book titled *The Wandering Investor*. This book takes the reader on a unique journey around the world in a discussion about various economies, Brendan's personal adventures along the way, business outlooks and observations for each country, lists of recommended activities in each country with a focus on outdoor adventure experiences, and lessons learned in terms of both travel and business. *The Wandering Investor* covers Brendan's travels across 17 countries spread out across six continents. *The Wandering Investor* is available through Brendan's publisher, BookBaby, as well as various other distributors such as Amazon and Barnes & Noble. The book is available in select libraries around the world.

Brendan is an avid reader. He primarily enjoys reading about finance, investing, world history, and economics. Brendan is a world traveler, having visited 36 countries at the time of this writing. He has been a lifelong fan of the Washington Wizards.

If you would like to connect with Brendan, you can find him on LinkedIn or e-mail him at Hughes2525@gmail.com.

Index

Printed in Great Britain
by Amazon

31075815R00136